QUALITATIVE RESEARCH

QUALITATIVE RESEARCH

A Guide to Design and Implementation

Fourth Edition

Sharan B. Merriam

Elizabeth J. Tisdell

JB JOSSEY-BASS™
A Wiley Brand

Cover design by
Cover image: ©

Published by Jossey-Bass
A Wiley Brand
One Montgomery Street, Suite 1000, San Francisco, CA 94104-4594—www.wiley.com, www.josseybass
.com/highereducation

Jossey-Bass books and products are available through most bookstores. To contact Jossey-Bass directly
call our Customer Care Department within the U.S. at 800-956-7739, outside the U.S. at 317-572-3986, or
fax 317-572-4002.

Wiley publishes in a variety of print and electronic formats and by print-on-demand. Some material
included with standard print versions of this book may not be included in e-books or in print-on-
demand. If this book refers to media such as a CD or DVD that is not included in the version you
purchased, you may download this material at http://booksupport.wiley.com. For more information
about Wiley products, visit www.wiley.com.

Library of Congress Cataloging-in-Publication Data

Merriam, Sharan B.
   Qualitative research : a guide to design and implementation / Sharan B. Merriam & Elizabeth J.
Tisdell. – Fourth edition.
        pages cm – (The Jossey-Bass higher and adult education series)
   Includes bibliographical references and index.
   ISBN 978-1-119-00361-8 (paperback)
   ISBN 978-1-119-00365-6 (ebk.)
   ISBN 978-1-119-00360-1 (ebk.)
   1. Education–Research–Methodology. 2. Education–Research–Case studies. 3. Case method.
4. Qualitative research. I. Tisdell, Elizabeth J. II. Title.
   LB1028.M396 2015
   370.72–dc23   2015005272

Printed in the United States of America

FOURTH EDITION

PB Printing SKY10020808_083120

The Jossey-Bass Higher and
Adult Education Series

CONTENTS

Preface

Qualitative research is a mature field of study with its own literature base, research journals, special interest groups, and regularly scheduled conferences. Indeed, staying current is a daunting task for any single individual. Van Maanen (2011) humorously describes trying to "keep up" with developments in ethnography, just one type of qualitative research:

> The ethnography industry now includes the ceaseless production of authoritative monographs, exhaustive reviews of the literature(s), method manuals, encyclopedias of concepts and theories, meta-critical expositions, themed anthologies, handbooks of door-stopping weight, established and quasi-established journal publications, formal presentations of talks and papers presided over by umpteen academic societies, online publications, blogs, topical chat-rooms, message boards, forums, social networking sites, and on and on. The answer then to how a single person can keep up without gagging is that he or she can't, for the potentially relevant materials are overwhelming, and new theories, new problems, new topics, new concepts, and new critiques of older work multiply with each passing year. It seems the best one can do is to selectively pursue and cultivate an ever-diminishing proportion of the potentially relevant work that comes one's way and assume an attitude of benign neglect toward the rest. (p. 146)

However, what *has* remained constant amidst the burgeoning of resources for doing qualitative research is the value of a practical guide for designing and implementing this type of research. *Qualitative Research: A Guide to Design and Implementation* represents our effort to explain qualitative research in an easy-to-follow narrative accessible to both novice and experienced researchers.

In essence, it is a practical guide without being just a "cookbook" for conducting qualitative research; readers also come to understand the theoretical and philosophical underpinnings of this research paradigm.

This edition of *Qualitative Research: A Guide to Design and Implementation* represents the latest iteration in thinking about and understanding qualitative research. The first edition, published in 1988, centered on qualitative *case study* research; the 1998 second edition featured *qualitative research,* with case study as a secondary focus. The 2009 third edition saw a further reduction in the attention to qualitative case studies. For this fourth edition the focus is largely on interpretive/constructivist qualitative research, of which qualitative case study is one common design, along with what we call a "basic" qualitative study, ethnography, grounded theory, narrative inquiry, and a phenomenological qualitative study. In fact, we have retained and updated the chapter on "types" of qualitative research because from our experiences teaching and conducting workshops, there is little clarity about the differences among these approaches for researchers new to qualitative research—hence, a chapter devoted to differentiating among these common types, as well as exploring their overlaps.

There are two other substantive changes to this fourth edition of *Qualitative Research: A Guide to Design and Implementation.* First, we have added a new chapter of research designs in which qualitative methods are heavily used, often with other more quantitative and/ or creative methods. This chapter reviews mixed methods, action research, critical research, and arts based research. The second substantive change in this edition is more attention to how technology permeates the process—as in, for example, online data sources and qualitative data analysis software packages.

This book continues to be positioned in applied fields of practice. Participants in our workshops and courses have come from nursing, social work, management, allied health, administration, counseling, religion, business gerontology, and human resource development, among others, as well as every subfield of education. Although our field of practice is adult education, and therefore there are many examples from education and adult education, we have made an effort to bring in examples from a variety of fields of practice. Certainly the design and implementation of a qualitative study is the same across these fields.

Another defining characteristic of this book is its how-to, practical focus, wherein the mechanics of conducting a qualitative study are presented in a simple, straightforward manner. Designing a qualitative study, collecting and analyzing data, and writing the research report are topics logically presented and liberally illustrated to assist the new researcher desiring some guidance in the process. The revisions in these chapters have greatly benefited from our having access to nearly a decade of additional resources published since the third edition; our own research; our supervision of dozens of qualitative dissertations; and, in particular, Sharan's conducting certificate programs in qualitative research methods in South Africa, Singapore, Malaysia, and South Korea. From these hands-on workshops have come techniques, resources, and strategies for assisting learners in understanding and conducting qualitative research. Thus for this fourth edition we draw upon recent literature in the field as well as our own experiences with qualitative research. The intended audiences for this book, then, are practitioners and graduate students in applied fields of practice who are interested in a basic understanding of how to design and conduct a qualitative study.

OVERVIEW OF THE CONTENTS

The organization of this text reflects the process of conducting a qualitative research investigation. Part One contains four chapters. The first is on the nature of qualitative research, the second covers several common types of qualitative research, and the third presents other designs in which qualitative methods constitute a major part of the methodology. The fourth explains the procedure for designing a qualitative study, from identifying a gap in the knowledge base, to forming a problem statement framed by the relevant literature, to selecting the particular qualitative design most appropriate for your question, to selecting a sample. Part Two consists of three chapters that detail data collection techniques. The three chapters in Part Three deal with analyzing the data collected; handling concerns about reliability, validity, and ethics; and writing the final report. We have also included in an appendix a qualitative methodology template created for graduate students who are designing a qualitative thesis or dissertation.

Chapter One positions qualitative research within research in general, discusses the roots of qualitative research in sociology and anthropology, and briefly describes early contributions in the development of qualitative research as a field itself. Next, the chapter reviews the philosophical/epistemological underpinnings of qualitative research as it contrasts with positivist (or quantitative), critical, and postmodern research traditions. Drawing from its philosophical foundations, the chapter defines and then presents the characteristics of qualitative research. It closes with a discussion of the investigator characteristics and skills needed to conduct a qualitative study.

Writers have organized the variety of types of qualitative studies into various traditions or approaches. Chapter Two reviews six of the more common types of qualitative studies found across applied fields of practice. The first type discussed is what we call a "basic" qualitative research study. This is by far the most common type of qualitative study found in education and most likely in other fields of practice; other texts on qualitative research often fail to address the fact that you can conduct a qualitative study without its being a particular type of qualitative study (such as a phenomenological study, a narrative inquiry, and so on). Other types of qualitative research share all the characteristics of a basic qualitative study but have an additional dimension. Other types and their unique characteristics discussed in this chapter are phenomenology, grounded theory, ethnography, narrative analysis, and qualitative case study research.

Chapter Three presents several more recent and increasingly more common types of research that have a major qualitative methods component, and have contributed to expanding the qualitative paradigm in the past decade. These include mixed method designs that make use of both qualitative and quantitative methods, action research, critical research, and arts based research (ABR). Action research is intended to solve a problem in practice and make something happen in the research process itself, whereas critical research is specifically intended to challenge power relations. Arts based approaches incorporate one or more multiple forms of art into the data collection and analysis process. There can be some overlap in these types of studies; for example, arts based approaches can be incorporated into action research, critical research, or other types of studies.

Knowledge of previous research and theory can help a researcher focus on the problem of interest and select the unit of analysis most relevant to the problem. Chapter Four explains what a theoretical framework is and shows how reviewing relevant literature contributes not only to identifying the study's theoretical framework but also to shaping the problem statement. The problem statement lays out the logic and purpose of the study and is critical to making informed decisions regarding sample selection (also covered in this chapter), data collection, and data analysis.

Data collection techniques are covered in the three chapters in Part Two. Chapters Five, Six, and Seven examine the three primary means of collecting data in qualitative research. Interviews, discussed in Chapter Five, can range in structure from a list of predetermined questions to a totally free-ranging interview in which nothing is set ahead of time. The success of an interview depends on the nature of the interaction between the interviewer and the respondent and on the interviewer's skill in asking good questions. Chapter Five also covers how to record and evaluate interview data.

Observations differ from interviews in that the researcher obtains a first-hand account of the phenomenon of interest rather than relying on someone else's interpretation. Chapter Six discusses what to observe, the interdependent relationship between observer and observed, and how to record observations in the form of field notes. Chapter Seven presents the third primary source of qualitative data: documents and artifacts. The term *document* is broadly defined to cover an assortment of written records, physical traces, and visual images. Although some documents might be developed at the investigator's request, most are produced independently of the research study and thus offer a valuable resource for confirming insights gained through interviews and observations. Chapter Seven covers various types of documents, their use in qualitative research, and their strengths and limitations as sources of data.

Many general texts on qualitative research devote more space to theoretical discussions of methodology and data collection than to the actual management and analysis of data once they have been collected. However, we have discovered in our many years of experience teaching and conducting qualitative research that the most difficult part of the entire process is *analyzing* qualitative data. We have also come to firmly believe that to learn how to do analysis, there is no substitute for actually engaging in analysis, preferably with one's own data. Nevertheless, in Chapter Eight we have tried to present as clear a discussion as possible on how to analyze qualitative data. The importance of analyzing data while they are being collected is underscored; some suggestions for analysis early in the study during data collection are also included. Management of the voluminous data typical of a qualitative study is another topic addressed in this chapter. The heart of the chapter presents an inductive analysis strategy for constructing categories or themes that become the findings of the study. The chapter also includes a discussion of the role of computer software programs in qualitative data analysis. The final section of this chapter reviews data analysis strategies particular to the types of qualitative research discussed in Chapter Two (such as phenomenology and narrative inquiry).

All researchers are concerned with producing valid and reliable findings. Chapter Nine explores the issues of validity and reliability in qualitative research. In particular, internal validity, reliability, and external validity are discussed, and strategies are offered for dealing with each of these issues. Also of concern to researchers is how to conduct an investigation in an ethical manner, which in turn impacts the trustworthiness of your study. Chapter Nine closes with a section on ethics, paying particular attention to ethical dilemmas likely to arise in qualitative research.

Many an educator has been able to design a study, collect relevant data, and even analyze the data, but then has failed to carry through in the important last step—writing up the results. Without this step, the research has little chance of advancing the knowledge base of the field or having an impact on practice. Chapter Ten is designed to help qualitative researchers complete the research process by writing a report of their investigation. The first half of the chapter offers suggestions for organizing the writing process—determining the audience for the report, settling on the main message, and outlining the overall report. The rest of the chapter focuses on the content of the report—its components and where to place them, how to achieve a good balance between description and analysis, and how to disseminate the study's findings.

Finally, the appendix presents a template created for graduate students and others who would like some guidance in what goes into a methodology chapter or proposal of a qualitative research study. This template is an outline of the component parts of a methodology chapter, explaining what needs to be included under each section. A modification of this outline could also be used for the methodology section of a qualitative research grant proposal.

ACKNOWLEDGMENTS

We want to acknowledge those who have contributed in various ways to this fourth edition. First, the three reviewers of the third edition provided extremely helpful suggestions for updating and organizing this fourth edition. We also want to thank participants in workshops on qualitative research in different parts of the world who raised wonderful questions and struggled with activities related to conducting small pilot studies—all of which enabled us to sharpen our thinking and instruction. We also want to give special thanks to our doctoral students, who, although they may have taken a number of courses in qualitative research, challenged us to improve our mentoring and advising as they worked through the process. We have, in fact, drawn examples from a number of their dissertations to illustrate aspects of the process. Finally, a very special thanks goes to Anne Greenawalt, a doctoral student in the Penn State Adult Education program, for her assistance with a wide range of research, technical, and organizational tasks related to getting the manuscript ready for publication.

SHARAN B. MERRIAM
Athens, Georgia

ELIZABETH J. TISDELL
Harrisburg, Pennsylvania

THE AUTHORS

Sharan B. Merriam is professor emerita of adult and continuing education at the University of Georgia in Athens, where her responsibilities included teaching graduate courses in adult education and qualitative research methods and supervising graduate student research. She received her B.A. degree (1965) in English literature from Drew University, her M.Ed. degree (1971) in English education from Ohio University, and her Ed.D. degree (1978) in adult education from Rutgers University. Before coming to the University of Georgia, she served on the faculties of Northern Illinois University and Virginia Polytechnic Institute and State University.

Merriam's main research and writing activities have focused on adult education, adult development and learning, and qualitative research methods. She has served on steering committees for the annual North American Adult Education Research Conference, the Qualitative Research in Education Conference at the University of Georgia, and the Commission of Professors of Adult Education. For five years she was coeditor of *Adult Education Quarterly*, the major research and theory journal in the field of adult education. She was also coeditor of a book series, *Professional Practices in Adult Education and Lifelong Learning*. She has won the Cyril O. Houle World Award for Literature in Adult Education for four different books. Various of her books have been translated into Chinese, Korean, Japanese, and French. Her most recent publications include *A Guide to Research for Educators and Trainers of Adults* (with Patricia Cranton, 2015), *Adult Learning* (with Laura Bierema, 2014), *Learning in Adulthood*, third edition (with Rosemary Caffarella and Lisa Baumgartner, 2007), *Non-Western Perspectives on Learning and Knowing* (2007), and *Third Update on Adult Learning Theory* (2008).

Based on her widespread contributions to the field of adult education, Merriam has been inducted into the International Adult and Continuing Education Hall of Fame and was the first to receive the American Association of Adult and Continuing Education's Career Achievement award. She regularly conducts workshops and seminars on adult learning and qualitative research throughout North America and overseas, including Brazil and countries in southern Africa, Southeast Asia, the Middle East, and Europe. She has been a senior Fulbright scholar to Malaysia, and a distinguished visiting scholar to universities in South Korea and South Africa.

Elizabeth J. Tisdell is professor of adult education at Penn State University–Harrisburg and the coordinator of graduate programs in adult education. Her teaching responsibilities include facilitating graduate courses in adult education, spirituality and culture in the health and medical professions, and in qualitative research methods. She also supervises graduate student research.

Tisdell received her B.A. in mathematics from the University of Maine in 1977, an M.A. in religion from Fordham University in 1979, and an Ed.D. in adult education from the University of Georgia in 1992. Prior to joining the faculty at Penn State, she was associate professor of adult and continuing education at National-Louis University in Chicago and served on the faculty at Antioch University, Seattle. She worked as a campus minister for the Catholic Church from 1979 to 1989 at both Central Michigan University and Loyola University–New Orleans.

Tisdell's main research and writing activities have focused on spirituality and culture in adult and higher education, diversity issues in adult education and medical education, and qualitative research methods. She is the author of *Exploring Spirituality and Culture in Adult and Higher Education* (Jossey-Bass, 2003). Her other scholarly works have appeared in numerous journals and edited books. Tisdell has served on steering committees for the annual North American Adult Education Research Conference, was the chair of the Commission of Professors of Adult Education from

2012 to 2014, and was coeditor of *Adult Education Quarterly* from 2006 to 2011. Tisdell enjoys exploring what is to be learned from spiritual pilgrimage, embodied in practices relating to yoga, music, and art, and from exploring both the wisdom in nature as well as the nature of wisdom.

QUALITATIVE RESEARCH

PART ONE

THE DESIGN OF QUALITATIVE RESEARCH

Education, health, social work, administration, and other arenas of social activity are considered applied social sciences or fields of practice precisely because practitioners in these fields deal with the everyday concerns of people's lives. Having an interest in knowing more about one's practice, and indeed in *improving* one's practice, leads to asking researchable questions, some of which are best approached through a qualitative research design. In fact, we believe that research focused on discovery, insight, and understanding from the perspectives of those being studied offers the greatest promise of making a difference in people's lives.

Engaging in systematic inquiry about your practice—doing research—involves choosing a study design that corresponds with your question; you should also consider whether the design is a comfortable match with your worldview, personality, and skills. It is thus important to understand the philosophical foundations underlying different types of research so that you can make informed decisions as to the choices available to you in designing and implementing a research study. The four chapters in Part One of this book provide the conceptual foundation for doing *qualitative* research and lay out some of the choices and decisions you will need to make in conducting a qualitative study.

The qualitative, interpretive, or naturalistic research paradigm defines the methods and techniques most suitable for collecting and analyzing data. Qualitative inquiry, which focuses on meaning in context, requires a data collection instrument that is sensitive to underlying meaning when gathering and interpreting data. Humans are best suited for this task, especially because interviewing, observing, and analyzing are activities central to qualitative research. Chapter One explores the foundations of qualitative research, defines this mode of inquiry, and identifies its essential characteristics.

Although all of qualitative research holds a number of assumptions and characteristics in common, there are variations in the disciplinary base that a qualitative study might draw from, in how a qualitative study might be designed, and in what the intent of the study might be. Thus a qualitative ethnographic study that focuses on culture could be differentiated from a narrative life history study or from a study designed to build a substantive theory. Chapter Two differentiates among six major types of qualitative studies commonly found in applied fields of study.

As the field of qualitative research continues to develop and expand, we thought it useful to include a chapter that reviews designs wherein qualitative methods are combined with other orientations. Chapter Three reviews mixed methods, action research, critical, and arts based research.

Other considerations have to do with identifying the theoretical framework that forms the scaffolding or underlying structure of your study. Reviewing previous thinking and research found in the literature can help illuminate your framework, as well as shape the actual problem statement and purpose of the study. Further, how you select your sample is directly linked to the questions you ask and to how you have constructed the problem of your study. These considerations are discussed in detail, with illustrative examples, in Chapter Four.

The four chapters that make up Part One of this book are thus designed to orient you to the nature of qualitative research and common types of qualitative research, as well as how to frame your question or interest, state your research problem, and select a sample. Part One paves the way for subsequent chapters that focus on data collection and data analysis.

CHAPTER ONE

WHAT IS QUALITATIVE RESEARCH?

This book is about qualitative research—what it is, and how to do it. But before we get into qualitative research, it's important to define what we mean by *research* itself. There are many definitions of research, but what they all have in common is the notion of inquiring into, or investigating something in a systematic manner. In everyday life we talk about "doing research" to inform our decisions and to decide on a particular course of action. For example, when it comes time to buy a new car, you might do some "research" by consulting *Consumer Reports* and a number of Internet sites that rate cars on quality, customer satisfaction, safety, and so on. All of this "research," in addition to test-driving several cars, will enable you to make your decision.

You as a reader probably found your way to this text because you have a more formal interest in research. Research is typically divided into the categories of *basic* and *applied*. Basic research is motivated by intellectual interest in a phenomenon and has as its goal the extension of knowledge. Although basic research may eventually inform practice, its primary purpose is to know more about a phenomenon. Al Gore, in his award-winning movie *An Inconvenient Truth*, shares quite a bit of basic research (such as the rate at which the polar ice caps have been melting) as evidence of global warming. This basic research of course has implications for what people might do to stem global warming.

Applied research is undertaken to improve the quality of practice of a particular discipline. Applied social science researchers generally are interested in speaking to an audience different from that of basic researchers. They hope their work will be used by administrators and policymakers to improve the way things are done. For example, a public health researcher might undertake a study to find out how healthier school lunch programs are affecting childhood obesity. The findings of this study would then inform legislators revising the policy, as well as school dieticians and administrators whose responsibility it is to implement the policy.

There are many forms of applied research. Evaluation studies constitute one form of applied research common to many of us in fields of social practice. The difference between evaluation and research, which are both forms of systematic inquiry, lies in the questions asked, not in the methods used, for the methods in each are essentially the same. Evaluation research collects data or evidence on the worth or value of a program, process, or technique. Its main purpose is to establish a basis for decision making, "to make judgments about the program, improve program effectiveness, and/or inform decisions about future programming" (Patton, 2015, p. 18). Other common forms of applied research are action research and appreciative inquiry, both of which focus on facilitating change. The goal of action research is to address a specific *problem* in a practice-based setting, such as a classroom, a workplace, a program, or an organization (Herr & Anderson, 2015). By contrast, appreciative inquiry is often used in organizational settings to tell stories of what is positive or appreciated and effective in those organizations, to facilitate innovation (Cooperrider, Whitney, & Stavros, 2008) rather than focusing on problems. Both of these kinds of research typically involve the participants in the research process, thus blurring the distinction between change processes and research. Further, while some training in research is helpful, both action research and appreciative inquiry are often conducted by people who are interested in facilitating change in their work, community, or family. They decide to "experiment" with the situation, while documenting what happens when trying a new strategy or intervention. Typically, many interventions or strategies are implemented by participants over time. The results and the unfolding process are continually documented, making apparent the process of finding either the most effective solutions to practice-based problems (action research) or what innovations arise when organizations focus on sharing positive appreciative stories among its members (appreciative inquiry).

In its broadest sense, research is a systematic process by which we know more about something than we did before engaging in the process. We can engage in this process to contribute to the knowledge base in a field (pure research), improve the practice of a particular discipline (applied research), assess the value of something (evaluation research), or address a particular, localized problem (action research).

THE NATURE OF QUALITATIVE RESEARCH

Most people know what an experiment is or what a survey is. We might know someone in a weight loss experiment in which some use diet alone, some use diet and exercise, and others use diet, exercise, and an appetite suppressant. This is an experiment to see which "treatment" results in the most weight loss. Randomly dividing participants into three groups will test which treatment has brought about the most improvement. Surveys are also familiar to us, as when we are stopped in the shopping mall and asked to respond to some survey questions about products we use, movies we've seen, and so on. Survey research describes "what is"; that is, how variables are distributed across a population or phenomenon. For example, we might be interested in who is likely to watch which television shows and their age, race, gender, level of education, and occupation.

There are a number of variations on these designs, but basically experimental approaches try to determine the cause of events and to predict similar events in the future. Survey or descriptive designs are intended to systematically describe the facts and characteristics of a given phenomenon or the relationships between events and phenomena. Sometimes these designs are grouped together and labeled "quantitative" because the focus is on how much or how many, and results are usually presented in numerical form.

Rather than determining cause and effect, predicting, or describing the distribution of some attribute among a population, we might be interested in uncovering the meaning of a phenomenon for those involved. Qualitative researchers are interested in understanding how people interpret their experiences, how they construct their worlds, and what meaning they attribute to their experiences. For example, rather than studying retired adults to find out the percentage and characteristics of those who take on part-time jobs after retirement, which could be done through a survey, we might be more interested in how people adjust to retirement, how they think about this phase of their lives, the process they engaged in when moving from full-time work to retirement, and so on. These questions are about *understanding* their experiences and would call for a qualitative design. While Braun and Clarke's (2013) distinction between qualitative and quantitative research is somewhat simplified, they write that "the most basic definition of qualitative research is that it uses *words* as **data** . . . collected and analyzed in all sorts of ways. Quantitative research, in contrast, uses *numbers* as data and analyzes them using statistical techniques" (pp. 3–4, emphasis in original).

WHERE DOES QUALITATIVE RESEARCH COME FROM?

Decades before what we now call "qualitative research" or "qualitative inquiry" became popular, anthropologists and sociologists were asking questions about people's lives, the social and cultural contexts in which they lived, the ways in which they understood their worlds, and so on. Anthropologists and sociologists went into "the field," whether it was a village in Africa or a city in the United States, observed what was going on, interviewed people in these settings, and collected and analyzed artifacts and personal and public documents relevant to understanding what they were studying. The written accounts of these studies were qualitative in nature. Bogdan and Biklen (2011) point out that Chicago sociologists in the 1920s and 1930s emphasized "the intersection of social context and biography" that lies at "the roots of contemporary descriptions of qualitative research as *holistic*" (p. 9).

> In addition, especially in the life histories Chicago School sociologists produced, the importance of seeing the world from the perspective of those who were seldom listened to—the criminal,

the vagrant, the immigrant—was emphasized. While not using the phrase, they knew they were "giving voice" to points of view of people marginalized in the society. (p. 10)

In addition to the work of anthropologists and sociologists, people in professional fields such as education, law, counseling, health, and social work have often been interested in specific cases for understanding a phenomenon. Piaget, for example, derived his theory of cognitive development by studying his own two children. Investigative journalism and even the humanities and the arts have also always been interested in portraying people's experiences in specific social contexts.

With regard to the development of what we now call qualitative research, two important mid-twentieth-century publications contributed to its emergence. In 1967, sociologists Barney Glaser and Anselm Strauss published *The Discovery of Grounded Theory: Strategies for Qualitative Research*. Rather than testing theory, their book made a case for building theory from *inductively* analyzing a social phenomenon. This book provided both a theoretical framework and practical strategies for doing this type of research. This book and subsequent work by Strauss and his colleagues continue to define and have an impact on our understanding of qualitative research.

The second publication we would point to as important in defining qualitative research was a monograph by Egon Guba published in 1978, titled *Toward a Methodology of Naturalistic Inquiry in Educational Evaluation*. A study was "naturalistic" if it took place in a real-world setting rather than a laboratory, and whatever was being observed and studied was allowed to happen "naturally." In naturalistic inquiry the investigator does not control or manipulate what is being studied. It is also discovery-oriented research, in which the findings are not predetermined.

The late 1970s and early 1980s saw a growing number of publications contributing to the understanding of this form of inquiry (see, for example, Bogdan & Taylor, 1975; Guba & Lincoln, 1981; Patton, 1978, 1981). Researchers in many fields outside the traditional disciplines of anthropology and sociology, such as education, health, administration, social work, and so on, began to adopt qualitative methods. Discipline-specific journals began publishing qualitative studies, and several journals devoted to qualitative research were established.

Today there are hundreds of books on various aspects of qualitative research, as well as journals and regularly held conferences devoted to qualitative research. In fact, there are now numerous paradigms and strategies of inquiry and analysis methods to choose from in designing a study, depending on the study's purpose and theoretical orientation (Lincoln, Lynham, & Guba, 2011). Although this is certainly good news in terms of presenting the researcher with a rich array of choices for doing qualitative research, making sense of all this material can be a daunting task for novice and experienced researchers alike!

PHILOSOPHICAL PERSPECTIVES

In the preceding section we presented a brief sketch of the emergence of what we today call qualitative research. An understanding of the nature of this type of research can also be gained by looking at its philosophical foundations. Unfortunately, there is almost no consistency across writers in how this aspect of qualitative research is discussed. Some talk about traditions and theoretical underpinnings (Bogdan & Biklen, 2011), theoretical traditions and orientations (Patton, 2015); others, about paradigms and perspectives (Denzin & Lincoln, 2011), philosophical assumptions and interpretive frameworks (Creswell, 2013), or epistemology and theoretical perspectives (Crotty, 1998). In true qualitative fashion, each writer makes sense of the underlying philosophical influences in his or her own way. In this section we share our understanding.

First, it is helpful to philosophically position qualitative research among other forms of research. Such a positioning entails what one believes about the nature of reality (also called ontology) and the nature of knowledge (epistemology). Most texts on qualitative research address philosophical foundations of this type of research in contrast to other types (Creswell, 2013; Denzin & Lincoln, 2011; Patton, 2015). Prasad's (2005) discussion of interpretive, critical, and "post" (as in postmodernism, poststructuralism, and postcolonialism) traditions is helpful here, as are typologies proposed by Carr and Kemmis (1995) and Lather (1992, 2006). Carr and Kemmis make distinctions among three forms of research—positivist, interpretive, and critical. To this typology Lather adds poststructural and postmodern.

A positivist orientation assumes that reality exists "out there" and that it is observable, stable, and measurable. Knowledge gained through the study of this reality has been labeled "scientific," and it included the establishment of "laws." Experimental research assumed a positivist stance. The rigidity of this perspective has given way to logical empiricism and postpositivism. Postpositivism recognizes that knowledge is relative rather than absolute but "it is possible, using empirical evidence, to distinguish between more and less plausible claims" (Patton, 2015, p. 106).

Interpretive research, which is the most common type of qualitative research, assumes that reality is socially constructed; that is, there is no single, observable reality. Rather, there are multiple realities, or interpretations, of a single event. Researchers do not "find" knowledge; they construct it. Constructivism is a term often used interchangeably with interpretivism. Creswell (2013) explains:

> In this worldview, individuals seek understanding of the world in which they live and work. They develop subjective meanings of their experiences. . . . These meanings are varied and multiple, leading the researcher to look for the complexity of views. . . . Often these subjective meanings are negotiated socially and historically. In other words, they are not simply imprinted on individuals but are formed through interaction with others (hence social constructivism) and through historical and cultural norms that operate in individuals' lives. (pp. 24–25)

In addition to social constructivism informing interpretive or qualitative research, phenomenology and symbolic interactionism are also important. Philosophers Edmund Husserl and Alfred Schutz presented phenomenology early in the twentieth century as a major orientation to social science. Patton (2015) explains that "by phenomenology Husserl (1913) meant the study of how people describe things and experience them through their senses. His most basic philosophical assumption was that *we can only know what we experience* by attending to perceptions and meanings that awaken our conscious awareness" (p. 116). The experience a person has includes the way in which the experience is interpreted. There is no "objective" experience that stands outside its interpretation. Symbolic interactionism, which is most often associated with George Herbert Mead, also focuses on meaning and interpretation, especially that which people create and share through their interactions. "The importance of symbolic interactionism to qualitative inquiry is its distinct emphasis on the importance of symbols and the interpretative processes that undergird interactions as fundamental to understanding human behavior" (Patton, 2015, p. 134).

Critical research goes beyond uncovering the interpretation of people's understandings of their world. Critical research has its roots in several traditions and currently encompasses a variety of approaches. Early influences include Marx's analysis of socioeconomic conditions and class structures; Habermas's notions of technical, practical, and emancipatory knowledge; and Freire's transformative and emancipatory education. A basic assumption of critical research is that "all thought is mediated by power relations that are historically and socially constructed" and that "Inquiry that aspires to the name 'critical' must be connected to an attempt to confront the injustice of a particular society" (Kincheloe, McLaren, & Steinberg, 2011, p. 164). Today, critical research draws from feminist theory, critical race theory, postcolonial theory, queer theory, critical ethnography, and so on. In critical inquiry the goal is to critique and challenge, to transform and empower. Crotty (1998, p. 113) writes that "It is a contrast between a research that seeks merely to understand and research that challenges . . . between a research that reads the situation in terms of interaction and community and a research that reads it in terms of conflict and oppression . . . between a research that accepts the *status quo* and a research that seeks to bring about change." Those who engage in critical research frame their research questions in terms of power—who has it, how it's negotiated, what structures in society reinforce the current distribution of power, and so on.

A fourth orientation in Lather's (1992, 2006) framework is poststructuralism or postmodernism. Research from a postmodern perspective is quite different from the previous three forms discussed, and there are many different and nuanced discussions of these "post" methodologies (Lather & St. Pierre, 2013); nevertheless, it is influencing our thinking about interpretive qualitative research and also critical research. A postmodern world is one where the rationality, scientific method, and certainties of the modern world no longer hold. According to postmodernists, explanations for the way things are in the world are nothing but myths or grand narratives. There is no single "truth" with a capital "T"; rather, there are multiple "truths." Postmodernists celebrate diversity among people, ideas, and institutions. By accepting the diversity and plurality of the world, no one element is privileged or more powerful than another. Congruent with this perspective, postmodern research is highly experimental, playful, and creative, and no two postmodern studies look alike. Grbich (2013) notes that "most forms of qualitative research now have an established postmodern position: for example, ethnography, grounded theory, action, evaluation research, phenomenology and feminist research. Postmodernism favors descriptive and individual inter-preted mini-narratives, which provide explanations for small-scale situations located within particular contexts with no pretentions of abstract theory, universality, or generalizability involved" (p. 8). This perspective is sometimes combined with feminist, critical theory, and queer approaches.

We summarize these four perspectives in Table 1.1. Across the top are the four perspectives just discussed—positivist/postpo-sitivist, interpretive/constructivist, critical, and postmodern/poststructural. Each perspective is viewed in terms of the *purpose* of research from this perspective, *types* of research found within each, and how each perspective views *reality*. This summary table is not meant to be interpreted as a rigid differentiation of these perspectives—in fact, there is overlap in actual research designs and orientations, such as in "critical ethnography" and "poststruc-tual feminist research"—but the table helps point out some of the assumptions. Lather (2006) has her students "play" with these categories—asking, "'If this research paradigm were a personality disorder . . . or a sport . . . or a drink'" (p. 36), what it might look like or be called—to help them understand the differences on another level. For example, a public event for each of these paradigms could be, for positivist, a marching band or classical ballet, which is precise and rule-dominated; for interpretive, a community picnic, which is cooperative, interactive, and human-istic; for critical, a March of Dimes telethon, because of its concern with marginal groups; and for postmodern, a circus,

TABLE 1.1. EPISTEMOLOGICAL PERSPECTIVES.

	Positivist/ Postpositivist	Interpretive/Constructivist	Critical	Postmodern/Poststructural
Purpose	Predict, control, generalize	Describe, understand, interpret	Change, emancipate, empower	Deconstruct, problematize, question, interrupt
Types	Experimental, quasi-survey, quasi-experimental	Phenomenology, ethnography, hermeneutic, grounded theory, naturalistic/qualitative	Neo-Marxist, feminist, participatory action research (PAR), critical race theory, critical ethnography	Postcolonial, poststructural, postmodern, queer theory
Reality	Objective, external, out there	Multiple realities, context-bound	Multiple realities, situated in political, social, cultural contexts (one reality is privileged)	Questions assumption that there is a place where reality resides; "Is there a there there?"

amusement park, or carnival, because of its multiplicity of perspectives and stimuli and no single reference point.

Differences among these four philosophical orientations as they would play out in a research study can be illustrated by showing how investigators from different perspectives might go about conducting research on the topic of the high school dropout—or, as it is sometimes referred to, noncompletion. From a positivist/postpositivist perspective you might begin by hypothesizing that students drop out of high school because of low self-esteem. You could then design an intervention program to raise the self-esteem of students at risk. You set up an experiment controlling for as many variables as possible and then measure the results.

The same topic from an interpretive or qualitative perspective would not test theory, set up an experiment, or measure anything. Rather, you might be interested in understanding the experience of dropping out from the perspective of the noncompleters themselves, or you might be interested in discovering which factors differentiate dropouts from those who may have been at risk but who nevertheless completed high school. You will need to interview students, perhaps observe them in or out of school, and review documents such as counselors' reports and personal diaries.

From a critical research perspective, you would be interested in how the social institution of school is structured such that the interests of some members and classes of society are preserved and perpetuated at the expense of others. You would investigate the way in which schools are structured, the mechanisms (for example, attendance, tests, grade levels) that reproduce certain patterns of response, and so on. You might also design and carry out the study in collaboration with high school noncompleters themselves. This collective investigation and analysis of the underlying socioeconomic, political, and cultural causes of the problem is designed to result in collective action to address the problem (if, indeed, noncompletion is identified as the problem by students themselves).

Finally, a postmodern or poststructural inquiry would question and "disrupt" the dichotomies (for example completer-noncompleter, successful-unsuccessful, graduate-dropout) inherent in the research problem. The "findings" of this postmodern study might be presented in the form of narratives, field notes, and creative formats such as drama and poetry. It would be important to present multiple perspectives, multiple voices, and multiple interpretations of what it means to be a high school dropout.

It should be pointed out that these four orientations to research might intersect in various studies. For example, one could combine a poststructural and feminist orientation, as English (2005) did with her analysis of learning in feminist nonprofit organizations; or a critical ethnography, as in Liu, Manias, and Gerdtz's (2012) study of medication communication between nurses and patients during nursing handovers on medical wards.

Getting started on a research project begins with examining your own orientation to basic tenets about the nature of reality, the purpose of doing research, and the type of knowledge to be produced through your efforts. Which orientation is the best fit with your views? Which is the best fit for answering the question you have in mind?

Definition and Characteristics of Qualitative Research

Given all of the philosophical, disciplinary, and historical influences on what has emerged as qualitative research, it's no wonder that the term defies a simple definition. There has even been some debate as to the best term to use—naturalistic, interpretive, or qualitative. Preissle (2006) recognizes the shortcomings of using *qualitative* but concludes that "the label has worked" because "it *is* vague, broad and inclusive enough to cover the variety of research practices that scholars have been developing. Thus we have journals and handbooks . . . that identify themselves as qualitative venues while other journals and handbooks have titles such as ethnography or interviewing that represent particular facets of qualitative practice" (p. 690).

Most writers advance definitions that reflect the complexity of the method. Denzin and Lincoln (2013), for example, begin their paragraph-long definition by saying "qualitative research is a situated activity that locates the observer in the world. Qualitative research consists of a set of interpretive, material practices that make the world visible" (p. 6). After several sentences on the practice of qualitative research, they conclude with "qualitative researchers study things in their natural settings, attempting to make sense of, or interpret, phenomena in terms of the meanings people bring to them" (p. 3). A more concise though several years older definition that we particularly like is by Van Maanen (1979): Qualitative research is "an umbrella term covering an array of interpretive techniques which seek to describe, decode, translate, and otherwise come to terms with the meaning, not the frequency, of certain more or less naturally occurring phenomena in the social world" (p. 520). Basically, qualitative researchers are interested in *understanding the meaning people have constructed*; that is, how people make sense of their world and the experiences they have in the world.

A definition of something as complex as qualitative research is not much more than a beginning to understanding what this type of research is all about. Another strategy is to delineate its major characteristics. As might be expected, different writers have emphasized different characteristics, although there is certainly some overlap. The following four characteristics are identified by most as key to understanding the nature of qualitative research: the focus is on process, understanding, and meaning; the researcher is the primary instrument of data collection and analysis; the process is inductive; and the product is richly descriptive.

FOCUS ON MEANING AND UNDERSTANDING

Drawing from the philosophies of constructionism, phenomenology, and symbolic interactionism, qualitative researchers are interested in how people interpret their experiences, how they construct their worlds, and what meaning they attribute to their experiences. The overall purposes of qualitative research are to achieve an *understanding* of how people make sense out of their lives, delineate the process (rather than the outcome or product) of meaning-making, and describe how people interpret what they experience. Patton (1985) explains:

> [Qualitative research] is an effort to understand situations in their uniqueness as part of a particular context and the interactions there. This understanding is an end in itself, so that it is not attempting to predict what may happen in the future necessarily, but to understand the nature of that setting—what it

> means for participants to be in that setting, what their lives are like, what's going on for them, what their meanings are, what the world looks like in that particular setting—and in the analysis to be able to communicate that faithfully to others who are interested in that setting. . . . The analysis strives for depth of understanding. (p. 1)

The key concern is understanding the phenomenon of interest from the participants' perspectives, not the researcher's. This is sometimes referred to as the *emic* or insider's perspective, versus the *etic* or outsider's view. An entertaining example of the difference in the two perspectives can be found in Bohannan's classic, *Shakespeare in the Bush* (1992). As she tells the story of *Hamlet* to elders in a West African village, they instruct her on the "true meaning" of the drama, based on their beliefs and cultural values.

RESEARCHER AS PRIMARY INSTRUMENT

A second characteristic of all forms of qualitative research is that *the researcher is the primary instrument for data collection and analysis*. Since understanding is the goal of this research, the human instrument, which is able to be immediately responsive and adaptive, would seem to be the ideal means of collecting and analyzing data. Other advantages are that the researcher can expand his or her understanding through nonverbal as well as verbal communication, process information (data) immediately, clarify and summarize material, check with respondents for accuracy of interpretation, and explore unusual or unanticipated responses.

However, the human instrument has shortcomings and biases that can have an impact on the study. Further, there is a particular theoretical framework or lens that informs a research study that the researcher makes visible. Rather than trying to eliminate these biases or "subjectivities," it is important to identify them and monitor them in relation to the theoretical framework and in light of the researcher's own interests, to make clear how they may be shaping the collection and interpretation of data. In a classic analysis of subjectivity in qualitative research, Peshkin (1988, p. 18) goes so far as to make the case that one's subjectivities "can be seen as virtuous, for it is the basis of researchers making a distinctive contribution, one that results from the unique configuration of their personal qualities joined to the data they have collected." Further, postmodernist and poststructural forms of qualitative research strive to make both the researcher's and participants' subjectivity visible (Lather & St. Pierre, 2013). While subjectivity is not the focus of most qualitative studies, it is important for researchers to deal with their own potential influences.

AN INDUCTIVE PROCESS

Often qualitative researchers undertake a qualitative study because there is a lack of theory or an existing theory fails to adequately explain a phenomenon. Therefore, another important characteristic of qualitative research is that the process is *inductive*; that is, researchers gather data to build concepts, hypotheses, or theories rather than deductively testing hypotheses as in positivist research. Qualitative researchers build toward theory from observations and intuitive understandings gleaned from being in the field. Bits and pieces of information from interviews, observations, or documents are combined and ordered into larger themes as the researcher works from the particular to the general. Typically, findings inductively derived from the data in a qualitative study are in the form of themes, categories, typologies, concepts, tentative hypotheses, and even theory about a particular aspect of practice.

This is not to say that the qualitative researcher has a blank mind devoid of any thoughts about the phenomenon under study. All investigations are informed by some discipline-specific theoretical framework that enables us to focus our inquiry and interpret the data. However, this framework is not tested deductively as it might be in an experiment; rather, the framework is informed by what we inductively learn in the field (for more on the role of the theoretical framework, see Chapter Four).

RICH DESCRIPTION

Finally, the product of a qualitative inquiry is *richly descriptive*. Words and pictures rather than numbers are used to convey what the researcher has learned about a phenomenon. There are likely to be descriptions of the context, the participants involved, and the activities of interest. In addition, data in the form of quotes from documents, field notes, and participant interviews, excerpts from videotapes, electronic communication, or a combination of these are always included in support of the findings of the study. These quotes and excerpts contribute to the descriptive nature of qualitative research.

OTHER CHARACTERISTICS AND COMPETENCIES

In addition to the characteristics common to all types of qualitative research, several others are more or less common to most forms of qualitative research. Ideally, for example, the design of a qualitative study is *emergent and flexible*, responsive to changing conditions of the study in progress. This is not always the case, however, as thesis and dissertation committees, funding agencies, and human subjects review boards often require the design of the study to be specified ahead of time. Sample selection in qualitative research is usually (but not always) nonrandom, *purposeful*, and small, as opposed to larger, more random sampling in quantitative research. Finally the investigator in qualitative research often spends a substantial amount of *time in the natural setting* (the "field") of the study, often in intense contact with participants.

Given the nature and characteristics of qualitative research, the following researcher competencies are desirable:

- *A questioning stance with regard to your work and life context.* Qualitative research is a means of answering questions, so you must first look with a questioning eye to what is happening in your life. Why are things the way they are?
- *High tolerance for ambiguity.* The design of a qualitative study is flexible, relevant variables are not known ahead of time, findings are inductively derived in the data analysis process, and so on. Thus one has to be comfortable with the ebb and flow of a qualitative investigation and trust in the process.
- *Being a careful observer.* Conducting observations is a systematic process, not a casual occurrence; you can increase your skill in observing through practice.
- *Asking good questions.* Interviewing is often the primary data collection strategy in qualitative studies. Getting good data in an

interview is dependent on your asking well-chosen open-ended questions that can be followed up with probes and requests for more detail.

- *Thinking inductively.* Data analysis requires the ability to think inductively, moving from specific raw data to abstract categories and concepts.
- *Comfort with writing.* Since findings are presented in words (sometimes also making use of images), not numbers as in quantitative research, a report of a qualitative study requires more writing. The final product is typically longer than a quantitative write-up.

Chapters in this book are designed to help develop these competencies. Chapter Four, for example, discusses how to raise questions that are appropriate for a qualitative study. Chapters on interviewing, observations, data analysis, and writing up qualitative research speak directly to the other competencies.

By way of a summary for this chapter, Table 1.2 displays a comparison of characteristics of qualitative research with the more familiar quantitative approach. Such a comparison helps illuminate some of the basic differences between the two types of research. However, as many experienced researchers can attest, this table sets up a somewhat artificial dichotomy between the two types; it should be viewed as an aid to understanding differences, not as a set of hard-and-fast rules governing each type of research. In the actual conduct of research, differences on several points of comparison are far less rigid than the table suggests.

SUMMARY

Qualitative research is a type of research that encompasses a number of philosophical orientations and approaches. The antecedents to what we call qualitative research today can be traced back to anthropology, sociology, and various applied fields of study such as journalism, education, social work, medicine, and law. The 1960s and 1970s saw a number of publications focusing on the methodology itself, such that by the last decades of the twentieth century qualitative research was established as a research methodology in its own right.

TABLE 1.2. CHARACTERISTICS OF QUALITATIVE AND QUANTITATIVE RESEARCH.

Point of Comparison	Qualitative Research	Quantitative Research
Focus of research	Quality (nature, essence)	Quantity (how much, how many)
Philosophical roots	Phenomenology, symbolic interactionism, constructivism	Positivism, logical empiricism, realism
Associated phrases	Fieldwork, ethnographic, naturalistic, grounded, constructivist	Experimental, empirical, statistical
Goal of investigation	Understanding, description, discovery, meaning, hypothesis generating	Prediction, control, description, confirmation, hypothesis testing
Design characteristics	Flexible, evolving, emergent	Predetermined, structured
Sample	Small, nonrandom, purposeful, theoretical	Large, random, representative
Data collection	Researcher as primary instrument, interviews, observations, documents	Inanimate instruments (scales, tests, surveys, questionnaires, computers)
Primary mode of analysis	Inductive, constant comparative method	Deductive, statistical
Findings	Comprehensive, holistic, expansive, richly descriptive	Precise, numerical

In this chapter we contrasted positivist/postpositivist (quantitative), interpretive (qualitative), critical, and postmodern approaches to research. We also briefly discussed the philosophies that most inform qualitative research, including constructivism, phenomenology, and symbolic interactionism. What all of these philosophies have in common is an emphasis on experience, understanding, and meaning-making, all characteristics of qualitative inquiry. In the final section of the chapter we defined qualitative research and delineated its major characteristics—the focus is on understanding the meaning of experience, the researcher is the primary instrument in data collection and analysis, the process is inductive, and rich description characterizes the end product.

CHAPTER TWO

SIX COMMON QUALITATIVE RESEARCH DESIGNS

In fields from education to social work to anthropology to management science, researchers, students, and practitioners are conducting qualitative studies. It is not surprising, then, that different disciplines and fields ask different questions and have evolved somewhat different strategies and procedures. Although *qualitative research* or *qualitative inquiry* remains the umbrella term, writers of qualitative texts have organized the diversity of forms of qualitative research in various ways. Patton (2015) discusses sixteen "theoretical traditions"; some, like ethnography and grounded theory, are familiar classifications, whereas others, such as semiotics and chaos theory, are less common. Creswell (2013) presents five "approaches": narrative research, phenomenology, grounded theory, ethnography, and case study. Tesch (1990) lists 45 approaches divided into designs (such as case study), data analysis techniques (such as discourse analysis), and disciplinary orientation (such as ethnography). Denzin and Lincoln (2011) include a number of chapters on major "strategies of inquiry" (p. xi), such as, among others, case study, ethnography, grounded theory, and participatory action research. As this brief overview suggests, there is no consensus as to how to classify "the baffling numbers of choices or approaches" to qualitative research (Creswell, 2013, p. 7).

Given the variety of qualitative research strategies, we have chosen to present six of the more commonly used approaches to doing qualitative research that we have encountered in our many years of experience advising doctoral students, teaching qualitative research courses, and conducting our own qualitative research: basic qualitative research, phenomenology, grounded theory, ethnography, narrative analysis, and qualitative case study. (Qualitative action research, which focuses on solving a problem in practice and implementing change during the research process, is increasingly common; we discuss this in the next chapter.) Because these types of qualitative research have some attributes in common, they fall under the umbrella concept of "qualitative." However, they each have a somewhat different focus, resulting in variations in how the research question may be asked, sample selection, data collection and analysis, and write-up. There can also be overlaps in these types of research, wherein a researcher may combine two or more, such as in an ethnographic case study. For now, we present these six approaches and then discuss some of the overlaps.

BASIC QUALITATIVE RESEARCH

A challenge especially to those new to qualitative research is trying to figure out what "kind" of qualitative research study they are doing and what their "theoretical framework" is. Our understanding of theoretical framework is discussed at length in Chapter Four, and it is different from what we mean by an epistemological framework; that is, a perspective on the nature of or types of knowledge explored by qualitative researchers. Qualitative research is based on the belief that knowledge is constructed by people in an ongoing fashion as they engage in and make meaning of an activity, experience, or phenomenon. (This is in contrast to quantitative research paradigms that tend to be based on the belief that knowledge is preexisting, waiting to be discovered.)

In our experience, in applied fields of practice such as education, administration, health, social work, counseling, business, and so on, the most common "type" of qualitative research is a basic interpretive study. Here, researchers simply describe their study as a "qualitative research study" without declaring it a particular *type* of qualitative study—such as a phenomenological, grounded theory, narrative analysis, or ethnographic study. Over the years there has been a struggle with how to label this common qualitative study using words such as *generic, basic,* and *interpretive*. Since all qualitative research is interpretive, and "generic" doesn't convey a clear meaning, we have come to prefer labeling this type of study a *basic qualitative study*.

A central characteristic of all qualitative research is that individuals construct reality in interaction with their social worlds. Constructivism thus underlies what we are calling a basic qualitative study. Here the researcher is interested in understanding the meaning a phenomenon has for those involved. Meaning, however, "is not discovered but constructed. Meaning does not inhere in the object, merely waiting for someone to come upon it. . . . Meanings are constructed by human beings as they engage with the world they are interpreting" (Crotty, 1998, pp. 42–43). Thus qualitative researchers conducting a basic qualitative study would be interested in (1) how people interpret their experiences, (2) how they construct their worlds, and (3) what meaning they attribute to their experiences. The overall purpose is to *understand* how people make sense of their lives and their experiences.

Although this understanding characterizes all of qualitative research, other types of qualitative studies have an *additional* dimension. For example, a phenomenological study seeks understanding about the essence and the underlying structure of the phenomenon. Ethnography strives to understand the interaction of individuals not just with others, but also with the culture of the society in which they live. A grounded theory study seeks not just to understand, but also to build a substantive theory about the phenomenon of interest. Narrative analysis uses the stories people tell, analyzing them in various ways, to understand the meaning of the experiences as revealed in the story. If the unit of analysis is a bounded system—a case, such as a person, a program, or an event—one would label such a study a "qualitative case study." These types of qualitative research are discussed in subsequent sections of this chapter. To some extent all forms of qualitative research are trying to uncover participants' understandings of their experiences.

Basic qualitative studies can be found throughout the disciplines and in applied fields of practice. They are probably the most common form of qualitative research found in education. Data are collected through interviews, observations, or document analysis. What questions are asked, what is observed, and what documents are deemed relevant will depend on the disciplinary theoretical framework of the study (see Chapter Four). An educational psychologist, for example, might be interested in understanding the teaching-learning transaction in a classroom, whereas a sociologist would be more interested in social roles and social interaction patterns in the same classroom. The analysis of the data involves identifying recurring patterns that characterize the data. Findings *are* these recurring patterns or themes supported by the data from which they were derived. The overall interpretation will be the researcher's understanding of the participants' understanding of the phenomenon of interest.

Book-length examples of basic qualitative studies are Levinson and Levinson's (1996) study of women's development, based on in-depth interviews with 15 homemakers, 15 corporate businesswomen, and 15 academics, or Tisdell's (2003) study of 31 adult educators and how spirituality informs both their own development and their emancipatory educator efforts as cultural workers. Journal-length examples of basic qualitative research studies can be found in the research journals of most fields. For example, Kim (2014) conducted a qualitative study to uncover the process Korean retirees engaged in in transitioning into a postretirement second career. Fernandez, Breen, and Simpson (2014) examined how women with bipolar disorder renegotiate their identities as a result of experiences of loss and recovery. As another example of a basic qualitative study, Merriam and Muhamad (2013) studied Malaysian traditional healers, identifying the roles they play in diagnosing and treating people with cancer.

In summary, all qualitative research is interested in how meaning is constructed, how people make sense of their lives and their worlds. The *primary* goal of a basic qualitative study is to uncover and interpret these meanings.

PHENOMENOLOGY

Because the philosophy of phenomenology also underlies qualitative research, some assume that all qualitative research is phenomenological, and certainly in one sense it is. Phenomenology is both a twentieth-century school of philosophy associated with Husserl (1970) and a type of qualitative research. From the philosophy of phenomenology comes a focus on the experience itself and how experiencing something is transformed into consciousness. Phenomenologists are not interested in modern science's efforts to categorize, simplify, and reduce phenomena to abstract laws. Rather, phenomenologists are interested in our "lived experience" (Van Manen, 2014, p. 26); such a focus requires us to go directly "'to the things themselves' . . . to turn toward phenomena which had been blocked from sight by the theoretical patterns in front of them" (Spiegelberg, 1965, p. 658). Phenomenology is a study of people's conscious experience of their life-world; that is, their "everyday life and social action" (Schram, 2003, p. 71). Van Manen (2014) explains it this way: "Phenomenology is the way of access to the world as we experience it prereflectively. Prereflective experience is the ordinary experience that we live in and that we live through for most, if not all, of our day-to-day existence" (p. 28).

Although all of qualitative research draws from the philosophy of phenomenology in its emphasis on experience and interpretation, one could also conduct a phenomenological study by using the particular "tools" of phenomenology. This type of research is based on

> the assumption that *there is an essence or essences to shared experience.* These essences are the core meanings mutually understood through a phenomenon commonly experienced. The experiences of different people are bracketed, analyzed, and compared to identify the essences of the phenomenon, for example, the essence of loneliness, the essence of being a mother, or the essence of being a participant in a particular program. The assumption of essence, like the ethnographer's assumption that culture exists and is important, becomes the defining characteristic of a purely phenomenological study. (Patton, 2015, pp. 116–117, emphasis in original)

The task of the phenomenologist, then, is to depict the essence or basic structure of experience. Often these studies are of intense human experiences such as love, anger, betrayal, and so on. Prior beliefs about a phenomenon of interest are temporarily put aside, or bracketed, so as not to interfere with seeing or intuiting the elements or structure of the phenomenon. When belief is temporarily suspended, consciousness itself becomes heightened and can be examined in the same way that an object of consciousness can be examined.

To get at the essence or basic underlying structure of the meaning of an experience, the phenomenological interview is the primary method of data collection. Prior to interviewing those who have had direct experience with the phenomenon, the researcher usually explores his or her own experiences, in part to examine dimensions of the experience and in part to become aware of personal prejudices, viewpoints, and assumptions. This process is called *epoche*, "a Greek word meaning to refrain from judgment. . . . In the Epoche, the everyday understandings, judgments, and knowings are set aside, and the phenomena are revisited" (Moustakas, 1994, p. 33). These prejudices and assumptions are then *bracketed* or temporarily set aside so that we can examine consciousness itself. Of course the extent to which any person can bracket his or her biases and assumptions is open to debate. This process from phenomenological research, however, has influenced all of qualitative research in that now it is common practice for researchers to examine their biases and assumptions about the phenomenon of interest before embarking on a study.

In addition to epoche or bracketing, there are other strategies unique to phenomenological research. *Phenomenological reduction* is the process of continually returning to the essence of the experience to derive the inner structure or meaning in and of itself. We isolate the phenomenon in order to comprehend its essence. *Horizontalization* is the process of laying out all the data for examination and treating the data as having equal weight; that is, all pieces of data have equal value at the initial data analysis stage. These data are then organized into clusters or themes. Moustakas (1994, p. 96) explains that in horizontalization, "there is an interweaving of person, conscious experience, and phenomenon. In the process of explicating the phenomenon, qualities are recognized and described; every perception is granted equal value, nonrepetitive constituents of experience are linked thematically, and a full description is derived." *Imaginative variation* involves viewing the data from various perspectives, as if one were walking around a modern sculpture, seeing different things from different angles.

The product of a phenomenological study is a "composite description that presents the 'essence' of the phenomenon, called the *essential, invariant structure (or essence)*" (Creswell, 2013, p. 82, emphasis in original). This description represents the structure of the experience being studied. "The reader should come away from the phenomenology with the feeling, 'I understand better what it is like for someone to experience that' (Polkinghorne, 1989, p. 46)" (Creswell, 2013 p. 62).

As mentioned earlier, a phenomenological approach is well suited to studying affective, emotional, and often intense human experiences. As an example, Trotman (2006) investigated imagination and creativity in primary school education. He asserts that this phenomenological research revealed "the ways in which these teachers value and interpret the imaginative experience of their pupils" and "suggests particular challenges that professional educators need to address if imaginative experience is to be legitimated and sustained as a worthwhile educational process" (p. 258). In another example, Ruth-Sahd and Tisdell (2007) investigated the meaning of intuitive knowing and how intuitive knowing influenced the practice of novice nurses. In a third example, Ryan, Rapley, and Dziurawiec (2014) conducted a phenomenological study of the meaning of coping in psychiatric patients. These three examples underscore the idea that a phenomenological qualitative study is well suited to studying emotions and affective states.

As with other forms of qualitative research, there are variations in how a phenomenological study is conducted. Moustakas (1994) and Spiegelberg (1965) have both delineated a process for doing such a study that might be helpful to researchers interested in exploring this method. Van Manen's (2014) recent book also provides some guidelines and also explores various strands and traditions that fall under the umbrella of "phenomenology." What is important here is understanding that phenomenology as a philosophy has had an impact on all of qualitative research; however, it is also a *type* of qualitative research with its own focus and methodological strategies.

ETHNOGRAPHY

Of the various types of qualitative research, ethnography is likely to be the most familiar to researchers. Its history can be traced to late nineteenth-century anthropologists who engaged in participant observation in the "field" (for a brief and interesting history, see Tedlock, 2011). Anthropologists "do" ethnography, a research process, as well as write up their findings as an ethnography, a product. Thus ethnography is both a process and a product. Although ethnography originated in the field of anthropology, nowadays researchers from many fields and disciplines may engage in an ethnographic study. Bracken (2011), for example, conducted an ethnographic study of adult education program planning in a feminist community-based organization in Mexico. There are now many forms of ethnography, including life history, critical ethnography, autoethnography (Muncey, 2010), performance ethnography, and feminist ethnography.

The factor that unites all forms of ethnography is its focus on human society and culture. Although *culture* has been variously defined, it essentially refers to the beliefs, values, and attitudes that structure the behavior patterns of a specific group of people. D'Andrade (1992) outlines the criteria used to determine what is called *cultural*:

> To say something is cultural is—at a minimum—to say that it is shared by a significant number of members of a social group; shared in the sense of being behaviorally enacted, physically possessed, or internally thought. Further, this something must be recognized in some special way and at least some others are expected to know about it; that is, it must be intersubjectively shared. Finally, for something to be cultural it must have the potential of being passed on to new group members, to exist with some permanency through time and across space. (p. 230)

Wolcott (2008, p. 22) concurs that culture, which "refers to the various ways different groups go about their lives and to the belief systems associated with that behavior," is the central defining characteristic of an ethnography.

To understand the culture of a group, one must spend time with the group being studied. As Van Maanen (1982, pp. 103–104) notes: "The result of ethnographic inquiry is cultural description. It is, however, a description of the sort that can emerge only from a lengthy period of intimate study and residence in a given social setting. It calls for the language spoken in that setting, first-hand participation in some of the activities that take place there, and, most critically, a deep reliance on intensive work with a few informants drawn from the setting."

Immersion in the site as a participant observer is the primary method of data collection. Interviews, formal and informal, and the analysis of documents, records, and artifacts also constitute the data set, along with a fieldworker's diary of each day's happenings, personal feelings, ideas, impressions, or insights with regard to those events.

At the heart of an ethnography is *thick description*—a term popularized by Geertz (1973). "Culture," Geertz writes, "is not a power, something to which social events, behaviors, institutions, or processes can be causally attributed; it is a context, something within which they can be intelligibly—that is, *thickly*—described" (p. 14). The write-up of an ethnography is more than description, however. While ethnographers want to convey the meanings participants make of their lives, they do so with some interpretation on their part (Wolcott, 2008). An award-winning book-length ethnography by Fadiman (1997) illustrates the power of thick description in a study of a Hmong child in the United States whose medical condition brought about the collision of two cultures' views of medicine and healing. The study also conveys the intensive and sustained immersion in the setting and the extensive data gathering necessary to produce a cultural interpretation of the phenomenon.

Anthropologists often make use of preexisting category schemes of social and cultural behaviors and characteristics to present their findings (see, for example, Murdock, 1983, and Lofland, Snow, Anderson, & Lofland, 2006). Qualitative researchers in other fields focusing on culture are likely to organize their findings into schemes derived from the data themselves. This is called the *emic* perspective, that of the insider to the culture, versus the *etic*, that of the researcher or outsider. Whatever the origin of the organizing concepts or themes, some sort of organization of the data is needed to convey to the reader the sociocultural patterns characteristic of the group under study. It is not enough to only describe the cultural practices; the researcher also depicts his or her understanding of the cultural meaning of the phenomenon.

Next to basic qualitative studies, ethnographic studies are quite common, and examples can be found in many journals and fields of practice. For example, ethnographic studies have been conducted of a women's flat-track roller derby league (Donnelly,

2014), a healthy Native American Indian family (Martin & Yurkovich, 2014), the Royal Ballet of London (Wainwright, Williams, & Turner, 2006), and Wall Street investment bankers (Michel, 2014). It might also be pointed out that just as is the case with phenomenological qualitative studies, sometimes studies are labeled "ethnographic" because of qualitative research's historic link to ethnography. However, to be an ethnographic study, the lens of *culture* must be used to understand the phenomenon.

GROUNDED THEORY

Grounded theory is a specific research methodology introduced in 1967 by sociologists Glaser and Strauss in their book *The Discovery of Grounded Theory*. As is true in other forms of qualitative research, the investigator as the primary instrument of data collection and analysis assumes an inductive stance and strives to derive meaning from the data. The result of this type of qualitative study is a theory that emerges from, or is "grounded" in, the data—hence, grounded theory. Rich description is also important but is not the primary focus of this type of study.

Charmaz (2000) articulates why Glaser and Strauss's book was so "revolutionary":

> It challenged (a) arbitrary divisions between theory and research, (b) views of qualitative research as primarily a precursor to more "rigorous" quantitative methods, (c) claims that the quest for rigor made qualitative research illegitimate, (d) beliefs that qualitative methods are impressionistic and unsystematic, (e) separation of data collection and analysis, and (f) assumptions that qualitative research could produce only descriptive case studies rather than theory development. (p. 511)

What differentiates grounded theory from other types of qualitative research is its focus on building theory (Corbin & Strauss, 2015). The type of theory developed is usually "substantive" rather than formal or "grand" theory. Substantive theory has as its referent specific, everyday-world situations such as the coping mechanisms of returning adult students, or a particular reading program that "works" with low-income children, or dealing with grief in the aftermath of a natural disaster. A substantive theory has a specificity and hence usefulness to practice often lacking in theories that cover more global concerns. Further, grounded theory is particularly useful for addressing questions about process; that is, how something changes over time.

Data in grounded theory studies can come from interviews, observations, and a wide variety of documentary materials. As with other types of qualitative research, grounded theory has its own jargon and procedures for conducting a study. First, data collection is guided by *theoretical sampling* in which "the analyst jointly collects, codes, and analyzes . . . data and decides what data to collect next and where to find them, in order to develop . . . theory as it emerges" (Glaser & Strauss, 1967, p. 45). Second, data are analyzed using *the constant comparative method* of data analysis. Basically, the constant comparative method involves comparing one segment of data with another to determine similarities and differences. Data are grouped together on a similar dimension. The dimension is tentatively given a name; it then becomes a category. The overall object of this analysis is to identify patterns in the data. These patterns are arranged in relationships to each other in the building of a grounded theory. (See Chapter Eight for more discussion on the constant comparative method.)

The constant comparative method of data analysis is widely used in all kinds of qualitative studies, whether or not the researcher is building a grounded theory. This perhaps explains the indiscriminate use of the term *grounded theory* to describe other types of qualitative research, or instances when researchers describe using grounded theory guidelines of data analysis and call it "a grounded theory study." This can be confusing to novice researchers. In fact, Charmaz (2011, p. 360) notes "To date, few grounded theory studies in social justice inquiry demonstrate theory construction. Many, however, show how grounded theory guidelines have sharpened thematic analysis." The inductive comparative nature of data analysis in grounded theory provides a systematic strategy for analyzing any data set. However, the constant comparative method of data analysis need not result in a substantive theory; we believe that it is best to call a study a "grounded theory study" only when a substantive theory results and is identified based on the data.

Building a substantive theory involves the identification of a *core category*, a third identifying characteristic of grounded theory. The core category is the main conceptual element through which all other categories and properties are connected. Strauss (1987, p. 36) explains that the core category "must be *central*, that is, related to as many other categories and their properties as is possible, . . . must appear frequently in the data . . . and must develop the theory." In addition to the core category, the theory consists of other categories, properties, and hypotheses. Categories, and the properties that define or illuminate the categories, are conceptual elements of the theory, all of which are inductively derived from or are "grounded" in the data. Hypotheses are the relationships drawn among categories and properties. These hypotheses are tentative and are derived from the study. They are not set out at the beginning of the study to be tested as in quantitative research.

As with other forms of qualitative research, the methodology of grounded theory has evolved over time; recent publications on grounded theory are from a constructionist's perspective (Charmaz, 2014) and a postmodern perspective (Clarke, 2005). And although originating with sociologists Glaser and Strauss, grounded theory studies can now be found in nearly all disciplines and fields of practice. Al Lily (2014) used a grounded theory methodology to explore how the international academic community of educational technology functions as a "tribe" in the same way that Saudi Arabian Bedouin tribes function culturally, politically, and socially. Stanley's (2006) grounded theory study of older adults' perceptions of well-being involved a core category of "perceived control" interrelated with a basic social process of "trading off." Grounded theory was also the methodology used in a study of rural Latino farmworkers' reasons for participation in a pesticides exposure study (Hohl, Gonzalez, Carosso, Ibarra, & Thompson, 2014).

NARRATIVE INQUIRY

"The oldest and most natural form of sense making" is that of stories or narratives (Jonassen & Hernandez-Serrano, 2002, p. 66). Stories are how we make sense of our experiences, how we communicate with others, and through which we understand the world around us. We watch news stories on television and the Internet, tell stories of our day at work, and read or view other people's stories through text or film. As Daiute (2014, p. xviii) explains, "The power of narrative is not so much that it is *about* life but that it interacts *in* life. Narrative is an ancient practice of human culture, enhanced today with technologies, personal mobilities, and intercultural connections." Narratives are how we share our daily lives, whether it be through cave drawings in ancient times or in a contemporary context, through Facebook, which Daiute calls "a massive contemporary epic narrative" (p. 2). Stories, also called "narratives," have become a popular source of data in qualitative research. The key to this type of qualitative research is the use of stories as data, and more specifically, first-person accounts of experience told in story form having a beginning, middle, and end. Other terms sometimes used for these stories of experience are biography, life history, oral history, autoethnography, and autobiography.

Since the early 1990s, stories have moved to center stage as a source of understanding the meaning of human experience. Numerous texts on narrative research—such as a five-volume series of narrative studies, the most recent being *The Meaning of Others: Narrative Studies of Relationships* (Josselson, Lieblich, & McAdams, 2007), a handbook on narrative analysis (Clandinin, 2007), and the journals *Narrative Inquiry* and *Journal of Narrative and Life History*— have contributed to the popularity of this type of qualitative research. First-person accounts of experience constitute the narrative "text" of this research approach. Whether the account is in the form of autobiography, life history, interview, journal, letters, or other materials that we collect, the text is analyzed for the meaning it has for its author.

Because the "text" of the story forms the data set for what is analyzed in this type of research, the philosophy of hermeneutics, which is the study of written texts, is often cited as informing narrative inquiry. Hermeneutic philosophy focuses on interpretation. Patton (2015) explains:

> Hermeneutics provides a theoretical framework for interpretive understanding, or meaning, with special attention to context and original purpose. . . . Hermeneutics offers a perspective for

interpreting legends, stories, and other texts. . . . To make sense of and interpret a text, it is important to know what the author wanted to communicate, to understand intended meanings, and to place documents in a historical and cultural context (Palmer, 1969). (pp. 136–137)

Patton (2002) points out that although hermeneutics "originated in the study of written texts . . . narrative analysis extends the idea of text to include in-depth interview transcripts, life history narratives, historical memoirs, and creative nonfiction." Further, "the hermeneutical perspective, with its emphasis on interpretation and context, informs narrative studies, as do interpretivist social science, literary nonfiction, and literary criticism (p. 115)." He also notes phenomenology's influence, as narratives are stories of lived experiences.

As with other forms of qualitative research, narrative inquiry makes use of various methodological approaches to analyzing stories (De Fina & Georgakopoulou, 2012; Riessman, 2007). Each approach examines, in some way, how the story is constructed, what linguistic tools are used, and/or the cultural context of the story. Biographical, psychological, and linguistic approaches are the most common. In Denzin's (1989, 2014) biographical approach, the story is analyzed in terms of the importance and influence of gender and race, family of origin, life events and turning point experiences, and other persons in the participant's life. The psychological approach concentrates more on the personal, including thoughts and motivations. This approach "emphasizes inductive processes, contextualized knowledge, and human intention. . . . [It] is holistic in that it acknowledges the cognitive, affective, and motivational dimensions of meaning making. It also takes into account the biological and environmental influences on development" (Rossiter, 1999, p. 78). A linguistic approach, or what Gee (2014) calls discourse analysis, focuses on the language of the story or the spoken text, and also attends to the speaker's intonation, pitch, and pauses. Gee offers eighteen questions by which one can build the analysis. Finally, a linguistic approach analyzes the structure of the narrative (Labov, 1982; Schiffrin, Tannen, & Hamilton, 2001). Here, one summarizes the substance of the narrative and identifies the events and their sequence of occurrence, the meaning of the actions, and the resolution or what finally happens.

The growing popularity of narrative as a means of accessing human action and experience has been accompanied by discussions as to how to best tell people's stories, the role of the researcher in the process, and how trustworthy these narratives are in terms of validity and reliability. Mishler (1995, p. 117) reminds us that "we do not *find* stories; we *make* stories." In fact,

> we retell our respondents' accounts through our analytic redescriptions. We, too, are storytellers and through our concepts and methods—our research strategies, data samples, transcription procedures, specifications of narrative units and structures, and interpretive perspectives—we construct the story and its meaning. In this sense the story is always coauthored, either directly in the process of an interviewer eliciting an account or indirectly through our representing and thus transforming others' texts and discourses. (pp. 117–118)

With so much attention to narrative analysis, there are many examples and variations on this type of qualitative study. For instance, a comprehensive discussion of narrative analysis is accompanied by an example from health geography—that is, how a person's health-related experiences are affected by physical place (Wiles, Rosenberg, & Kearns, 2005); Brockenbrough (2012) afforded his five male participants "multiple opportunities to recount and construct their life stories" as Black queer male teachers in an urban school (p. 746); McAdams, Josselson, and Lieblich (2013) edited a book recounting narrative studies of people at transition points in their lives, such as dealing with divorce in mid-life, transitioning from school to the world of work, recovering from heroin addiction, and so on; in another example, Wilensky and Hansen (2001) had nonprofit executives tell "stories" to uncover their beliefs, values, and assumptions about their work. Finally, Piersol (2014) employed narrative inquiry to gain a deeper understanding of how interpersonal relations might inform outdoor educators' relationship with the land; that is, how participants "listened" to place, thus strengthening ecological relations.

QUALITATIVE CASE STUDIES

The term "case study" is often used interchangeably with "qualitative research," especially when researchers new to qualitative research feel pressure to label their inquiry as something more than just "a qualitative study." However, as with the other types of qualitative research already discussed (phenomenology, ethnography, grounded theory, narrative inquiry), a *qualitative case study* has some defining characteristics that are in addition to what it shares with other forms of qualitative research. Part of the confusion lies in the fact that some case studies employ both qualitative and quantitative methods (see the "mixed methods" discussion in Chapter Three). However, in this chapter on "Types of Qualitative Research" we will limit our discussion to case studies that are exclusively *qualitative* in design. Thus qualitative case studies share with other forms of qualitative research the search for meaning and understanding, the researcher as the primary instrument of data collection and analysis, an inductive investigative strategy, and the end product being richly descriptive.

Modern case study research has antecedents in anthropology, sociology, and psychology. Further, lawyers, doctors, social workers, and even detectives can be involved in researching a "case." But it wasn't until the evolution of qualitative research methods that case studies received attention from a methodological perspective. Back in the 1960s and 1970s, textbooks on research methods were all about variations of experimental designs and statistical methods. Some of these texts included a final catch-all chapter titled "Case Studies" wherein it was acknowledged that there existed the occasional historical or in-depth descriptive study of a phenomenon. By the 1980s, Stake (1988), Yin (1984), Merriam (1988), and others were writing about case study research as a methodology.

A *case study* is an in-depth description and analysis of a bounded system. Part of the confusion surrounding case studies is that the process of conducting a case study is conflated with both the unit of study (the case) and the product of this type of investigation. Yin (2014), for example, defines case study in terms of the research process. "A case study is an empirical inquiry that investigates a contemporary phenomenon (the 'case') within its real-life context, especially when the boundaries between phenomenon and context may not be clearly evident" (p. 16). As Yin (2014) observes, case study is a design particularly suited to situations in which it is impossible to separate the phenomenon's variables from their context. Stake (2005), however, focuses on trying to pinpoint the unit of study—the case. Wolcott (1992) sees it as "an end-product of field-oriented research" (p. 36) rather than a strategy or method.

Of course each of these approaches reveals something about case studies and contributes to a general understanding of the nature of this kind of research. We have concluded, however, that the single most defining characteristic of case study research lies in delimiting the object of study: the case. As Stake suggests, "much qualitative research aims at understanding one thing well: one playground, one band, one Weight Watchers group" (2010, p. 27). Further, case study is less of a methodological choice than "a choice of what is to be studied" (Stake, 2005, p. 443). The "what" is a *bounded system* (Smith, 1978), a single entity, a unit around which there are boundaries. You can "fence in" what you are going to study. The case, then, could be a single person who is a case example of some phenomenon, a program, a group, an institution, a community, or a specific policy. Some examples include Sprow Forté's (2013) case study of a financial literacy program aimed at Latina mothers, Coady's (2013) study of the adult health learning of participants in a particular community-based cardiac rehabilita-tion program in Nova Scotia, and Perry's (2008) case study of the national health policy of Ghana. Miles, Huberman, and Saldaña (2014) think of the case as "a phenomenon of some sort occurring in a bounded context" (p. 28). They graphically present it as a circle with a heart in the center. The heart is the focus of the study, and the circle "defines the edge of the case: what will not be studied" (p. 28).

The unit of analysis, *not* the topic of investigation, characterizes a case study. For example, a study of how older adults learn to use computers would probably be a qualitative study but not a case study because the unit of analysis would be the learners' experi-ences, and an indefinite number of older adult learners and their experiences using computers could be selected for the study. For it to be a case study, *one* particular program or *one* particular classroom of learners (a bounded system), or *one* particular older learner selected on the basis of typicality, uniqueness, success, and so forth, would be the unit of analysis. Stake (2006, p. 1) explains:

> A case is a noun, a thing, an entity; it is seldom a verb, a participle, a functioning. Schools may be our cases—real things that are easy to visualize. . . . Training modules may be our cases—amorphous and abstract, but still things, whereas "training" is not. Nurses may be our cases; we usually do not define "nursing activity" as the case. "Managing," "becoming effective," "giving birth," and "voting" are examples of functioning, not entities we are likely to identify as cases. For our cases, we may select "managers," "production sites," "labor and delivery rooms," or "training sessions for voters." With these cases we find opportunities to examine functioning, but the functioning is not the case.

If the phenomenon you are interested in studying is not intrinsically bounded, it is not a case. One technique for assessing the boundedness of the topic is to ask how finite the data collection would be; that is, whether there is a limit to the number of people involved who could be interviewed or a finite time for observations. If there is no end, actually or theoretically, to the number of people who could be interviewed or to observations that could be conducted, then the phenomenon is not bounded enough to qualify as a case.

Since it is the *unit of analysis* that determines whether a study is a case study, this type of qualitative research stands apart from the other types described in this chapter. The other types of qualitative research—such as ethnography, phenomenology, narrative, and so on—are defined by the focus of the study, not the unit of analysis. And in fact, since it is the unit of analysis—a bounded system—that defines the case, other types of studies can be combined with the case study. Ethnographic case studies are quite common, for example, wherein the culture of a particular social group is studied in depth. In addition, one could build grounded theory within a case study, or present a person's "story," hence combining narrative with case study.

Although our definition of a qualitative case study as "an indepth description and analysis of a bounded system" is congruent with other definitions (Bogdan & Biklen, 2011; Creswell, 2013; Patton, 2015; Stake, 2005), some readers may find Creswell's detailed definition helpful. For him, "case study research is a qualitative approach in which the investigator explores a bounded system (a *case*) or multiple bounded systems (cases) over time, through detailed, in-depth data collection involving *multiple sources of information* (e.g., observations, interviews, audiovisual material, and documents and reports), and reports a case *description* and case-based themes" (2013, p. 97; emphasis in original).

Finally, case studies can be historical, as in the history of an organization or program; biographical, wherein "the researcher conducts extensive interviews with one person for the purpose of collecting a first-person narrative" (Bogdan & Biklen, 2011, p. 63); or comparative. Comparative case studies, also called multicase or multisite case studies, involve collecting and analyzing data from several cases and can be distinguished from the single case study that may have subunits or subcases embedded within (such as students within a school). Taylor (2006), for example, wished to explore learning in nonformal community sites. He looked at state parks as one case and home improvement centers as a second case, comparing what the two had in common in terms of planning and instruction of the educational activity. Another example of a comparative case study is Collins's (2001) and Collins and Hansen's (2011) well-known study of what distinguished companies that sustained top performance over fifteen years from mediocre-performing companies. Eleven companies that went from good to great that met rigorous selection criteria were studied in comparison with average-performing companies. As Miles, Huberman, and Saldaña (2014) point out, the more cases included in a study, and the greater the variation across the cases, the more compelling an interpretation is likely to be. "By looking at a range of similar and contrasting cases, we can understand a single-case finding, grounding it by specifying how and where and, if possible, why it carries on as it does. We can strengthen the precision, the validity, and the stability of the findings" (p. 33). The inclusion of multiple cases is, in fact, a common strategy for enhancing the external validity or generalizability of your findings (see Chapter Nine).

When the Types of Qualitative Research Overlap

The types of qualitative research we have discussed here are the most common, and they are quite distinct from each other in the ways that we have described. However, there are many more particular types of qualitative research, and some qualitative studies that are a combination of types that we have described above. For example, sometimes a researcher might conduct an ethnographic case study, by focusing on the cultural dimension (ethnography) of a particular program (a specific case). Or a researcher could combine grounded theory with case study. An ethnographic study could also make use of narrative interviews as part of the data collection, which is something that Tedlock (2011) considers in her discussion of narrative ethnography.

There are many ways that a qualitative researcher could design a study. How a researcher does so is determined in part by both the theoretical framework of the study (further described in Chapter Four), and the purpose of the study as shown in its focus and research questions. Given that there is no single correct way to define or describe a qualitative study, it is up to the researcher, in determining how and what to label her study, to make a clear justification, drawing on the qualitative research literature as well as her or his own intentions for the research. There are numerous handbooks, edited books, and textbooks in print that include chapters on various types of qualitative research (see, for example, Clandinin, 2007; Creswell, 2013; Denzin & Lincoln, 2011; Knowles & Cole, 2007). When determining the specific type of qualitative study for your investigation, it is helpful to examine numerous sources of literature in order to sort out the nuances in justifying your particular selection.

Summary

In this chapter we briefly discussed six types of qualitative research. These were chosen from among a number of types of qualitative research because they are commonly found in social sciences and applied fields of practice. Figure 2.1 offers a summary of the types of qualitative research discussed in this chapter. A basic qualitative

FIGURE 2.1. TYPES OF QUALITATIVE RESEARCH

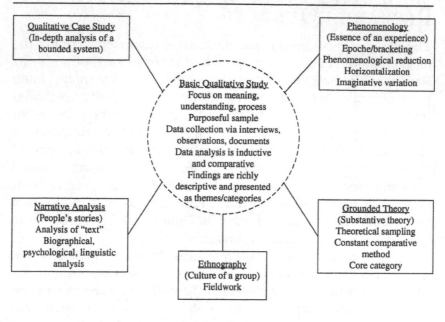

study is the most common form and has as its goal understanding how people make sense of their experiences. Data are collected through interviews, observations, and documents and are analyzed inductively to address the research question posed.

The other types of qualitative research discussed in this chapter share exactly the same characteristics of a basic qualitative study, which is why we placed the basic qualitative study in the center of Figure 2.1. However, although each of the other types shares these characteristics, each also has an *added* dimension. A phenomenological study is interested in the essence or underlying structure of a phenomenon; ethnography focuses on a sociocultural interpretation; grounded theory strives to build a substantive theory, one "grounded" in the data collected; narrative analysis uses people's stories to understand experience; and a qualitative case study is an in-depth analysis of a bounded system.

CHAPTER THREE

EXPANDING THE QUALITATIVE PARADIGM
Mixed Methods, Action, Critical, and Arts Based Research

Imagine that you are interested in community development in your local neighborhood, and you need some information about the community at the same time that you are hoping to increase community involvement. You are interested in designing a type of research project to facilitate this process. In the last chapter we discussed six of the most common types of qualitative research, but none of them really will help you get all the information you need or will necessarily help to facilitate community involvement. There are other types of research designs that could help with this, that are either fully qualitative or have a strong qualitative component. In this chapter, we discuss several approaches to research that have become increasingly popular in the last few years.

We begin by discussing mixed methods approaches (that have both quantitative and qualitative components) and then move on to a discussion of action research and its varieties. Third, we discuss openly ideological forms of critical qualitative research (informed by neo-Marxist, critical, feminist, queer, dis/ability, critical race theory, or postmodern/poststructural/post-colonial theoretical frames that explicitly attempt to analyze and challenge power relations). Finally, we end with a brief discussion of arts based approaches to research. While these types of research with qualitative components are not quite as common as those discussed in the last chapter, they have become increasingly more popular, and many recent dissertations and journal articles make use of such approaches; in fact, some journals are devoted to these approaches to research. No current text on qualitative research would be complete without a consideration of these research methodologies.

Mixed Methods Research

One approach to developing a study about community development in your neighborhood—in which you would gather information and, ideally, facilitate community involvement—is to conduct a mixed methods research study. You might begin by developing a quantitative survey exploring people's attitudes and interests, their involvement in community issues, and what they are most concerned about, as well as including the usual demographic queries. This would give you some important general information, and you might be able to explore statistically significant differences in concerns and involvement based on gender, race, or economic status. But such a survey wouldn't tell you anything about how those who are most interested in being involved in the community perceive how to get things done or to facilitate its development. Hence you might choose to also include a qualitative component whereby you interview a certain subset of survey respondents based on purposeful criteria. You might do individual interviews simply to gather such information, or focus group interviews if you were also interested in engaging people in interaction. This is one example of a mixed methods research study.

There are different ways to discuss mixed methods research. Creswell (2015) highlights that it can be discussed from a philosophical stance, "in which epistemology and other philosophical assumptions take center stage. It can also be presented as a methodology, that is, as a research process originating from a broad philosophy and extending to its interpretation and dissemination" (p. 1). He acknowledges that different authors discuss mixed methods in different ways, but his own stance is to look at it as a method. As such, he defines mixed methods research as:

> an approach to research in the social, behavioral, and health sciences in which the investigator gathers both quantitative (closed-ended) and qualitative (open-ended) data, integrates the two and then draws interpretations based on the combined strengths of both sets of data to understand research problems. (Creswell, 2015, p. 2)

Our purpose here in this introductory book on qualitative research is primarily to discuss the use of mixed methods research for its qualitative components, and hence as a method in the way that Creswell (2015) describes. We first provide a brief history of the development of mixed methods approaches and then discuss the types of mixed methods designs.

A BRIEF HISTORY OF MIXED METHODS RESEARCH

Mixed methods approaches to research have developed and been accepted over time. Creswell and Plano Clark (2011) discuss the *formative period* as the late 1960s and early 1970s, when there began to be a combination of quantitative surveys and interviews to answer research questions.

They term the next stage, in the later 1970s and 1980s, as the *paradigm debate* period. These debates focused on the differences in epistemological assumptions of qualitative and quantitative research. As was discussed in Chapter One, qualitative research is generally based on the assumption that "reality" is constructed by individuals, in light of their experiences; hence, in this view, there is not one reality but many realities. By contrast, some argue that the positivist underpinning of quantitative research is based on a belief that there *is* one reality that can be measured. Hence during this debate period (and currently still for some scholars), there were *the purists*, who argue that quantitative and qualitative methods should not be combined because they have incompatible epistemological underpinnings. Others counterargue that it is possible to conduct a quantitative study exploring general trends and tendencies without fully embracing a positivist worldview. These *situationalists* "adapt their methods to the situation," whereas "*pragmatists* believe that multiple paradigms can be used to address research problems" (Creswell & Plano Clark, 2011, p. 26).

The next period, during the 1990s, resulted in procedural developments in fleshing out different types of mixed methods approaches to research, whereas the more recent period, from roughly 2000 to the time of this writing, Creswell and Plano Clark (2011) term "the advocacy and expansion period." This period has been characterized by not only an expansion of possibilities of mixed methods approaches but also a perception of such approaches as a methodology in their own right. This more recent period has resulted in the appearance of handbooks and journals devoted to mixed methods research. Further, funding sources have provided guidelines for doing mixed methods research, with the National Institutes of Health (NIH) taking the lead in 1999. The National Science Foundation in 2003 conducted a workshop on qualitative research methods and touted the benefits of a mixed methods approach (Creswell & Plano Clark, 2011), and since then numerous funding sources call for mixed methods research proposals.

Types of Mixed Methods Research

There are many types of mixed methods research. Creswell (2015) discusses three primary designs: a convergent design, an explanatory sequential design, and an exploratory sequential design. In a convergent design, both the qualitative and quantitative data are collected more or less simultaneously; both data sets are analyzed and the results are compared. For example, Kerrigan (2014) made use of a "convergent parallel mixed method case study" (p. 341) of four different community colleges (each of which served as a "case") to explore the relationship of organizational capacity and the use of data-driven decision making. In doing so she drew largely on the leadership literature and the literature on forms of capital. First, she used purposeful criteria to select the four cases. Next, she invited all administrators at the director level and above and selected faculty (based on certain criteria) to fill out a quantitative survey. During the same period she also interviewed a select group of faculty and administrators about their data-driven decision making. She analyzed both sets of data within each case and across cases, and found that "community colleges' organizational capacity for data-driven decision-making is a function of human and social capital, but not physical capital" (p. 346), with physical capital being access to and an understanding of technology. This is an example not only of a convergent design study but also of a mixed methods comparative case study.

In what Creswell (2015) refers to as the explanatory sequential design, the quantitative data are collected first; the collection of the qualitative data follows, generally with the purpose of *explaining* the results or a particular part of the findings in more depth. One example is Tisdell, Taylor, and Sprow Forté's (2013) mixed methods study examining the teaching beliefs and pedagogical practices of 245 financial literacy educators and how they attempt to educate about financial matters in working class and cultural communities. They first conducted a quantitative survey. Then interviews were conducted with 15 of those respondents who indicated high attention to cultural issues on the survey; the interviews focused on what they actually did in practice. Hence the quantitative data provided information about *what* the beliefs and espoused educational practices of financial literacy educators were, in general, including their level of attention to cultural issues. But the qualitative interviews provided cultural stories and examples of *how* these beliefs, specifically about cultural issues, played out in their pedagogy.

In the exploratory mixed methods research design (Creswell, 2015), the qualitative data are collected first, and then a survey is created based on an analysis of the qualitative data. One generally employs this method of research when little is known about a particular population or subject, and the qualitative data are used *to explore* and define the topic in order to create a survey instrument to gather data from a larger sample. An example is Jodi Jarecke's (2011) dissertation study of third-year medical students' perceptions of teacher-learner relationships in the clinical environment and how they relate to students' perceptions of teaching and learning in their own future role as educators. (The third year is typically when medical students move from the classroom to the clinic.) While there had been some studies of third-year medical students, there was none about faculty-student relationships. Hence Jarecke initially interviewed thirteen students in their third year and then developed a survey, based on issues and themes that were raised during the interviews, that was distributed to all third-year students at a single institution. She found that relationships were affected by contextual factors, relating to time, the clinical hierarchy, and the particular clinical rotation content area. Further, faculty-student relationships were extremely important in determining students' specialty area.

Often one form of data in a mixed methods study is more primary than another (Plano Clark et al., 2013). For example using the topic posed at the beginning of this chapter, we could design the community development study of a local neighborhood predominantly as a qualitative case study, in which we primarily conduct observations, analyze documents, and interview neighborhood residents. In the middle of the project it might appear that a quantitative survey with a broader group of participants might yield some important further data. So what began as a qualitative case study becomes a qualitative mixed method case study, but the qualitative data remains primary. In this scenario the quantitative component is nested within the design of what is predominantly a qualitative case study design. Plano Clark et al. (2013) refer to these as embedded designs, defined as:

> having an unequal priority in terms of the relative importance of the quantitative and qualitative components for addressing the study's research questions. Researchers choose an embedded approach when their research questions include primary and secondary questions, where one question (e.g., the primary question) calls for a quantitative approach and the other question (e.g., the secondary question) calls for a qualitative approach. (p. 223)

Given that this book is primarily about qualitative research methods, most of the mixed methods studies we refer to here in this chapter and use as examples are embedded designs in which the quantitative components are nested within primarily qualitative designs. Our point here is to discuss the ways in which researchers have used qualitative and quantitative components together to yield a richer understanding of the subject under study. For further information on mixed methods research, we recommend readers to any of the excellent resources that have been cited here.

ACTION RESEARCH

Action research is a form of practitioner research. It not only seeks to understand how participants make meaning or interpret a particular phenomenon or problem in their workplace, community, or practice, but it also usually seeks to engage participants at some level in the process in order to solve a practical problem. Social workers, teachers, and health professionals often engage in action research to improve their practice (Stringer, 2014). For example, a teacher might begin to wonder whether or not a particular intervention will improve the math skills of her students. She might develop an intervention strategy and study its effects over time, simultaneously engaging students in the process.

Practitioners also engage in action research in organizations, for social or community development, and for social change. The research design emerges over time, as one engages with the participants, and together researcher and participants decide on next steps in working toward coming up with solutions to the problem. In considering an example, let's return to the study posed at this chapter's opening about community development in your local neighborhood, at the same time that you are hoping to increase community involvement. You could easily design such a study through an action research methodology. What might such a study look like?

You could begin by gathering six key leaders in the community and conducting a focus group interview to explore what these leaders see as key issues in the community and how they think the community might work together to facilitate its own development. You would likely try to engage these key leaders as co-researchers to help design the next phase of study and to discuss what kinds of data need to be collected in the community. As a researcher and with the leaders' permission, you would audiotape this interaction and transcribe and analyze it as data. Imagine that during this opening focus group interview these leaders decide that the next step should be for them to conduct interviews with community members; they do so, and then all of you reconvene to analyze some of what was found so far. In the next stage, together you might decide to do a survey to get some more large-scale quantitative data about the community. Imagine that through the interviews and the survey you find that one thing that people seem to emphasize is the need to engage the youth of the neighborhood in positive change for the community; a few people suggest a community art project. So after figuring out how to find the money to fund such a project, one subgroup decides to engage a community artist to work with youth to create a series of community murals. This subgroup then studies the process of engaging youth in this mural creation.

The point here is that in action research studies, the research design continues to unfold as researcher and participants collect and analyze data and make decisions for the next phase of the study. Lead researchers work with participants as co-researchers at every phase of the study.

PRINCIPLES OF ACTION RESEARCH

Action research as a theory and approach to research began to develop in the 1940s out of psychologist Kurt Lewin's work on group relations. While Lewin wasn't necessarily the first to use action research—people have been informally doing action research since the dawn of time—"he was the first to develop a theory of action research that made it a respectable form of research in the social sciences" (Herr & Anderson, 2015, p. 12). Since the time Lewin developed the theory, action research has been used in many different situations with many different configurations to solve practical problems; indeed, that is its purpose. There are different types of action research, but all forms of it share several principles. Herr and Anderson's (2015) explanation of action research is a useful starting point for examining some of these principles: "Action research is oriented toward some action or cycle of actions that organizational or community members have taken, are taking, or wish to take to address a particular problematic situation" (p. 4).

A first principle, then, of action research is that it focuses on a "problematic situation" in practice. Hence its purpose is to either solve this practical problem or at least to find a way to further enhance what is already positive in a practice situation; it is always focused on the improvement of practice.

A second principle of action research is that the design of the study is emergent; as Herr and Anderson (2015) state, it is "oriented toward some action or cycle of actions" (p. 4) in which researchers and participants engage to improve practice. Hence the design of an action research study typically unfolds while the study is in process through a spiral cycle of planning, acting, observing, and reflecting (Kuhne & Quigley, 1997). The researcher(s) initially *plan* what they are going to do as a first step; in the next phase they *act* or implement what they have initially planned; in the third phase they *observe* what happened as a result of the action; and in the fourth phase they *reflect* on what they will do next as a result of the data they have collected and analyzed in this first cycle. Typically the reflection phase becomes the next planning phase. Usually this reflective phase also engages the participants as co-researchers in the next steps for the study.

A third principle of action research is that, to at least some extent, researchers engage participants as co-investigators. Action research is generally not done *on* participants; it is done *with* participants. This is why Herr and Anderson (2015) emphasize that action research is about engaging in action that "organizational or community members have taken, are taking, or wish to take." (p. 4) to change some aspect of their situation. The degree to which participants act as co-investigators varies in action research projects, and they can also be more involved in some phases than in others. Often participants are not that interested in writing up the study, for example. Further, the setting might dictate to some degree the extent to which participants can act fully as co-researchers. However, one key to the success of an action research project is the extent to which there is participant buy-in and active participation. As Stringer (2014) notes, "active participation is the key to feelings of ownership that motivate people to invest their time and energy to help shape the nature and quality of the acts, activities and behaviors in which they engage" (p. 31). If one wants to make something happen in a community, or a workplace, or in an area of professional practice, one key to doing so is participants' active participation.

A fourth principle of action research is that the degree to which the lead researcher (the one who is eventually responsible for the study) is an insider or outsider to the community under study makes a difference and must be a consideration in any action research study (Herr & Anderson, 2015). One can conduct an action research study as an insider to an organization, or as an outsider, or some configuration of the two that may emerge over time. One could be a complete insider; teacher researchers, for example, typically conduct research with students in their own classes to improve some aspect of their teaching. They are complete insiders both to the school and to their own classroom. One could also be a collaborative researcher with a teacher doing a similar study. For example, a researcher from a university might engage with a teacher or group of teachers as co-researchers to engage in a certain approach to literacy. So if the university researcher were an outsider, this scenario represents an outsider collaborating with an insider. In our community development study example, if you are a member of the community you are an insider, but you might not necessarily be a leader in the community at the beginning of the study, and at the outset you may be a sort of marginal insider—you live in the community but may have not had a significant involvement with the community. However, you are an insider taking on a lead role as a researcher *with* other community members to get the study done and to make something happen in the community, and you may become a more important part of a group of community leaders in the process. If one is a complete outsider to an organization, it is important to try to collaborate with at least one insider in some way in order to be able to engage more authentically with participants who have a vested interest in improving their practice. No matter what stance one takes as a researcher, it is important to remember this: "action research seeks to develop and maintain social and interpersonal interactions that are nonexploitive and enhance the social and emotional lives of all people who participate" (Stringer, 2014, p. 23).

A final principle of action research is that researchers and co-investigators collect and analyze multiple forms of data in a systematic way as the research process unfolds. Most action research studies make use of only qualitative data collection methods. However, as we have seen, participants as co-researchers could also decide they want to conduct a quantitative survey as part of their data collection methods, though it is rare in action research studies that participants choose to do so. What all *qualitative* action research studies have in common is that they make use of only qualitative data collection methods, such as interviews, focus groups, observations, and analysis of documents or artifacts. Many qualitative action research studies begin with in-depth interviews of participants as part of the planning process and then engage participants as co-researchers in a problem-solving process, and often conclude with individual or focus group interviews reflecting on the process. Stuckey (2009), for example, conducted an action research study of participants with Type 1 diabetes and the role of creative expression as they made further meaning of their diabetes. She conducted individual interviews, then engaged the participants in a series of group creative expression activities of their own choosing, and at the end of the process conducted individual interviews.

In sum, there are distinct principles of action research that hinge on making something happen, that focus on solving real problems in practice, and that engage participants, at least to some extent, so that the research meets their needs. Most action research studies are qualitative action research studies, since most collect only qualitative forms of data; however, as we have seen, it is possible to include a quantitative component in an action research study.

TYPES OF ACTION RESEARCH

There are many types of action research that are variously named: *teacher research, collaborative action research, cooperative inquiry, appreciative inquiry, critical action research, feminist action research,* and *participatory action research* (Herr & Anderson, 2015). There are some distinctions among these types, but most of the differences can be accounted for in the theoretical framework that informs the action research study, as well as the degree to which participants are involved in the overall design and implementation of the study.

In reviewing some of the developments of action research and its varieties, Kemmis, McTaggert, and Nixon (2014) distinguish the types of action research in light of Habermas's three types of knowledge:

1. Technical action research guided by an interest in improving control over outcomes;

2. Practical action research guided by an interest in educating or enlightening practitioners so they can act more wisely and prudently;

3. Critical action research guided by an interest in emancipating people and groups from irrationality, unsustainability and injustice. (p. 14)

This is a useful framework for considering some of the main differences in the types of action research.

While it is certainly possible to do a technical action research project—perhaps an intervention strategy for teaching math with the sole purpose of improving standardized test scores—such action research projects are clearly unusual. Most action research projects fall into what Kemmis et al. (2014) refer to as either "practical action research" or "critical action research."

Teachers and professors often conduct qualitative action research studies in their own classrooms to improve their practice. These are most often examples of what Kemmis et al. (2014) refer to as "practical action research" studies. In the 1990s, such forms of action research were often referred to as "teacher research" or "teacher action research"; now they are more often called "practitioner inquiry" or "collaborative action research" (Cochran-Smith & Lytle, 2009). The point of teacher action research is the improvement of teaching practice at the same time that the teacher-researcher develops into more of a reflective practitioner and creates new knowledge about and with her or his students. Such teacher action research projects typically emerge as teachers become curious about or have "puzzling moments" in their practice (Ballenger, 2009, p. 1). As a result of such puzzling moments, a teacher might begin to implement a new strategy or method of teaching by making use of the plan-act-observe-reflect cycle to implement change. Some teachers do so by partnering with university researchers, and others do so on their own or with other teacher groups. In these forms of action research, there is generally less of an emphasis on engaging K–12 students directly as co-researchers, although teachers solicit their input; rather, the emphasis is more on the voice of collaborative teacher groups or on the unfolding knowledge and professional development in the teacher's practice.

Other forms of practical action research are focused more on organizational change, sometimes on behalf of a particular subgroup within an organization. Banerjee (2013), for example, conducted an action research dissertation study of early career scientists to develop leadership within their organization. She herself did the research as an insider to the organization; as such she was aware that early career scientists within the organization often feel isolated, and her study developed partly to ameliorate this need as well as to develop their leadership. Two different action research teams, made up of these early career scientists and their mentors, met monthly over a two-year period. In this case she was looking for these scientists to get involved in continuing to design the project (a co-researcher role) even as they engaged in a leadership development project. As the researcher, she took responsibility for convening the groups and supporting the process (and writing up the report), but the participants determined their own projects. She found that they developed adaptive leadership capabilities to get their projects done, which was supported by the learning culture of the group itself.

Another player on the action research stage, particularly in education and other applied fields of practice, is appreciative inquiry (AI), which emerged from the field of organizational development. Some would argue that AI differs from action research in that it does not focus on solving a *problem* in practice per se. According to Cooperrider, Whitney, and Stavros (2008), its focus is more on what is positive in an organization and on initiating interventions by highlighting the positive, according to the 4D (discovery, dream, design, and destiny) model. In particular, they state: "AI interventions focus on the speed of imagination and innovation instead of negative, critical, and spiraling diagnoses commonly used in organizations. The discovery, dream, design, and destiny model links the energy of the positive core to change never thought possible" (p. 3). AI studies are often done in health care organizations. For example, Richer, Ritchie, and Marchionni (2009) conducted an AI study with health care workers to discover and implement innovative ideas related to cancer care. Later, this same group of researchers conducted a critical literature review analyzing studies that have used AI in health care settings (Richer, Ritchie, & Marchionni, 2010). While AI does focus on what is positive in organizations as opposed to what is problematic, given that it is process oriented and initiates a change process, we consider it a form of what Kemmis et al. (2014) call "practical action research."

There is a wide body of literature that discusses what Kemmis et al. (2014) refer to as "critical action research." Critical action research studies are specifically about attempting to challenge power relations based on societal structures of race, gender, class, sexual orientation, or religion. From a theoretical perspective, such research studies are informed by critical theory or pedagogy, feminist theory, critical race theory, or other theoretical orientations that are specifically focused on challenging power relations. Some critical action research studies are also participatory action research studies, in which the participants in the study act to a great degree as co-researchers. In other critical action research studies, there are more limitations on the extent to which participants can act as co-researchers. For example, in most formal education settings there are some limitations on the extent to which students can be involved in determining curriculum or their final (graded) evaluation in the course. But in critical action research studies, teachers typically work with students so that they can have some say and control over what they are learning.

Siha's (2014) critical action research study serves as an example. Siha, a community college writing professor, conducted a critical action research study making use of critical pedagogy in his writing composition class, based on the thinking of Paulo Freire (Horton & Freire, 1990). He wanted his students to begin to write about things that they cared about and that mattered in their lives, as they learned about different types of writing—the kind of writing that was expected by an academic culture that requires "standard English" versus the kind of language that they might engage in at home or on the street. In his teaching, he emphasized that one form of language use or writing is not necessarily "better" than another; rather, they needed to know which type to use in which setting, and in the community college writing setting or in any formal writing, they generally had to make use of the standards of writing and language determined by the "power culture." In emphasizing this, he was trying to highlight to some degree that writing and language "standards" are determined by those who are part of the hegemonic culture, and these standards are not better or worse than their home language; they just need to know which to use in which setting.

As part of the planning phase, he engaged participants in an initial educational narrative writing assignment in which they highlighted the kinds of writing and topics in which they were interested. After analyzing these papers as documents and as part of the group planning process, he and the student participants then opted to make use of smaller writing groups as a critical pedagogy technique to use for feedback related to a series of five different types of writing assignments. Students learned to question assumptions and analyze power issues in relation to writing and language, and they engaged in processes that helped them become more involved in their education and learn to build better writing skills in the process. He and each of the students analyzed the writing, and at the end of the study Siha conducted individual interviews with students. This is an example of a critical action research study, in which students participated to some degree as active participants and had a say in determining the direction of writing assignments, but not to the same degree that they might in a participatory action research study.

Practitioners and community members sometimes take on an action researcher role and conduct participatory action research (PAR) studies in their own communities to specifically challenge power relations and initiate change in their communities. Our proposed community development study, described earlier as an action research project, could easily be considered a PAR study. In almost all PAR studies, such researchers are either insiders of the communities where they are conducting such studies or are specifically asked by a community to help them engage in a PAR study. Kemmis et al. (2014) highlight that in critical PAR studies, participants are "profoundly interested" in their practices "and in whether the conditions under which they practice are appropriate" (p. 6). Hence it is easy to involve such participants in a PAR study; in fact, it is usually their idea, and they initiate the study specifically to engage with others to make those conditions better. Kemmis et al. (2014) provide numerous examples of critical PAR studies in their work.

Critical PAR studies can affect and transform people from both an individual and a societal perspective. Pyrch (2007) argues that PAR helps people to move beyond fear—or in spite of fear—to take action, and that taking control of fear is liberating in itself. He describes his own journey of doing so in much of his work in Canada and then discusses the connection between PAR and popular education as adult education, noting: "For me, the community development concept is a combination of adult learning and social action for the purpose of educating people for collective cooperative enterprises for local control of local affairs" (p. 208). Many people either do not believe that they can join with others to exercise control of local affairs or are too afraid to even think they can. Moving beyond that fear, that lack of awareness, or both is part of what PAR is about. This too can sometimes have policy implications. Carney, Dundon, and Ní Léime (2012), for example, describe how their PAR study in Ireland with community activist groups affected policy decisions as people moved beyond fear. Indeed, this is ultimately the purpose of PAR studies: to engage people in taking action on their own behalf as part of their own communities.

In sum, there are many types of action research studies. Most such studies fall into what Kemmis et al. (2014) refer to as "practical action research" or "critical action research" studies. In addition, most make use of only qualitative data collection methods; though occasionally some action researchers or collaborative teams will opt to collect some forms of quantitative data, this is quite unusual in action research studies. While all action research studies attempt to engage participants to meet their own needs and interests, the extent to which participants actually become co-researchers varies with the type of action research study and the stage of the study. Participatory action research studies most fully engage participants as co-researchers. As we have seen, both critical and participatory action research studies are intended to challenge structured power relations such as those based on social class, race, gender, sexual orientation, or religion. But there are also other forms of critical research that are not specifically critical or participatory action research studies. It is to these types of qualitative research studies that we now turn.

CRITICAL RESEARCH

In our preceding discussion, we talked about one form of critical research—critical *action* research (and participatory action research, which is a form of critical research). But thinking more generally about critical research, what makes it specifically *critical* is the theoretical framework that informs the study; in the case of critical action research studies, the point is specifically to help people understand and challenge power relations in the process of the study and to make something happen *while the study is going on*. There are many other types of qualitative studies informed by critical or feminist theory, queer theory, critical race theory, dis/ability, or poststructural/postmodern/postcolonial theory (collectively called "critical studies) that do not necessarily *intend* to specifically make something happen or solve a problem in practice while the study is going on. The point is that these types of studies are collectively *critical* in the sense of the theoretical framework that informs the study and in their analysis of power relations. It is *analyzing the data*, in light of the theoretical framework and the power relations of society that inform how people make meaning, that makes the study critical. We will discuss the role of the theoretical framework in qualitative research studies more thoroughly in the next chapter, but because critical research studies are now so common, in light of what Yvonna Lincoln (2010) refers to as "the critical turn" in qualitative social science research, we will discuss them in some depth here.

GOALS AND TYPES OF CRITICAL RESEARCH

In critical inquiry the goal of the study *in its findings or results* is to critique and challenge, to transform, and to analyze power relations. In most critical studies, the hope is often that people will take action as a result of the study. As Patton (2015, p. 692) observes, what makes critical research critical is that "it aims to critique existing conditions and through that critique bring about change." Thus *critical research* is not a "type" of qualitative research in the same sense as the others covered in the last chapter. Rather, critical research is about a worldview, and this worldview and the tools of analysis from this perspective can be applied to many types of qualitative research. Thus, for example, one could do a critical ethnography or a critical narrative study. A critical lens can also be used for interpreting data in a basic qualitative study, a grounded theory study, or a case study. The point is that in design of the study and in the analysis of the study, the researcher would be specifically examining the nature of power relations.

Critical research has its roots in several traditions and, as currently practiced, encompasses a variety of approaches. Early influences include Marx's analysis of socioeconomic conditions and class structures, Habermas's notions of emancipatory knowledge, and Freire's transformative and emancipatory education. Kincheloe and McLaren (2000) center critical research in critical hermeneutics: "In its critical theory-driven context, the purpose of hermeneutical analysis is to develop a form of cultural criticism revealing power dynamics within social and cultural texts" (p. 286).

Critical research has become a broad term that covers a number of orientations to research, all of which seek to not just understand what is going on, but also to critique the way things are in the hopes of bringing about a more just society. Critical research can be combined with other qualitative methodologies. Charmaz (2011), for example, suggests combining a critical stance toward social justice with the analytical tools of grounded theory. As another methodological combination, critical ethnography attempts to interpret the culture but also to expose cultural systems that oppress and marginalize certain groups of people (Madison, 2012). In critical autoethnography a researcher uses data to analyze how structures of power inherent in culture inform some aspect of her or his own story. Wright (2008), for example, analyzed how her working class roots along with her gender and "intellectual obsession" relate to how she became a researcher and an academic.

As noted earlier, critical qualitative research studies can be informed by critical theory, feminist theory, critical race theory, queer theory, or poststructural/postmodern/postcolonial theory. Critical theory tends to focus on the analysis of social class; critical race theory highlights race; feminist frames tend to focus on gender; queer theory on sexual orientation; postcolonial studies analyze colonial relations. Postmodern/poststructural frames analyze how all forms of power influence research—in Foucault's

(1980) sense that power is "capillary," or everywhere—at the same time that such theoretical perspectives tend to question categories and fixed notions of truth or knowledge.

Indeed, *power dynamics* are at the heart of critical research although, as implied earlier, typically researchers often have a specific interest about particular structural power relations—such as gender in feminist studies, or race in critical race studies—or in the intersections of social structures, such as that of race and gender in studies informed by Black feminist thought (Hill Collins, 2008). Questions are asked about who has power, how it's negotiated, what structures in society reinforce the current distribution of power, and so on. Critical perspectives generally assume that people unconsciously accept things the way they are, and in so doing, reinforce the status quo. Others may act in seemingly self-destructive or counterproductive ways in resisting the status quo. In critical studies, the assumption is that power in combination with hegemonic social structures results in the marginalization and oppression of those without power. Critical research seeks to make these dynamics visible so that people can challenge power relations.

Critical research focuses less on individuals than on context. Critical educational research, for example, queries the context in which learning takes place, including the larger systems of society, the culture, and institutions that shape educational practice, and the structural and historical conditions framing practice. Questions are asked regarding whose interests are being served by the way the educational system is organized, who really has access to particular programs, who has the power to make changes, and what outcomes are produced by the way in which education is structured. Thus *critical qualitative research* raises questions about how power relations advance the interests of one group while oppressing those of other groups, and about the nature of truth and the construction of knowledge.

A delightful and now classic example of critical research is Burbules's (1986) analysis of the children's book *Tootle*. This is a good example of applying a critical lens to a text. Burbules reveals how the seemingly innocent story of a baby locomotive learning to be an adult locomotive can be read as a parable of schooling, work, and adulthood—and how the oppressive structures of class and gender are reinforced in our society. Three more recent examples of critical qualitative research are by Davidson (2006), English (2005), and Robertson, Bravo, and Chaney (2014). Using a critical and queer theoretical lens, Davidson (2006) presents a case study of a bisexual Latino male; English's (2005) study of women working internationally for social justice employed postcolonial theory, which examines those who are marginalized due to race, gender, and ethnic group as a result of colonization. Robertson, Bravo, and Chaney (2014) examine Latino/Latina students' experiences of racism at a predominantly White university from a critical race theory perspective, and how they found counter spaces to navigate this predominantly White milieu. There are numerous critical research studies, and entire journals are specifically devoted to publishing critical forms of social research.

Attending to Positionality and Reflexivity in Critical Research

So far we have emphasized the fact that it is the theoretical framework and the analysis of societal power relations that makes a study critical. But there are also methodological issues, particularly related to the role of the researcher in conducting studies, that are theoretically grounded in any critical perspective analyzing power relations that need to be considered in critical qualitative studies (Steinberg & Cannella, 2012). A basic assumption of critical theory, feminist theory, dis/ability theory, critical race theory, queer theory, and postcolonial/poststructural/postmodern theory is that the world is informed by structured power relations based on race, gender, class, sexual orientation, dis/ability, or religion. In essence, the assumption is that power relations are everywhere, including in the research study itself. While all forms of qualitative research address issues such as building rapport with participants in qualitative data collection, in critical research more attention is given to an examination of power relations in the research act itself.

We made the point earlier that, aside from critical action research studies, in other types of critical research studies researchers generally do not necessarily intend to make change happen during the study itself. However, there is a certain assumption in most critical forms of research that change is happening all the time, and when participants are asked questions in interviews or in other forms of data collection about their experiences related to gender, race, class, or sexual orientation, the very act of talking about issues changes their consciousness about these things and hence invites change (Kemmis et al., 2014). Thus change is accepted as a given in critical forms of qualitative research; however, except in the case of critical action research studies (and at times in critical ethnography), the point isn't really to study how people or groups change in the research process. Rather, it's to analyze issues relating to power relations in participants' lives. Of course, most critical researchers hope that the participants or others will do something and engage in action as a result of the study. But most critical researchers also recognize and attempt to grapple with power relations within the study while they are doing it (Koro-Ljungberg, 2012).

Discussions of critical research tend to highlight three major interrelated issues in considering the relationship the researcher has with participants: insider/outsider issues; positionality issues; and, as a result of both of these intersecting factors, the importance of researcher reflexivity. Lincoln (2010, citing Fine, 1994) refers to the work on these issues collectively as "working the hyphen" and explains that "working the hyphen refers to studying the Self-Other conjunction" (p. 5)—in essence, the researcher-participant relationship and how one affects the other in the research process. To some extent we have talked about insider/outsider issues in our earlier discussion of action research. But critical researchers of all types need to grapple with these issues, to consider how whether or not one is an insider or outsider affects the research process. For example, if one is doing a study as an academic university researcher of how high school teachers try to attend to power relations in classrooms, and one has never been a high school teacher, then one does the research as a complete outsider. If one has been a high school teacher in the past but now teaches at a university, one may have a mix of insider and outsider status in the view of the participants. These insider/outsider status issues can affect whether one has access to participants, as well as to the kinds of stories they will tell the researcher.

An extension of this notion of insider/outsider status is the issue of researchers' positionality—their race, gender, social class background, and sexual orientation—particularly with respect to the study purposes. For example, doing a research study about gay men might be easier if one is a gay man; getting access and developing trust with participants is often more natural if relevant aspects of one's positionality are similar to those under study. Vicars (2012) highlights this in his study of gay men's childhood and adolescent reading practices that related to their identity development. He conducted the research as a gay man, and he writes that "without insider access, it would have proved difficult to find gay men in education that would have been willing and prepared to talk openly about their experiences" (p. 468). This is not to say that researchers' positionality needs to always match that of the participants. And as Johnson-Bailey (2004) explains, in her experience of doing a critical narrative study with Black women returning to higher education, there are always ways one's positionality does not match participants'; she was an insider with her participants in regard to race and gender, but with some participants she was an outsider in relation to social class and color. The point is that participants in studies of marginalized groups (by race, gender, class, sexual orientation) are often suspicious of those who are members of the dominant culture doing research *on* people of oppressed groups. They often worry about what the researcher's agenda is and how they will be portrayed as participants. The point of critical research is generally to do research *with* people, not *on* people.

While all qualitative researchers would argue that it is important to tend to researcher reflexivity, critical researchers in particular emphasize this because of the power relations inherent in the research act itself. In their recent study of the role of reflexivity in social work researchers, Probst and Berenson (2014) note: "Reflexivity is generally understood as awareness of the influence the researcher has on what is being studied and, simultaneously, of how the research process affects the researcher. It is both a state of mind and a set of actions" (p. 814). This implies that qualitative research is a dialectical process that affects and changes both the participants and the researcher, at least to some extent. In the critical sense of qualitative research—and if one is serious about challenging power relations both in the world and in the research process itself—it is incumbent upon the critical researcher to be reflexive: to consider issues such as positionality and insider/outsider stances in research and to try to own their effects in the process in so far as this is possible. A word of caution is in order here, though, in finding balance in the write-up: as Pillow (2003) observes, one can go over-board in discussing these issues, so that it appears that the study is more about the researcher than the participants and the findings of the study. Nevertheless, this issue of researcher reflexivity in critical research and how the researcher deals with it in a report is part of what also contributes to making critical research studies critical.

Arts Based Research

Qualitative research is fundamentally about examining how people make meaning. Most typically, researchers have analyzed what people *say* (in interviews or in written documents) and what people *do* by observing them and writing down field notes. Hence most qualitative researchers analyze data that are *words*. But people do not make meaning or express it only through words; they also do so by art, in visual art, in symbol, in theater based art, and through photography, music, dance, story, or poetry. Since the advent of the new millennium, there has been much more of an emphasis on how creative expression can be a part of qualitative research efforts in what has come to be referred to as arts based research (ABR). Barone and Eisner (2012) discuss the limitations of using narrative words alone, and note that "arts based research is the effort to extend beyond the limiting constraints of discursive communication in order to express meanings that would otherwise be ineffable" (p. 1).

Researchers can make use of arts based practices at different phases of the research study or at all phases. As Leavy (2015) explains, "ABR practices are a set of methodological tools used by qualitative researchers across the disciplines during all phases of social research, including data collection, analysis, interpretation, and representation" (pp. 2–3). The point of incorporating art into research is partly in recognition of the fact that people make meaning and express it in different ways. However, as artists and many teachers know, people also often make meaning in new and *even deeper* ways when asked to express something through symbol, photography, visual art, music, metaphor, dance, poetry, or other forms of creative expression (Bailey & Van Harken, 2014). Artists know this and regularly do so in their creative process. But people who do not see themselves as artists or "good" at art can also make deeper meaning through arts based forms of expression—perhaps because doing so taps into a different part of the brain (Zeki, 2000). In any case, a researcher can engage in arts based research and not identify as an artist; one can also incorporate arts based activities into aspects of a research project with people who do not identify as artists. Researchers do so because its use generally invites deeper meaning making, and meaning making is the focus of qualitative research.

There are debates about whether or not arts based research is a unique form of research (Barone & Eisner, 2012; Leavy, 2015). Some argue it is not, in and of itself; one can make use of arts based approaches in a myriad of ways in basic interpretive studies, ethnographies, narrative studies, grounded theory approaches, case studies, or critical or action forms of research. Nevertheless, others argue that arts based research has its own methodology and extends the paradigm of qualitative research. To some extent the poles of the argument hinge on (1) whether the purpose of the arts based approach is as a data collection and/or presentation method, or (2) whether the whole purpose of the research is really to study artists and/or the artistic process. Hence, for the sake of simplicity, we break our discussion of arts based approaches down into these two primary areas.

Use of the Arts in Data Collection and Research Presentation

Many researchers make use of arts based approaches more as part of their data collection methods, to a lesser or greater extent, and sometimes in the presentation of the findings to clarify a point. In these instances the studies' purposes are not really about the art or the image; the images in this sense are more typically used as an elicitation device during interviews. In speaking about the use of photos in research, Harper (2002) explains that photo elicitation is "the simple idea of inserting a photograph into a research interview" (p. 13); he goes on to note that any visual image—such as cartoons, paintings, symbols, graphic images or objects—can be inserted into an interview. Participants are invited to talk about the image during the interview to see how they make meaning of it. If it is a researcher-generated image, the images are typically used to elicit meaning about particular types of experiences. For example, Matteucci (2013) used photos of the flamenco music and dance experience with tourists who had gone to the southern part of Spain specifically to engage in flamenco music and dance classes. He chose the photos himself for two primary reasons: he was interested in exploring particular aspects of tourists' perceptions and experiences of flamenco music and dance as depicted in these photos, and participants were in this region for only a brief time, so taking their own photos would have been time-prohibitive.

More often, researchers use participant-gathered or participant-created photos or visual images as an elicitation device in data gathering, which we discuss further in Chapter Seven. If the participant simply found an image or object and brought it to the interview, the researcher might ask not only what it means but also how it was chosen; if the participant created it, the researcher might ask what the creative experience was like. For example, Lachal et al. (2012) conducted a study with obese adolescents to examine the role of food in family relationships. They gave these adolescents a disposable camera with the directions to take a photo of the family table following a meal before the table was cleared; they were told no one was to be in the pictures. They interviewed the adolescents about how meals unfolded in their family and the nature of family relationships around food; the picture was used as an elicitation device.

In these uses of arts based approaches as data collection, the studies are about the subject itself and typically not primarily about the images per se. Matteucci's (2013) study was about tourists' experiences of taking flamenco music and dance classes; Lachal et al.'s (2012) study was to examine the role of food in family relationships. The use of images was only an elicitation device to see how participants make meaning of their experience.

In some studies that make use of arts based approaches, the role of the art or image making takes on a more central role. This is often the case in action research studies when participants are asked to create some sort of drawing, collage, or symbol to express something. Stuckey (2009) and her participants, in her action research study about the role of creative expression in making further meaning of diabetes, together decided to first create an image in one session and then take photographs in another. They also discussed the image-making and the photo-gathering experience in the sessions themselves. These sessions were not only about how they made meaning of diabetes; they were also about how the role of creative expression facilitated the meaning-making process (Stuckey & Tisdell, 2010). In the final interviews participants were invited to create an art piece to depict their whole experience. In this case, the study was about their further meaning-making of diabetes through engaging in the creative process. The study was still more about how they made meaning of their diabetes, but the role of creative expression did take center stage.

Qualitative researchers employ arts based approaches to research not only in the data collection methods but also in the presentation of the findings. Lodico, Spaulding, and Voegtle (2010), for example, discuss a program evaluation study of a youth summer camp academic enrichment program; the researchers had some of the youth create photographs of what their experience was like and used the photos as a way of presenting some of the major findings of the study, but the study was more about the evaluation of the youth summer camp program.

Of course, arts based inquiry is more than just using or creating images; it often involves the more creative use of words, such as in the use of poetry or in creating a performance out of participants' words. Ward (2011), for example, conducted a narrative study of four students with disabilities. She described how she used poetic writing from the students' narratives in "bringing the message forward" (p. 355) to solve the research dilemmas she ran into along the way. In her conclusion she writes that the effect of using poetry "foregrounded the students' stories, enabling focus on the meaning and threads of their experiences and creating coherent storylines, verisimilitude, and evocative text to engage the reader in reflection and deeper understanding."

Researchers sometimes use participants' words or work to create some sort of performance to engage with the larger public about the findings of the study. Davis (2014) for example, created an ethnodrama of young adults' stories of transitioning from high school to adult basic education in GED programs, which was performed as readers' theater to create discussion about the life experiences of such young adults in these educational programs. An even more dramatic example of arts based research as presentation is in "how Eve Ensler transformed her interviews with victims of sexual violence into a play, *The Vagina Monologues*, that has been performed in hundreds of locations" (Lodico, Spaulding, & Voegtle, 2010, p. 201).

There are many other examples of how researchers have drawn on the arts to more creatively present the findings of their study to different audiences, rather than strictly presenting themes of findings in an academic journal. This is where, to some extent, some arts based approaches are often critical in their orientation, in that the findings are meant to effect change in people by raising consciousness about the issues under study. Those who draw on the findings of a study to engage with poetic license in this way (Barone & Eisner, 2012) have found that their approach raised some issues. Some were concerned about the trustworthiness of findings, or the ethics of doing so; hence most who discuss arts based approaches to research specifically address such questions (Barone & Eisner, 2012; Leavy, 2015). Further, researchers who present findings in this manner generally have their participants' permission to do so, or specifically work with their participants to engage in such a production. In addition, when findings are presented as poetry or even creative prose, in either a research article or writing for a more general audience, the author-researchers are generally transparent about what they are doing in trying to take a more creative approach that will appeal to a more general audience.

ARTS BASED RESEARCH ABOUT ARTISTS AND ARTISTIC PROCESSES

In most of the examples just provided, the purpose of the research was to explore how participants make meaning of a particular phenomenon or experience, not about the art itself. But there are qualitative research projects that are specifically intended to study artists or the processes of creating and/or presenting some form of art.

These studies take various forms. Some studies focus more on artists and their art as a form of knowledge creation or education. Zorrilla (2012), for example, studied how the art and practice of German-born Uruguayan conceptual artist Luis Camnitzer functioned as a form of public pedagogy. From the time Camnitzer was a child and escaped the Nazi regime with his family, he has lived his life in a constant state of exile from oppressive regimes. He uses his art to raise consciousness about oppression. Zorrilla's specific purpose was to examine both how Camnitzer thought about his role as someone engaged in a form of public pedagogy, as well as how his art functions as a form of education. She carried out her study by conducting interviews with Camnitzer and with art curators who had shown his work, as well as by analyzing Camnitzer's writings and his art. Zorrilla's specific point was to examine the artist and the artistic process.

Leavy (2015), in her book about arts based approaches, specifically discusses situations in which the researchers engage the arts for the purposes of producing art or for examining how art contributes to the knowledge construction process. She has separate chapters on qualitative approaches in creating visual arts, dance, and movement; music; drama and performance studies; poetry; and fictional and autobiographical writing in narrative studies. One good example of using drama and poetry is Hanley and View's (2014) critical race theory study using interviews with African American, Latino/Latina, and Native Americans to create poetry and drama that challenges the dominant narrative on race and culture. Their purpose was explicitly to create a performance using participants' words to engage communities about issues related to race and ethnic identity and the role of creativity in the creation of counter-narrative.

Many arts based research studies about artists and/or the artistic process are written as autoethnographies in which the researcher is examining aspects of her or his cultural identity through engagement in one or more of the arts. Quite a provocative example is Manovski's (2014) use of multiple art forms including poetry, visual art, and especially music to examine intersecting aspects of her identity around race, gender, sexuality, and national origin.

Many arts based research projects are partly about how participants produce new knowledge through the engagement of arts in their process of doing it; hence they are often PAR projects. An interesting recent example is Tyler's (in press) study of an organizational development project with a faith-driven and community-based nonprofit organization group, My Brother's Keeper (also known as MBK), in inner-city Baltimore, which provides various services to the community at large. Her purpose was to integrate storytelling and the creation of a mosaic, a landscape of integrated images created by and with the community, as a form of presentational knowing, to see how these activities affected the organization's strategic visioning and planning processes. She first gathered together 30 participants from the community. She asked them to imagine it was ten years from now and the larger community was thriving, partly due to MBK's role. She then asked them to tell a story, in pairs, about what had contributed to the success. From there she asked them to come up with an image, which they shared with the larger group. Eventually, over the course of time, from these images the community chose those that were the most salient, drew them, and then laid them out in a sequence that made sense to serve as sort of a vision to the community. Then they created a mosaic from the drawings. Tyler describes the process and the impact on the organization; the key factor was participants' buy-in and ownership of the project. Evidence for this was the fact that they installed the mosaic at the entrance of the agency's dining room, so every day their visioning is imprinted and reinscribed in time and space, and in the hearts, minds, and spirits of those who use the space (see Figure 3.1). As Tyler observes, doing such

FIGURE 3.1. MY BROTHER'S KEEPER MOSAIC.

Source: Tyler (in press). Reprinted with permission.

projects is exciting, it makes use of multiple ways of knowing, and the reward is great; but such projects also require time and patience and the invitation of the community. Indeed, there are numerous interesting examples of such approaches for which the creation of art and its impacts was central to the purpose of the qualitative or action research study.

SUMMARY

In this chapter we explored newer forms of qualitative research or research with a strong qualitative component. We began by discussing mixed methods research, which makes use of both qualitative and quantitative research methods. Then we discussed various kinds of action research studies, pointing out that most often such studies make use of only qualitative methods, but that they can occasionally incorporate quantitative components. Third, we discussed critical research studies, which are intended to examine and hopefully challenge power relations, and ended the chapter by considering arts based approaches to qualitative research, pointing out that there can be overlap among some of these types of research. For example, arts based approaches can be incorporated into action research, critical research, or other types of studies.

These types of designs have contributed to expanding the qualitative paradigm of research. They have become increasingly more common in the last two decades; many dissertation studies now make use of mixed methods, action research, and arts based research, or are designed specifically as critical research studies intended to challenge power relations. There are also now specific journals devoted to one or more of these research designs that make use of qualitative research methods, which indicates how common such designs are becoming in further expanding the influence of the qualitative paradigm.

CHAPTER FOUR

DESIGNING YOUR STUDY AND SELECTING A SAMPLE

Rarely would anyone starting out on a trip just walk out the door with no thought of where to go or how to get there. The same is true when beginning a research study. You need some idea of what you want to know and a plan for carrying it out. This map, or research design, is "*a logical plan for getting from here to there,* where *here* may be defined as the initial set of questions to be answered, and *there* is some set of conclusions (answers) about these questions" (Yin, 2014, p. 28, emphasis in original).

This chapter begins with how you select a topic for a research study, followed by how to focus this topic and shape it into a research problem. The research problem reflects your theoretical framework. We explain what a theoretical framework is and what the role of a literature review is in establishing this framework and forming the problem statement. Although defining the research problem, identifying the theoretical framework, and reviewing the literature are explained in sequence here, in reality they are very much interactive processes, as we hope to make clear. Once the research problem is defined, your next task is to select the sample to be studied—a process also covered in this chapter.

SELECTING A TOPIC

How do you select a topic for a qualitative research study? The first place to look is your daily life—your work, family, friends, community. What are you curious about? What is happening or has occurred at work that puzzles you? Why are things the way they are?

What happens when something changes at work, in your family, in your neighborhood? Look around. What is interesting to you that you do not quite understand? For example, you might observe that all your efforts to include certain students in classroom discussions have failed. You might wonder about any number of factors related to this situation. Is there something about these students that makes them reluctant to participate? Is it the methods you use to try to include them? Is there something about the classroom atmosphere? Your feelings about these students? Thus out of personal, practical experience can come research questions. Following are several examples of how our daily lives can generate a topic for research:

- Paul, a hospice counselor, wondered how the grieving experience of older adults could also be a significant learning experience, one that is transformative (Moon, 2011).
- Amelia had been working in adult basic education. She became fascinated with the stories and experiences of how young adults who had left high school transition into adult education programs (Davis, 2014).
- Alfred had been teaching writing and composition at a community college. He was interested in how to teach in a way that would engage students and help them both learn to write and feel as if they were making change in the world and in their lives (Siha, 2014).
- Robin had worked as a museum educator. She observed that some docents were quite good at their jobs. She wondered how volunteer docents, often with a minimum of training, became experts (Grenier, 2009).

In applied fields of practice such as education, management, social work, health professions, and so on, the vast majority of research topics come from one's personal interest in the field and from the work setting itself. A research topic can also come from other sources. Current social and political issues offer numerous possibilities. For example, one might become interested in the learning and practices of health care providers in light of the changes in health care and the pressures of evidence based medicine (Timmermans & Oh, 2010). Out of their concern and interest in these issues, Armstrong and Ogden (2006) conducted a qualitative study of how practicing physicians deal with such changes and how these changes altered their behavior. Another example from social and political discourse is related to the 2008 financial crisis and the increased public discussion of the limited financial literacy of many adults. This increased public discussion prompted Tisdell, Taylor, and Sprow Forté (2013) to conduct a study to examine the teaching beliefs of financial literacy educators and how they attempt to educate about financial matters in working class communities.

A topic might come from the literature, especially previous research or theory in an area. Something you read in your association newsletter, a paper you write for a course assignment, or even leisure reading may be the source of a question that can evolve into a research study. Completed research studies are a good source because nearly every research study has a section with suggestions for future research, many of which could be approached qualitatively. Theory might also suggest topics. Much of the theoretical literature in adult education, for example, states that adults are self-directed and therefore prefer to participate in planning, implementing, and evaluating their own learning. However, data-based studies of adult learners have revealed that some do not want—or know how—to take control of their own learning. Since these two notions are inconsistent, a problem arises. Is self-direction a precondition of adult learning, or is it one of the goals of an adult learning activity? What differentiates self-directed learners from those who are not? What about the context of learning that may or may not promote self-direction? Is self-directed learning—as opposed to, say, collaborative learning—desirable?

Although not as common in qualitative research as it is in quantitative research, a research problem can be derived from a theory by questioning whether a particular theory can be sustained in practice. Even architects of grounded theory (see Chapter Two) concede that qualitative research can be used to elaborate and modify existing theory by the rigorous "matching of theory against data" (Strauss & Corbin, 1994, p. 273). For example, Wenger's (1998) theory of communities of practice posits that learning is a social activity in which we collectively make meaning as we mutually engage in some activity. Further, that learning changes who we are, our identity. To explore Wenger's theory, you could select a community of practice to study, as did Allen (2013) in his ethnographic case study of how social media mediates the boundary between a workplace-based community of practice and the external professional community of Microsoft SharePoint.

So research topics most often come from observing and asking questions about your everyday activities. They can also come from social and political issues, from the literature on a topic, or from theory. These areas of course intersect; for example, there are always social and political issues embedded in one's work setting. So, too, you are likely to encounter theories in reading the literature in your field. A crucial factor in deciding what topic you would like to research is to be *genuinely* curious and interested in finding the answers to your questions. This interest, even passion, will carry you through the process more than any other single factor. Once you have a topic, the next step is to shape it into a research problem.

THE RESEARCH PROBLEM

It would be a fruitless undertaking to embark on a research journey without first identifying a research problem. Most people understand what it means to have a "problem." A problem in the conventional sense is a matter involving doubt, uncertainty, or difficulty. A person with a problem usually seeks a solution, some clarification, or a decision. So, too, with a research problem. For Dewey (1933), a problem is anything that "perplexes and challenges the mind so that it makes belief . . . uncertain" (p. 13).

The first task, then, in conducting a qualitative study is to raise a question about something that perplexes and challenges the mind. It has often been said that research is more art than science. In comparing qualitative research to the art form of dance, Janesick (1994) says of this important first step, "All dances make a statement and begin with the question, What do I want to say in this dance? In much the same way, the qualitative researcher begins with a similar question: What do I want to know in this study? This is a critical beginning point. Regardless of point of view, and quite often because of our point of view, we construct and frame a question for inquiry" (p. 210).

The thing you are curious about, then, forms the core of the research problem, or the problem statement. It reflects your particular theoretical framework; more precisely, it represents a gap in the knowledge base. As Kilbourn (2006) points out:

> Statements such as "I want to explore . . ." and "This study will examine . . ." do not tell a reader what the problem of the study is; rather, they say what the study will do, and although what the study will do is equally critical, a reader first wants to know the problem that will be the focus of the research. (p. 538)

In crafting the research problem, you move from general interest, curiosity, or doubt about a situation to a specific statement of the research problem. In effect, you have to translate your general curiosity into a problem that can be addressed through research.

The structure of a problem statement, which essentially lays out the logic of the study, can be compared to a funnel shape—broad at the top and narrow at the bottom. At the "top" you identify the general area of interest. Is it students who are the first in their family to attend college? Dealing with diversity in the workplace? Math anxiety? Online learning? You acquaint the reader with what this topic is all about; you introduce key concepts, what has already been studied with regard to this topic, and why it is an important topic; that is, why anyone should care about it.

Moving along, you then narrow the topic, directing the reader toward the specific question you have. At this juncture you also point out the lack of information—*the knowledge gap*—with regard to this particular aspect of the topic. Perhaps nothing in the literature addresses your question, or there may be some research but, for reasons you make clear, it is inadequate or flawed in some important way. You have just led your reader down the funnel to the point where the necessity for the study is obvious. What needs to be done becomes the precise purpose of your study. You typically point out the lack of research related to the exact topic, and then problem statements often conclude with the statement, "The purpose of this study is to . . ." The purpose statement is a restatement of the "gap" in the knowledge base. Once you've talked about the topic and perhaps what we do know, you point out what we don't know—for example, "Despite the fact that there is much discussion on embodied learning in the literature, there is a paucity of data-based published research studies on how people actually learn through the body." This gap in our knowledge (how people learn through the body) then becomes the purpose statement; the purpose statement might also identify a particular group of people to be studied. For example, with regard to the gap in our knowledge about how people learn through the body, the purpose statement might be: "The purpose of this study is to identify the embodied learning processes of martial arts teachers."

The purpose statement is often followed by a set of research questions. These questions reflect the researcher's thinking on the most significant factors to study. Maxwell (2013) suggests researchers ask themselves "what questions are most central to your study? How do these questions form a coherent set that will guide your study? You can't study everything interesting about your topic; start making choices. Three or four main questions are usually a reasonable amount for a qualitative study, although you can have additional subquestions for each of the main questions" (p. 84). For example, with reference to the embodied learning study above, research questions might be (1) How do martial arts instructors recognize that embodied learning is taking place? (2) What are the steps or stages in the process of embodied learning? (3) How do martial arts instructors foster or promote embodied learning?

Research questions also determine how data are to be collected. In qualitative research they often identify areas of inquiry for what to observe in a field observation, or what topics to ask about in an interview. Research questions are *not* usually specific interview questions; research questions are broader, identifying areas to ask questions about. Research questions that guide a qualitative inquiry should not be confused with the general question, curiosity, or puzzlement that gave rise to the study in the first place (and that is reflected in the problem statement and purpose of the study). For example, in Bierema's (1996) study of executive women, her overall question or purpose was to understand how these women learned enough about the culture to break through the glass ceiling. Questions that guided the study were, "What formal and informal learning do women experience to develop their understanding of organizational culture? What barriers do women encounter in their climb up the corporate ladder? What are executive women's strategies for coping and excelling in corporate environments?" (p. 149).

In summary, the problem statement is a carefully crafted essay that lays out the logic of the research study. In a thesis or dissertation, the problem statement comes after a section usually titled "Introduction to the Problem" or "Background of the Problem." This introductory section can be any length but usually runs five to ten pages. It is where you can give us the details about the topic, what we know, what research has been done, what concepts and theories are important, and so on. You basically take the reader's hand and lead him or her through the topic to get to the place where *you* want to land; that is, the particular question that you have about the phenomenon. The problem statement is kind of a summary of this introductory section and can be as short as a half page—one or two pages being quite common. In a journal article, the problem statement, introduction to the problem, and sometimes the literature review are often interwoven together. Nevertheless, the important components of any problem statement should be present.

There are three important components to the problem statement. First is the *context* of the study; that is, what is the area or topic you are interested in and about which you have a particular question? This is the easy part of the problem statement, because writing anything about some topic identifies the context of the study. A second component is the identification of the *gap* in the knowledge base—what we don't know that your research will address. The third component is making it clear, either implicitly or explicitly, that this is a *significant* problem to address. There is some urgency about addressing this problem. Why is it important to know the answer to your question? Why is it important to fill in the knowledge gap? The problem statement ends with the purpose statement and research questions.

Exhibit 4.1 is an example of a problem statement of a study of dealing with emotions in the adult classroom. The first paragraph establishes the context of the study—the well-researched and established link between emotional states and learning. The sentence beginning "The literature in the fields of adult education and

Exhibit 4.1. Problem Statement: Engaging Moments: Adult
Educators Reading and Responding to Emotion
in the Classroom.

Statement of the Problem

Research in neuroscience indicates that emotional states
are the starting point for all learning (Damasio, 1994a,   *Context*
1999, 2003; LeDoux, 1996, 1999, 2002). There are
thousands of states, each containing a unique mix of
potential behaviors, feelings, and 16 emotions that can
either enhance or impede learning. The literature in the
fields of adult education and learning readily acknowledges   *Significance*
that emotions influence the learning process (Argyris,
Putnam, & Smith, 1985; Dirkx, 2001; Heron, 1999;
Lovell, 1980; MacKeracher, 2004; Merriam et al., 2007;
More, 1974), however there is surprisingly little research
and/or literature on how this process plays out in the adult *Gap*
classroom. This study sought to understand and thickly
describe the nature of the experiences of a group of adult
educators and how they go about reading and responding
to learners' emotional states in practice.

Purpose Statement and Research Questions

The purpose of this study was to better understand the   *Purpose*
practices of adult educators in reading and responding to
emotional states exhibited by learners. The study was
guided by the following questions:

1. What indicators do adult educators use to read and determine
   emotional states?
2. What actions do adult educators take in response to learners'
   emotional states?
3. What is the reasoning behind the actions taken?

Source: Buckner (2012). Reprinted with permission.

---

learning" speaks to the significance of this study—that is, knowing
more about this link can only enhance our learning. Next the "gap"
in our knowledge is clearly identified—we know little about how
emotions play out in the adult classroom. This gap in our knowledge
is then turned into the purpose of the study—that is, the research will
directly address this gap in our knowledge base. The purpose
statement is followed by three research questions.

In the example in Exhibit 4.2, Valente (2005) sets up the problem statement regarding older adults' self-directed learning and their health care. The first paragraph establishes the context of the study—health care needs of older adults in a managed care system. In both the first and second paragraphs there are references to the significance of the problem: health educators recommend a more "active role for the patient in their own health care" and older adults are particularly at risk in this system. The *gap* in our knowledge is that we know little about how older adults are using self-directed learning for their health care. This gap then becomes the purpose of the study followed by five research

EXHIBIT 4.2. PROBLEM STATEMENT: THE ROLE OF SELF-DIRECTED
LEARNING IN OLDER ADULTS' HEALTH CARE.

Statement of the Problem

Growing numbers of older adults are placing increasing demands on medical services systems and, subsequently, will affect the future direction of health care policy. In *Context* response to the increasing numbers, costs, and health care needs of older adults, the medical establishment has changed patient-care policies. For example, managed care provider reimbursement policies have created incentives to move patients quickly through the health care system and have pressured physicians to limit office visit time for dialogue and health education. In response to these *Significance* changes, health educators have been promoting an active role for patients in their own health care (Berman & Iris, 1998; Keller & Fleury, 2000; National Centers for Chronic Disease Prevention & Health Promotion, 2002).

The importance of understanding factors contributing *Significance* to health maintenance is especially relevant for older adults, as it is this segment of the population who are most at risk. Those older adults who have taken control of their health care are self-directing their own learning. However, little is known about how older adults are using self- *Gap* directed learning to gain access to health information and how this information is affecting their health care.

(*continued*)

Exhibit 4.2   (*Continued*)

Statement of the Problem

Purpose of the Study

The purpose of this study was to understand the role of self-directed learning in older adults' health care. The research questions that guide this study are as follows:	*Purpose*

1. What motivates older adults to take control of their learning regarding health care?
2. What health care behaviors are controlled by self-directed learners?
3. What contextual factors are controlled by self-directed learners?
4. What is the process of self-directed learning of one's health care?
5. How does self-directed learning affect one's health care?

Source: Valente (2005). Reprinted with permission.

questions exploring different aspects of the overall (and more general) purpose.

Finally, Exhibit 4.3 is a worksheet that you may find helpful in setting up your research problem. As with all problem statements, you first identify the topic that you are interested in. This is the broad top of the funnel structure. As you move on in explaining what this topic is about and what *is* known about your topic, and then what is not known (the "gap" in our knowledge), you move to the narrow end of the funnel. Somewhere in this movement you indicate why this is an important problem to be researched. Finally, at the narrowest end of the funnel, you take the gap you have already identified and write a purpose statement explicitly stating how your study will address this gap. This purpose statement is often followed by research questions.

The Theoretical Framework

A colleague of ours once commented that if she could have figured out what a theoretical framework was early on, she could have cut a year off of her graduate studies! Indeed, the theoretical or conceptual framework (terms used interchangeably by many writers)

EXHIBIT 4.3. PROBLEM STATEMENT WORKSHEET.

In your field, what topic is of interest to you that you could shape into a research study?

What are some of the things we *do* know about this problem/topic from the literature?

What is the *gap* in our knowledge/understanding of this phenomenon? That is, what is missing from the literature on this topic? This is the *problem* of your study. (Although we know x, y, z about this phenomenon, we *do not know* . . .)

Take the "gap" in our knowledge and turn it into a purpose statement. Complete this sentence:

The purpose of this study is to

What are the specific research questions that elaborate your research purpose?

of a study and where theory fits into a research study continue to mystify and frustrate many a novice (and sometimes experienced) researcher. Yet it is often the lack of a clearly articulated theoretical framework—or weak theorizing in general—that results in a study proposal or report being rejected by selection committees and publication outlets. Unfortunately, although it is relatively easy to spot the lack of a theoretical framework, it is considerably more difficult to explain what it is and how to go about incorporating it into your study.

What Is a Theoretical Framework?

Part of the struggle in identifying the theoretical framework in a qualitative study is that qualitative research is designed to inductively build rather than to test concepts, hypotheses, and theories. Because of this characteristic, many mistakenly believe that theory has no place in a qualitative study. Further, some who write about qualitative research speak of theory as it relates to the particular methodology one uses and that methodology's epistemological underpinnings (Crotty, 1998; Denzin & Lincoln, 2011).

Yet another point of confusion is that the terms *theoretical framework* and *conceptual framework* are often used interchangeably in the literature. We prefer *theoretical framework* because a theoretical framework seems a bit broader and includes terms, concepts, models, thoughts, and ideas as well as references to specific theories; further, conceptual frameworks are often found in the methodology chapter or section of a quantitative study wherein the concepts and how they are to be operationalized and *measured* are presented.

Although it is good to explore your ideas about the nature of knowledge and its construction (epistemology) and the logical links to how you conduct research (methodology), this is more often discussed in the section on methodology; this is not how we and others think about the theoretical framework of a particular study.

We concur with Schwandt's (1993, p. 7) statement that "Atheoretical research is impossible." A theoretical framework underlies all research. Theory is present in all qualitative studies because no study could be designed without some question being asked (explicitly or implicitly). How that question is phrased and how it is worked into a problem statement reflect a theoretical orientation.

Just what is a theoretical framework? A theoretical framework is the underlying structure, the scaffolding or frame of your study. This underlying structure consists of concepts or theories that inform your study (Maxwell, 2013). The theoretical framework is derived from the orientation or stance that you bring to your study, and every study has one. As Anfara and Mertz (2015, p. xv) observe, a theoretical framework "is any empirical or quasi-empirical theory of social and/or psychological processes, at a variety of levels (e.g., grand, midrange, explanatory), that can be applied to the understanding of phenomena." They also write that theoretical frameworks are the "lenses" to study phenomena. Examples of what they mean by "lenses" to study phenomena might include "Vygotskian learning theory, micro-political theory, class, reproduction theory, job-choice theory, and social capital" (p. xv). In Anfara and Mertz's edited book titled *Theoretical Frameworks in Qualitative Research,* chapter authors discuss their use of theoretical frameworks in their qualitative research. Frameworks range from transformational learning theory to Kübler-Ross's grief model to Black feminist thought and liminality theory from anthropology.

IDENTIFYING YOUR THEORETICAL FRAMEWORK

There are several ways to identify what your theoretical framework is. First, what is your disciplinary orientation? Each of us has been socialized into a discipline (such as education, psychology, business, and the like) with its own vocabulary, concepts, and theories. This disciplinary orientation is the lens through which you view the world. It determines what you are curious about, what puzzles you, and hence, what questions you ask that, in turn, begin to give form to your investigation. Looking at the same classroom, for example, different researchers might ask different questions about it. An educator might ask questions about the curriculum, the instructional strategies, or the learning activities. A psychologist might be curious about the self-esteem or motivation of certain students, a sociologist about the social interaction patterns or roles that different participants assume, an anthropologist about the culture of the classroom—its rites and rituals.

One of the clearest ways to identify your theoretical framework is to attend to the literature you are reading that is related to your topic of interest. What are the titles of journals? What key words do you use to search databases for information? At the very least, you will be looking into the literature to see whether the study you are thinking of doing has already been done. In your search, what are the recurring concepts, models, and theories? Who are the major writers, theorists, and researchers in this area? (See the following section on reviewing the literature for a fuller discussion of this process.)

The framework of your study will draw upon the concepts, terms, definitions, models, and theories of a particular literature base and disciplinary orientation. This framework in turn will generate the "problem" of the study, specific research questions, data collection and analysis techniques, and how you will interpret your findings. Nearly 30 years ago, Schultz (1988) explained this process with regard to vocational education research: "Any research problem may be approached from more than one theoretical perspective. . . . The choice of a theoretical model/conceptual framework . . . will guide the research process in terms of the identification of relevant concepts/constructs, definition of key variables, specific questions to be investigated, selection of a research design, choice of a sample and sampling procedures, data collection strategies . . . data analysis techniques, and interpretation of findings" (p. 34).

All aspects of the study are affected by its theoretical framework. The theoretical framework in relation to the specific research problem to be investigated can be pictured as a set of interlocking frames. As illustrated in Figure 4.1, the outermost frame—the theoretical framework—is the body of literature, the disciplinary orientation that you draw upon to situate your study. This framework indicates to the reader the topic you are interested in. The theoretical framework for Buckner's study, mentioned earlier, is the role of emotions in learning; for Valente's study it is self-directed learning. Drawing from the literature wherein the theoretical framework is lodged, you identify what is known about the topic (citing appropriate literature), what aspect of the topic

Figure 4.1. The Theoretical Framework.

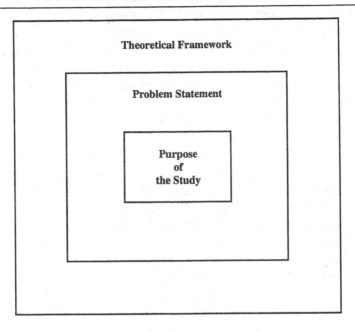

you are going to focus on, what is not known (the gap in the knowledge base), why it is important to know it, and the precise purpose of the study. All of this information is pulled from the larger frame of the study in order to construct the problem statement itself (see the previous section on problem statements). Thus the problem statement is represented by a second frame that is firmly lodged within the overall framework. Finally, the exact purpose of the study is within the problem statement and can be pictured as the third, innermost frame in this set of interlocking frames.

The theoretical framework, problem statement, and purpose can be illustrated in a study of Korean workers who, postretirement, transition into second careers (Kim, 2014). The author begins by stating that a rapidly aging, globalized economy such as Korea "has created different employment trends and work lives, which in turn require adults to adapt to changes in their careers" (p. 4). Kim then presents data showing the increase in labor force participation of those over 55, including a 41 percent employment rate for people age 65 to 69, even though the official—and in some situations mandatory—retirement age is 60. She points out that "postretirement employment after voluntary retirement is a relatively new phenomenon in Korea," one that has not yet been adequately studied" (p. 4). The literature that *frames* the study (and hence the *theoretical framework*) is career development theory. She reviews and critiques this literature, deciding that several well-known models seem best suited to the more "predictable career mobility typical of employees in organizations in the 20th century," and that the developmental-contextual approach emphasizing "the variability of the process" in conjunction with the fast-changing context of the 21st century (p. 5) is best suited to frame her study.

The *problem* of her study, or the gap in what is known about this phenomenon, is stated as follows: "Little is known about how individuals experience their career transition processes within the realm of postretirement employment" (p. 5).

In addition to determining how the problem and purpose are shaped, "our observations as researchers are framed in some ways rather than others, which makes perception itself theory-laden. Theory allows seeing what we would otherwise miss; it helps us anticipate and make sense of events" (Thornton, 1993, p. 68). That is to say that the things we observe in the field, the questions we ask of our participants, and the documents we attend to are determined by the theoretical framework of the study. It also determines what we do not see, do not ask, and do not attend to. Or, as Mertz and Anfara (2015) point out, one's theoretical framework both reveals and conceals meaning and understanding—something researchers should be aware of.

The sense we make of the data we collect is equally influenced by the theoretical framework. That is, our analysis and interpretation—our study's findings—will reflect the constructs, concepts, language, models, and theories that structured the study in the first place. As Wolcott (2005, p. 180) observes, there is a "need for every researcher to be able to place his or her work within some broader context," and one's theoretical framework is that broader context. This is usually done in the "Discussion" section of a research study. In the study of the career transition process of middle-aged workers to postretirement employment just cited, for example, the findings are situated back in the career development literature. Situating the findings back in the literature tells the reader exactly how the particular study has addressed the gap in our knowledge; this gap was identified in setting up the problem (see previous mention).

As we noted at the beginning of this section on the theoretical framework, confusion arises about the place of theory in qualitative research because qualitative research is inductive, leading to interpretive or analytical constructs, even to *theory*. The argument could be made, however, that most qualitative research inherently shapes or modifies existing theory in that (1) data are analyzed and interpreted in light of the concepts of a particular theoretical orientation, and (2) a study's findings are almost always discussed in relation to existing knowledge (some of which is theory), with an eye to demonstrating how the present study has contributed to expanding the knowledge base. For example, Merriam discusses how a qualitative study of HIV-positive young adults implicitly tested Erikson's eight-stage model of life-span development (Merriam, 2015). She asked how the threat of death affected movement through stages of development and found that the movement was not as linear or sequential as Erikson's theory implies. Even those who set out to develop a grounded theory (see Chapter Two) do not enter the study with a blank mind, with no notion of what to think about or look for. For example, Al Lily's (2014) grounded theory study of how the international academic community of educational technologies functions as a tribe is framed by the social and anthropological literature on actual Saudi Arabian Bedouin tribal habits and practices.

This section presents a case for theory permeating the entire process of qualitative research. The very questions you raise derive from your view of the world. In research, this view is lodged in a disciplinary base and can be identified through attending to the literature you review in preparation for the study. A discussion of how and why you review the literature follows.

REVIEWING THE LITERATURE

One way to identify and establish the theoretical framework of a qualitative study is to review the relevant literature. By literature we mean the theoretical or conceptual writing in an area (the "think" pieces) and the empirical data-based research studies in which someone has gone out and collected and analyzed data. In practice, designing a study is not a linear process of reading the literature, identifying the theoretical framework, and then writing the problem statement. Rather, the process is highly interactive. Your question takes you to some of the literature, which sends you back to looking anew at the phenomenon of interest. In trying to shape the problem, you go back again to the literature, and so on. In essence, you carry on a dialogue with previous studies and work in the area.

Typically, the first question you ask in this dialogue is whether there is any literature on the topic. If so, does it confirm that you are onto a problem that needs researching, or has your idea already been researched to death? In a chapter aptly titled "Terrorized by the Literature," Becker (2007) speaks to everyone's fear of discovering that a "carefully nurtured idea was in print before they thought of it (maybe before they were born) and in a place they should have looked" (p. 136). Claiming that there is no literature on a topic can only mean that no one thinks the topic is worth studying, there is no way to study it, or, more than likely, you have searched too narrowly. In our experience there is always some related literature. An investigator who ignores prior research and theory risks pursuing a trivial problem, duplicating a study already done, or repeating others' mistakes. Then the goal of research—contributing to the knowledge base of the field—may never be realized. According to Cooper (1984, p. 9), "the value of any single study is derived as much from how it fits with and expands on previous work as from the study's intrinsic properties." And if some studies seem more significant than others, it is "because the piece of the puzzle they solve (or the puzzle they introduce) is extremely important."

WHY REVIEW THE LITERATURE?

Investigators who do not take the time to find out what has already been thought or researched may be missing an opportunity to make a significant contribution to their field. Indeed, one function of the literature review is to provide the foundation for contributing to the knowledge base. No problem in one field exists in isolation from other areas of human behavior. Consequently, there is always some research study, some theory, some thinking related to the problem that can be reviewed to inform the study at hand.

While many novice researchers find the idea of doing a literature review rather intimidating, Montuori (2005) discusses how conducting a literature review can be a rather creative activity. He highlights the fact that a literature review is like engaging with those who have gone before you who have also been fascinated with a similar topic. Doing a literature review is like participating in a dialogue with that community; you can highlight what the assumptions have been and add your own special spin to the discussion. It is a way of contributing to the knowledge construction process related to the topic.

Besides providing a foundation—*a theoretical framework*—for the problem to be investigated, the literature review can demonstrate how the present study advances, refines, or revises what is already known. It is important for the researcher to know how his or her study deviates from what has already been done. A literature review can do more than set the stage for a study, however. The process can contribute to formulating the problem and answering specific design questions. Knowing what hypotheses have been advanced and tested previously, how terms have been defined, and what assumptions have been dealt with by other investigators can simplify the researcher's task; knowing what research designs have been used before, and with what success, can save time and money. For qualitative studies, researchers can benefit from knowing how well certain data collection techniques used in previous related studies may or may not have yielded meaningful data.

Previous research is often cited in support of the way the study is framed, how concepts are defined, and so on. Previous literature can also be drawn upon to make the case that the present study is necessary, urgent, and important to undertake.

Finally, a commanding knowledge of previous studies and writing on a topic offers a point of reference for discussing the contribution the current study will make to advancing the knowledge base in this area. The researcher literally situates his or her findings in the previous literature, pointing out the exact nature of this particular study's contribution.

In the typical research study, references to previous literature—sometimes even the same citation—may appear in three places. First, previous literature and writing are cited in the introduction, perhaps judiciously quoted from, to build the case for doing the present study. A quote from a well-known authority about the importance of a problem and the need for research in the area will shore up the researcher's position. Underscoring the paucity of research on a topic by citing the few existing studies is also persuasive.

The second place for a literature citation is in a section or chapter often called the "Literature Review" or "Previous Research." Here the literature is synthesized and critiqued; the work that has been done on the topic, its strengths, and its shortcomings are highlighted. In an article-length report of a study, previous literature is often integrated into the development of the problem for study.

Third, the discussion of the findings of a study, found at the end of a research report, *always* contains references to the literature. In the discussion the researcher points out what the study contributes to the knowledge base of the field by showing how the study's findings extend, modify, or contradict previous work. In this discussion the researcher situates the findings of the study within the literature base on the topic, pointing out what new insights have been found, what aspects of theory have been challenged, and so on.

Although there is little doubt that a literature review can strengthen a research study, determining the best time to conduct the review is a matter of some debate. Most writers would agree that the task of becoming familiar with the background of a topic is best undertaken early in the research process; a literature review's impact on problem formulation is an interactive process. At one end of a continuum is a researcher reviewing the literature to find a problem; at the other end is a researcher reviewing the literature to see whether an identified problem has previously been studied. Somewhere in the middle is the investigator who has some notion about what he or she wants to research and consults the literature for help in focusing the problem. Although a literature review helps in problem formation regardless of design, in grounded theory studies in particular, there is a range of opinion as to when the literature should be consulted. Glaser (1978) feels it is best to wait until after data have been collected. However, Glaser is clear that even in inductive, grounded theory studies, it is essential to read widely. He suggests reading in substantive areas somewhat different from the research area at first, then reading in the researcher's own area as the project gets under way. The activity is then highly relevant, for the researcher can "skip and dip, thereby gaining greater coverage, since he now has a clear purpose for covering his field, which is to integrate his generated theory with the other literature in the field" (Glaser, 1978, p. 32). However, weighing the possibility of being unduly influenced by previous work versus the possibility that an early review of the literature could enhance even a grounded theory study, most qualitative researchers would consult the literature earlier rather than later in the process. In our personal experience, having a command of the literature early in the process greatly facilitates the shaping of the research problem and, simultaneously, decisions related to carrying out the study.

CONDUCTING AND WRITING UP A LITERATURE REVIEW

How is a literature review conducted? This topic is covered in more depth in other sources (Cranton & Merriam, 2015; Galvan, 2012; Imel, 2011). Nevertheless, a summary of the process here may be helpful. First, the scope of the search is determined by how well defined the research problem is, as well as the researcher's prior familiarity with the topic. If you as a prospective researcher have only a vague sense of a problem you want to investigate, a good way to start would be to conduct an overview of the topic. In this way you can identify major studies, theories, issues, and so on. The next step is to check bibliographies, indexes, and abstracts that reference specific aspects of a topic.

Once you have collected a set of references and abstracts, you must decide which full-length resources should be obtained. You can use the following criteria:

- Is the author of the source an authority on the topic, one who has done much of the empirical work in the area, or one who has offered seminal theory upon which subsequent research and writing has been based? If so, that author's work will be quoted by others and listed in bibliographies on the topic.

- When was the article or book or report written? As a rule, the most recent work in an area should be included in a review.
- What exactly was written about or tested? If a particular resource or research study is highly relevant to your present research interest, it should be included even if the "who" and "when" criteria are not met.
- What is the quality of the source? A thoughtful analysis, a well-designed study, or an original way of viewing the topic likely indicates a significant piece of literature. In historical or documentary analysis, the quality of primary and secondary sources is a major criterion for inclusion in the database.

Once you have decided which sources you want to look at more closely, you must obtain the full document. As you review a source, be scrupulously diligent about recording the full bibliographic reference. If you write down a particularly good quote or idea, record the page number. Many a researcher has spent hours going back to look for an author's first initial, volume number, date, or page number of a reference! Begin developing an annotated bibliography. This will be something you can add to and draw from as you begin putting together the rationale for your study.

Knowing when to stop reviewing the literature is as important as knowing where and how to locate sources. There are two ways you can determine whether you have done enough. One is to recognize that you have covered all of the relevant literature in the area. Your first glimpse of this end point happens when you turn to the reference list at the end of an article or report and discover that you are familiar with all of the references listed. You may even have read them all. When this happens two or three times, you can feel that you have accounted for most, if not all, of the relevant literature. This is a saturation point. The second clue is a bit more subjective—you realize you know the literature. You can cite studies, people, dates, theories, historical trends, and so on. You have a command of the literature. It is time to quit reviewing.

A literature review is a narrative essay that integrates, synthesizes, and critiques the important thinking and research on a particular topic. Having collected and reviewed the relevant sources, the researcher still faces the task of writing up the review into a coherent narrative essay. There are probably as many organizing possibilities as there are authors. Most literature reviews are organized according to particular themes found in the literature reviewed. A review of the literature on learning styles, for example, might contain sections on conceptualizations of learning style, instruments that measure learning style, populations that have been used in learning style research, and so on. Sometimes reviews are organized as a mixture of early important works reviewed chronologically, followed by a thematic organization characteristic of most of the more recent work on a topic.

Regardless of the organization, a crucial component of any literature review is the critical assessment of the research and literature included. The reader wants to know what *you* think of the literature, its strengths as well as its weaknesses, whether or not it constitutes a major breakthrough in the thinking on the topic, what it adds to the knowledge base, and so on. As a caveat, new researchers are sometimes reluctant to critique the research in a field, especially if an author is well-known and respected. However, it's important to point out that a critique does not mean being negative, but rather assessing the strengths and weaknesses of a particular theory or research study and, in particular, how the piece advances (or does not) the thinking about the topic you are investigating.

In summary, a familiarity with previous research and theory in the area of study is necessary for situating your study in the knowledge base of the field. A review of the literature can also yield information that will be helpful when you make design decisions. Further, the literature is crucial to identifying the overall theoretical framework of your study, as well as shaping the problem statement.

SAMPLE SELECTION

Once the general problem has been identified, the task becomes to select the unit of analysis—the sample. Within every study there are numerous sites that could be visited, events or activities that could be observed, people who could be interviewed, documents that could be read. The researcher thus needs to choose what, where, when, and whom to observe or interview.

The two basic types of sampling are probability and nonprobability sampling. Probability sampling (of which simple random sampling is the most familiar example) allows the investigator to generalize results of the study from the sample to the population from which it was drawn. Since generalization in a statistical sense is not a goal of qualitative research, probabilistic sampling is not necessary or even justifiable in qualitative research (see Chapter Nine for more discussion on generalizability). Thus nonprobability sampling is the method of choice for most qualitative research. Anthropologists, for example, have long maintained that non-probability sampling methods "are logical as long as the field-worker expects mainly to use his data not to answer questions like 'how much' and 'how often' but to solve qualitative problems, such as discovering what occurs, the implications of what occurs, and the relationships linking occurrences" (Honigmann, 1982, p. 84). Thus the most appropriate sampling strategy is nonprobabilistic—the most common form of which is called *purposive* (Chein, 1981) or *purposeful* (Patton, 2015). Purposeful sampling is based on the assumption that the investigator wants to discover, understand, and gain insight and therefore must select a sample from which the most can be learned. Chein (1981) explains, "The situation is analogous to one in which a number of expert consultants are called in on a difficult medical case. These consultants—also a purposive sample—are not called in to get an average opinion that would correspond to the average opinion of the entire medical profession. They are called in precisely because of their special experience and competence" (p. 440).

Patton (2015) argues that "the logic and power of qualitative purposeful sampling derives from the emphasis on in-depth understanding of specific cases: *information-rich cases.* Information-rich cases are those from which one can learn a great deal about issues of central importance to the purpose of the inquiry, thus the term *purposeful sampling*" (p. 53, emphasis in original).

To begin purposive sampling, you must first determine what selection criteria are essential in choosing the people or sites to be studied. Some qualitative researchers, such as LeCompte and Schensul (2010), also use the term *criterion-based selection*. In criterion-based selection you first decide what attributes of your sample are crucial to your study and then find people or sites that meet those criteria. The criteria you establish for purposeful sampling directly reflect the purpose of the study and guide in the identification of information-rich cases. You not only spell out the criteria you will use, but you also say why the criteria are important. For example, in Bierema's (1996) study of executive women in corporate settings, she decided that to ensure that the women were top-level executives, they would have to be from Fortune 500–type corporate environments (one criterion); they had to have achieved executive-level status, which meant that they would have responsibility for a business unit with supervisory, policy development, or organizational strategy responsibilities (a second criterion). Third, she reasoned that they had to have been with the same company for at least five years "to ensure that each participant understood the corporate culture" (p. 150).

TYPES OF PURPOSEFUL SAMPLING

A number of writers have differentiated among different types of purposeful sampling (Creswell, 2013; Miles, Huberman, & Saldaña, 2014; Patton, 2015). Some of the more common types are typical, unique, maximum variation, convenience, and snowball or chain sampling. Using a population of high school graduates for illustration, a discussion and example of each of these types follows.

A typical sample would be one that is selected because it reflects the average person, situation, or instance of the phenomenon of interest. When using a typical purposeful sampling strategy, you want to "highlight what is typical, normal, and average" (Patton, 2015, p. 268). When selecting a site that is "typical" (as in a case study for example), "the site is specifically selected because it is not in any major way atypical, extreme, deviant, or intensely unusual" (p. 284). Using a profile of the average or typical high school graduate, any who fit this profile could be included in a typical purposeful sample.

A unique sample is based on unique, atypical, perhaps rare attributes or occurrences of the phenomenon of interest. You would be interested in them because they are unique or atypical. With regard to high school graduates, you might select one who has become a professional athlete.

Maximum variation sampling was first identified by Glaser and Strauss (1967) in their book on grounded theory. A grounded theory, it was reasoned, would be more conceptually dense and potentially more useful if it had been "grounded" in widely varying instances of the phenomenon. "Any common patterns that emerge from great variation are of particular interest and value in capturing the core experiences and central, shared dimensions of a setting or phenomenon" (Patton, 2015, p. 283). Sometimes this strategy involves looking for "negative" or "disconfirming" instances of the phenomenon (Miles, Huberman, & Saldaña, 2014, p. 36). Maximum variation sampling of high school graduates would involve identifying and seeking out those who represent the widest possible range of the characteristics of interest for the study.

Convenience sampling is just what is implied by the term—you select a sample based on time, money, location, availability of sites or respondents, and so on. Although some dimension of convenience almost always figures into sample selection, selection made on this basis alone is not very credible and is likely to produce "information-poor" rather than information-rich cases. A convenience sample of high school graduates might begin with your own teenagers and their friends.

Snowball, chain, or network sampling is perhaps the most common form of purposeful sampling. This strategy involves locating a few key participants who easily meet the criteria you have established for participation in the study. As you interview these early key participants, you ask each one to refer you to other participants. "By asking a number of people who else to talk with, the snowball gets bigger and bigger as you accumulate new information-rich cases" (Patton, 2015, p. 298). High school graduates would name other graduates who exemplify the characteristics of interest in the study.

Finally, some qualitative research designs incorporate an ongoing sample selection process commonly referred to as *theoretical sampling*. This type of sampling begins the same way as purposeful sampling. First put forward by Glaser and Strauss (1967), "theoretical sampling is the process of data collection for generating theory whereby the analyst jointly collects, codes, and analyzes his data and decides what data to collect next and where to find them, in order to develop his theory as it emerges" (p. 45). The researcher begins with an initial sample chosen for its obvious relevance to the research problem. The data lead the investigator to the next document to be read, the next person to be interviewed, and so on. It is an evolving process guided by the emerging theory—hence, *theoretical* sampling. Analysis occurs simultaneously with identifying the sample and collecting the data. As data are being collected and theoretical constructs begin to evolve, the researcher might also look for exceptions (negative-case selection) or variants (discrepant-case selection) to emerging findings.

"TWO-TIER" SAMPLING

Unlike the other types of qualitative research presented in Chapter Two (basic qualitative study, phenomenology, ethnography, grounded theory, narrative), two levels of sampling are usually necessary in qualitative case studies. First, you must select the case to be studied. Then, unless you plan to interview, observe, or analyze all the people, activities, or documents within the case, you will need to do some sampling *within* the case.

As we discussed in Chapter Two, a case is a single unit, a bounded system. And as Stake (1995) points out, sometimes selecting a case turns out "to be no 'choice' at all. . . . It happens when a teacher decides to study a student having difficulty, when we get curious about a particular agency, or when we take the responsibility of evaluating a program. The case is given" (p. 3). Other times, we have a general question, an issue, a problem that we are interested in, and we feel that an in-depth study of a particular instance or case will illuminate that interest.

To find the best case to study, you would first establish the criteria that will guide case selection and then select a case that meets those criteria. For example, if your interest is in programs that are *successful* in addressing learning disabilities, you would establish criteria for what constitutes a successful program; then you would select a program that meets those criteria. This program would be the case. For multicase or comparative case studies, you would select several "cases" based on relevant criteria. One of the criteria might be that you want as much variation as possible; hence you would be employing a maximum variation sampling strategy in the selection of your cases. Using the successful learning disabilities program example, you might seek out programs that are successful in a wide range of socioeconomic neighborhoods or that address a wide range of disabilities or grade levels.

Thus the researcher first identifies the case—the bounded system, the unit of analysis—to be investigated. The case can be as varied as a second-grade classroom, the training department of a company, a system-wide model science program, or a patient education clinic at a local hospital. Within every case there are numerous sites that could be visited (as in the model science program), events or activities that could be observed, people who could be interviewed, and documents that could be read. A sample within the case needs to be selected either before the data collection begins or while the data are being gathered (ongoing or theoretical sampling). Random sampling can be used within the case; indeed, this is one strategy that can be employed for addressing validity (see Chapter Nine). More commonly, however, purposeful sampling as outlined earlier is used to select the sample within the case, just as it is used to select the case itself. However, a second set of criteria is usually needed to purposefully select whom to interview, what to observe, and which documents to analyze.

Thus the questions, concerns, and purposes of qualitative studies lead to forms of nonprobability sampling in determining the sample of instances, locations, people, and times to be included. Purposive or purposeful sampling usually occurs before the data are gathered, whereas theoretical sampling is done in conjunction with data collection. The size of the sample within the case is determined by a number of factors relevant to the study's purpose. In case studies, then, there are usually two levels of sampling; first the case is selected, then people, events, sites, and so on *within* the case are selected. For both levels of sampling, criteria need to be established to guide the process. Using the successful learning disabilities program as an example, the criteria for selecting the program (the case) might be the following: the program will have been in existence for a minimum of five years; 60 percent of its students are able to join regular classes after one year in the program; the program deals with learning disabilities in reading and math only. Once the program has been selected, you will need to determine whom to interview (unless you plan to interview everyone) and what to observe. Criteria for selecting the interview sample might include all administrators, teachers who have been with the program at least five years, students representing various ages, length in the program, and particular learning disabilities.

How Many in the Sample?

Invariably, the question of how many people to interview, how many sites to visit, or how many documents to read concerns—more likely, haunts—the novice qualitative researcher. Unfortunately for those with a low tolerance for ambiguity, there is no answer. It always depends on the questions being asked, the data being gathered, the analysis in progress, and the resources you have to support the study. What is needed is an adequate number of participants, sites, or activities to answer the question posed at the beginning of the study (in the form of the purpose statement). Lincoln and Guba (1985) recommend sampling until a point of saturation or redundancy is reached. "In purposeful sampling the size of the sample is determined by informational considerations. If the purpose is to maximize information, the sampling is terminated when no new information is forthcoming from new sampled units; thus *redundancy* is the primary criterion" (p. 202, emphasis in original).

Reaching a point of saturation or redundancy means that you begin hearing the same responses to your interview questions or seeing the same behaviors in observations; no new insights are forthcoming. It is impossible to know ahead of time when saturation might occur. In order to recognize that your data is saturated, you must engage in analysis along with data collection. As discussed more fully in Chapter Eight, data analysis is best done simultaneously with data collection.

If you are submitting a proposal to a funding agency, dissertation committee, or other oversight board for approval or support, you can offer a tentative, approximate number of units to be included (that is, people, sites, cases, activities, and so on), knowing full well that this will be adjusted in the course of the investigation. Patton (2015) recommends specifying a minimum sample size "based on expected reasonable coverage of the phenomenon given the purpose of the study" (p. 314).

SUMMARY

We began this chapter by explaining how to select a topic for study. Once a topic has been selected, it needs to be shaped into a research *problem.* Defining the research problem is a key step in any type of research. You can examine your own practice, review the literature, or look to current social problems for questions that can be shaped into a research problem. The statement of the problem presents the logic of the study and includes identifying the context of the study, the gap in our knowledge of the topic, and a rationale for the importance or significance of addressing this gap through research. The statement of the problem concludes with a very specific purpose statement followed by research questions.

Also discussed in this chapter is the theoretical framework of a study; that is, the underlying structure upon which all other aspects of the study rest. Previous literature plays an important role in the formation of a study's theoretical framework, and we reviewed the benefits of conducting a literature review, the steps in doing it, and the place of the review in the overall research process. Establishing the theoretical framework and reviewing the literature, which we discussed sequentially in the chapter, are, in reality, quite intertwined. From a review of the literature a researcher discovers what research exists on a topic and how theory and previous research may help frame the study at hand. Likewise, a researcher is guided to a specific body of literature by the emerging problem, by issues that arise during data collection and analysis, and by the need to interpret findings in light of previous research.

Selecting the sample is dependent upon the research problem. In qualitative research, the most appropriate sampling strategy is nonprobability sampling. Purposeful and theoretical sampling are well-known and widely used nonprobability sampling strategies in qualitative research. There are also times when sample selection occurs twice, as in a qualitative case study wherein the case is selected first, followed by people, events, and documents within the case. The chapter closes with a brief discussion of sample size.

PART TWO

COLLECTING QUALITATIVE DATA

Data are nothing more than ordinary bits and pieces of information found in the environment. They can be concrete and measurable, as in class attendance, or invisible and difficult to measure, as in feelings. Whether or not a bit of information becomes data in a research study depends solely on the interest and perspective of the investigator. The way in which rainwater drains from the land may be data to a soil scientist, for example, but not even noticed by the homeowner. Likewise, activity patterns in a school cafeteria, while holding little research interest to students, staff, or faculty, may be of great interest to someone studying students' behavior outside the formal classroom setting.

Data conveyed through words have been labeled qualitative, whereas data presented in number form are quantitative. Qualitative data consist of "direct quotations from people about their experiences, opinions, feelings, and knowledge" obtained through interviews; "detailed descriptions of people's activities, behaviors, actions" recorded in observations; and "excerpts, quotations, or entire passages" extracted from various types of documents (Patton, 2015, p. 14).

Part Two is about collecting data through interviews, observations, and documents or, in Wolcott's (1992) "common, everyday terms" (p. 19), data collection is about asking, watching, and reviewing. It should be kept in mind, however, that "the idea that we 'collect' data is a bit misleading. Data are not 'out there' waiting collection, like so many rubbish bags on the pavement. For a start, they have to be noticed by the researcher and treated as data for the purposes of his or her research" (Dey, 1993, p. 15). The data collection techniques used, as well as the specific information considered to be data in a study, are determined by the researcher's theoretical orientation, by the problem and purpose of the study, and by the sample selected (see chapters in Part One for a discussion of these factors).

In education, if not in most applied fields, interviewing is probably the most common form of data collection in qualitative studies. In some studies it is the *only* source of data. Chapter Five focuses on interviews: the different types of interviews, good interview questions, and how to record and evaluate interview data; considerations of the interviewer and respondent interaction are also discussed.

Conducting observations is the topic of Chapter Six. The different roles an observer can assume, what to observe when on site, how to record observations, and the content of field notes are topics discussed in this chapter.

The third technique covered in Part Two is mining data from documents and artifacts. The term *documents* is used broadly in this book to refer to printed and other materials relevant to a study, including public records, personal documents, popular culture and popular media, visual documents, and physical artifacts. A distinction is also made between the common reference to documents as materials existing naturally in the context of the study versus researcher-generated documents. Limitations and strengths of documents are considered, as well as special considerations in dealing with online data sources.

The three chapters in Part Two thus present the means by which you can address the problem and specific research questions you established in the design of your qualitative study. Interview transcripts, field notes from observations, and documents of all types, including online data, can help you uncover meaning, develop understanding, and discover insights relevant to the research problem.

CHAPTER FIVE

CONDUCTING EFFECTIVE INTERVIEWS

Sharan and a colleague were collecting data for a study of older adult learning in Malaysia. As the headman of a rural village escorted us to the home of an elderly woman who had agreed to talk with us, a crowd of villagers gathered around us, and one young man asked, "Are you from CNN? We want to be interviewed too."

Interviewing has so pervaded popular media that we have become "the 'interview society,' where everyone gets interviewed and gets a moment in the sun" (Fontana & Frey, 2005, p. 695). Talk shows, social media, 24-hour news cycles, and print media rely on interviews, verbal or written, to construct their story. But unlike "the spontaneous exchange of views in everyday conversations," a research interview "is a conversation that has a structure and a purpose" (Brinkmann & Kvale, 2015, p. 5). Interviewing for research purposes is a systematic activity that you can learn to do well. Its popularity as a data collection technique is attested to by dozens of books on interviewing, including Fielding's (2008) four-volume series and a recent handbook (Gubrium, Holstein, Marvasti, & McKinney, 2012). In this chapter we explore interviewing as a data collection technique in qualitative research. We discuss several types of interviews as well as related topics: asking good questions, beginning the interview, recording and evaluating interview data, and the nature of the interaction between interviewer and respondent.

INTERVIEW DATA

In most forms of qualitative research, some and occasionally all of the data are collected through interviews. DeMarrais (2004) defines a research interview as "a process in which a researcher and participant engage in a conversation focused on questions related to a research study" (p. 55). The most common form of interview is the person-to-person encounter, in which one person elicits information from another. Group or collective formats can also be used to obtain data. Both person-to-person and group interviews can be defined as a conversation—but a "conversation with a purpose" (Dexter, 1970, p. 136). The main purpose of an interview is to obtain a special kind of information. The researcher wants to find out what is "in and on someone else's mind" (Patton, 2015, p. 426). As Patton explains:

> We interview people to find out from them those things we cannot directly observe. . . . We cannot observe feelings, thoughts, and intentions. We cannot observe behaviors that took place at some previous point in time. We cannot observe situations that preclude the presence of an observer. We cannot observe how people have organized the world and the meanings they attach to what goes on in the world. We have to ask people questions about those things.
>
> The purpose of interviewing, then, is to allow us to enter into the other person's perspective. (p. 426)

Interviewing is necessary when we cannot observe behavior, feelings, or how people interpret the world around them. It is also necessary to interview when we are interested in past events that are impossible to replicate. For example, school psychologists might be interested in the reaction of students who witnessed a teacher being attacked at school. Likewise, a catastrophic event such as a nuclear accident or natural disaster cannot be replicated, but its effects on a community might be the focus of a qualitative case study. Interviewing is also the best technique to use when conducting intensive case studies of a few selected individuals, as Bateson (1990) did in interviewing five women for her book, *Composing a Life*. Conversely, interviewing can be used to collect data from a large number of people representing a broad range of ideas. Terkel's

(2001) book on the mystery of death and dying is based on dozens of interviews with people from all walks of life. In short, the decision to use interviewing as the primary mode of data collection should be based on the kind of information needed and whether interviewing is the best way to get it. Dexter (1970) summarizes when to use interviewing: "Interviewing is the preferred tactic of data collection when . . . it will get better data or more data or data at less cost than other tactics!" (p. 11). We would add that depending on the topic, interviewing is sometimes the *only* way to get data.

TYPES OF INTERVIEWS

There are a number of ways different types of interviews can be categorized. In this section we first discuss types of interviews in terms of the amount of structure, followed by different types of interviews emanating from different theoretical stances. We also discuss focus group and online interviewing.

BY STRUCTURE

The most common way of deciding which type of interview to use is by determining the amount of structure desired. Table 5.1 presents three types of interviews, which vary according to the amount of structure inherent in the interview. If placed on a continuum, the range of structure varies from highly structured, questionnaire-driven interviews to unstructured, open-ended, conversational formats. In *highly structured* interviews, sometimes called standardized interviews, questions and the order in which they are asked are determined ahead of time.

The most structured interview is actually an oral form of the written survey. The U.S. Census Bureau and marketing surveys are good examples of oral surveys. The problem with using a highly structured interview in qualitative research is that rigidly adhering to predetermined questions may not allow you to access participants' perspectives and understandings of the world. Instead, you get reactions to the investigator's preconceived notions of the world. Such an interview is also based on the shaky assumptions that respondents share a common vocabulary and that the questions will be interpreted in the same way by all respondents. The

TABLE 5.1.   INTERVIEW STRUCTURE CONTINUUM.

Highly Structured/ Standardized	Semistructured	Unstructured/Informal
• Wording of questions is predetermined • Order of questions is predetermined • Interview is oral form of a written survey • In qualitative studies, usually used to obtain demographic data (age, gender, ethnicity, education, and so on) • Examples: U.S. Census Bureau survey, marketing surveys	• Interview guide includes a mix of more and less structured interview questions • All questions used flexibly • Usually specific data required from all respondents • Largest part of interview guided by list of questions or issues to be explored • No predetermined wording or order	• Open-ended questions • Flexible, exploratory • More like a conversation • Used when researcher does not know enough about phenomenon to ask relevant questions • Goal is learning from this interview to formulate questions for later interviews • Used primarily in ethnography, participant observation, and case study

major use of this highly structured format in qualitative research is to gather common sociodemographic data from respondents. That is, you may want to know everyone's age, income, history of employment, marital status, level of formal education, and so on. You may also want everyone to respond to a particular statement or to define a particular concept or term.

For the most part, however, interviewing in qualitative investigations is more open-ended and less structured. Less-structured formats assume that individual respondents define the world in unique ways. Your questions thus need to be more open-ended. A less-structured alternative is the *semistructured* interview. As is illustrated in Table 5.1, the semistructured interview is in the middle, between structured and unstructured. In this type of interview either all of the questions are more flexibly worded or the interview is a mix of more and less structured questions. Usually, specific information is desired from all the respondents, in which case there is a more structured section to the interview. But most of the interview is guided by a list of questions or issues to be explored, and neither the exact wording nor the order of the questions is determined ahead of time. This format allows the researcher to respond to the situation at hand, to the emerging worldview of the respondent, and to new ideas on the topic.

The third type of interview is one that is *unstructured* and informal. These are particularly useful when the researcher does not know enough about a phenomenon to ask relevant questions. Thus there is no predetermined set of questions, and the interview is essentially exploratory. One of the goals of the unstructured interview is, in fact, learning enough about a situation to formulate questions for subsequent interviews. Thus the unstructured interview is often used in conjunction with participant observation in the early stages of a qualitative study. It takes a skilled researcher to handle the great flexibility demanded by the unstructured interview. Insights and understanding can be obtained in this approach, but at the same time an interviewer may feel lost in a sea of divergent viewpoints and seemingly unconnected pieces of information. Totally unstructured interviewing is rarely used as the sole means of collecting data in qualitative research. In most studies the researcher can combine all three types of interviewing so that some standardized information is obtained, some of the same open-ended questions are asked of all participants, and some time is spent in an unstructured mode so that fresh insights and new information can emerge.

By way of illustrating the kinds of questions you might ask in each of the types of interviews—highly structured, semistructured, or unstructured—let us suppose you are studying the role of mentoring in the career development of master teachers. In a highly structured interview you might begin by giving each respondent a definition of mentoring and then asking the person to identify someone who is a mentor. In a semistructured interview you would be more likely to ask each teacher to describe his or her understanding of mentoring, or you might ask the teacher to think of someone who is a mentor. In an unstructured interview you might ask the respondent to share how he or she got to be a master teacher. More direct, but still rather unstructured, would be a question about the people, influences, or factors that have helped to shape the respondent's career.

BY PHILOSOPHICAL AND DISCIPLINARY ORIENTATION

As a means of collecting information, interviewing has been with us for centuries. Census taking, surveying, and opinion polling have long been and still are measurement-oriented forms of interviewing. More informal interpretive interviewing arose in the early decades of the twentieth century, primarily in sociology (Fontana & Frey, 2005). From the latter decades of the twentieth century to the present day, interviewing has been discussed and analyzed from numerous philosophical perspectives. There is now feminist interviewing, postmodern interviewing, cross-cultural interviewing, and so on.

One of the clearest analyses of the link between philosophical orientation and type of interview is by Roulston (2010). She identifies six conceptions of interviewing, each lodged in a different theoretical framework. Neo-positivist interviews are those in which a "skillful interviewer asks good questions, minimizes bias through his/her neutral stance, generates quality data and produces valid findings" (p. 52). What she calls "romantic" conceptions of interviewing are interviews in which the researcher "makes no claim to being objective" (p. 58), analyzes and reveals subjectivities, and strives "to generate the kind of conversation that is intimate and self-revealing" (p. 56). This type of interview draws from phenomenology, psychoanalysis, feminist research, and psychosocial theories.

Roulston's (2010) third type of interview is constructionist, in which *how* the interview data are constructed receives attention through such tools as discourse analysis, narrative analysis, and conversation analysis. The fourth type of interview in her typology is the postmodern interview. Congruent with postmodern and poststructural theory, the aim of the interview is not to come up with a single perception of the self, since there is no essential self; rather, there are "various non-unitary performances of selves," and the presentations of these data are made via creative performances (p. 63).

The final two types of interviewing, transformative and decolonizing, share a critical theory philosophical orientation in which issues of power, privilege, and oppression are made visible. In what Roulston (2010) calls transformative interviewing, the researcher "*intentionally* aims to challenge and change the understandings of participants" (p. 65, italics in original). In the decolonizing interview, concern is with "restorative justice" for indigenous peoples

(p. 70); a key to the decolonizing interview is to privilege an indigenous research agenda that "involves the processes of decolonization, transformation, mobilization, and healing" (p. 68).

Other writers categorize interviews based more on disciplinary perspectives. For example, the "ethnographic" interview from anthropology focuses on culture; that is, the type of information elicited from an interview is data about the culture of a group, such as its rites and rituals, myths, hierarchies, heroes, and so on. Spradley's book *The Ethnographic Interview* (1979) is considered a classic in the field. A second often-discussed disciplinary-based type of interview is the phenomenological interview. Phenomenology is a philosophy that informs all of qualitative research to some extent (see Chapter One). However, one could also do a specifically phenomenological study (see Chapter Two), in which case one would do phenomenological interviewing, meaning that the researcher attempts to uncover the essence of an individual's "lived" experience (Seidman, 2013); such an interview "focuses on the deep, lived meanings that events have for individuals, assuming that these meanings guide actions and interactions" (Marshall & Rossman, 2016, p. 153). It is common practice in phenomenological research for researchers to write about their own experiences of the phenomenon or to be interviewed by a colleague in order to "bracket" their experiences prior to interviewing others.

FOCUS GROUP INTERVIEWS

Fully a year before any U.S. presidential election, focus group interviews of voters are held by candidates' staffs, by the media, by citizens' groups, and so on to ferret out voters' views on issues, policies, and candidates. This is an extension of the widespread use of focus groups in marketing research begun in the 1950s in which businesses test consumer preferences and promote particular products. The use of focus groups as a social science research method can be traced back even further, to social psychological studies of group dynamics begun in the early decades of the twentieth century, followed by sociologist Robert K. Merton and associates' publication of *The Focused Interview* (Merton, Riske, & Kendall, 1956). "A primary difference between focus group research and other types of research, such as surveys, individual interviews, and laboratory experiments is that data collection occurs in and is facilitated by, a group setting" (Stewart & Shamdasani, 2015, p. 17). Whether in marketing or social science research (and now with virtual groups) focus group interviewing remains a popular data collection strategy.

As a method of collecting data in qualitative research, a focus group is an interview on a topic with a group of people who have knowledge of the topic. Since the data obtained from a focus group is socially constructed within the interaction of the group, a constructivist perspective underlies this data collection procedure. Hennink (2014) explains: "Perhaps the most unique characteristic of focus group research is the interactive discussion through which data are generated, which leads to a different type of data not accessible through individual interviews. During the group discussion participants share their views, hear the views of others, and perhaps refine their own views in light of what they have heard" (pp. 2–3).

The composition of a focus group depends on the topic to be discussed. As with individual interviewing, purposeful sampling should be used to include people who know the most about the topic. Although there are no hard and fast rules about how many to include in a group, most writers suggest somewhere between six and ten participants, preferably people who are strangers to each other. It is also recommended that the moderator or interviewer of the group be familiar with group processes and with the range of possible roles as moderator (Barbour, 2008; Hennink, 2014; Krueger & Casey, 2015; Stewart & Shamdasani, 2015).

Finally, "focus groups work best for topics people could talk about to each other in their everyday lives—but don't" (Macnaghten & Myers, 2004, p. 65). Obviously, a focus group is a poor choice for topics that are sensitive, highly personal, and culturally inappropriate to talk about in the presence of strangers. Of course, it's not always obvious ahead of time how appropriate a topic might be. Crowe (2003) reports successful use of focus groups to create culturally appropriate HIV prevention material for the deaf community. Jowett and O'Toole (2006) report an interesting analysis of two focus groups—one of mature students and their attitude toward participation in higher education, and one of young women and their views of feminism. They found that the mature students' focus group was a failure but the young women's group was a success.

The authors had not anticipated "how ingrained the sense of inadequacy is for some people who have felt excluded from education" (p. 462), nor how the power imbalance among members of the mature students' group and between the researcher and the group inhibited participation. Finally, Stewart and Williams (2005) explore the practical and ethical issues of conducting synchronous and asynchronous *online* focus groups.

Thus, as with any other data collection method, focus groups are appropriate to be used when this is the best way to get the best data that addresses your research question. And as with any other method, the advantages need to be weighed against the disadvantages; one also needs to develop the skills necessary for using this technique.

ONLINE INTERVIEWS

There is no question that the Internet has changed the world. It has also increased the possibilities for the myriad ways that one can collect data through online venues in conducting qualitative research through various information communication technologies (ICTs) and computer mediated communication (CMC) tools (Salmons, 2015). Qualitative data are collected from or through email, blogs, online discussion groups, Skype, tweets, texts, and various forms of social media. Here we discuss issues in conducting online interviews.

One can conduct online interviews *synchronously* (in real time) through various CMC tools such as Skype or Adobe Connect. These are typically verbal interviews with a video component that are more like face-to-face interviews; one can also conduct voice-to-voice real-time interviews over the telephone. One can also conduct interviews *asynchronously* (where there is a lag time) over email or on an online discussion group; asynchronous interviews tend to be text-based or written interviews. There are strengths and weaknesses to both synchronous and asynchronous venues. As will be discussed in more detail later, in general it is helpful to build rapport with participants when conducting qualitative interviews. Rapport building can be slightly more challenging in text-only asynchronous venues (such as email), when visual cues are missing (James & Busher, 2012). Further, participants may not respond to email queries or not respond to certain questions over email that they would likely answer in synchronous video or voice-to-voice formats. On the other hand, text-based interviews over email provide the researcher with a ready-made transcript, making it easy to document what was said, though the nonverbal cues and pauses in conversation are missing. Such an email "transcript" can save the researcher time and money in transcription costs.

Given the availability of various information and communications technology (ICT) tools for conducting online interviews in either synchronous or asynchronous formats, Salmons (2015), in her book on online interviews, presents a framework for considering what she refers to as "e-interview research" (p. 4). She invites the researcher to explore key questions in eight interrelated categories: (1) aligning the purpose of the research with the design; considering issues related to (2) choosing data collection methods and (3) one's position as a researcher; determining (4) the e-interview style, (5) the type of ICT tools to use, (6) sampling issues, (7) ethical issues, and (8) actually collecting the data. While qualitative researchers always need to consider similar issues in all qualitative studies, Salmons proposes questions and issues specifically related to the online environment.

There is a growing discussion of the availability of various ICT tools for conducting online interviews, many of which are reviewed by Salmons (2015) and others, talking mainly about individual interviews. Tuttas (2015) focuses more specifically on lessons learned from using real-time audiovisual web conferencing technology to carry out focus group interviews with nurses from geographically dispersed locations in the United States. While she ultimately chose to use Adobe Connect, she considers the strengths and weaknesses of various web conferencing technology venues (Skype, ooVoo, GoTo-Meeting, and Adobe Connect) for her focus group interviews, which can provide some guidance for some of the available options.

Like any data collection method, conducting online interviews has its strengths and weaknesses. One of the obvious strengths is that the researcher is no longer constrained by geography in considering participants. A researcher could interview participants across the world, and could perhaps even conduct focus group interviews where all parties can see each other. Another strength is that many CMC venues allow video recordings to be made, which can be helpful if one wants to explore or review nonverbal cues later. Some obvious weaknesses are that not everyone has access to various CMC tools or the knowledge of how to use them. Further, technology is always subject to breakdowns. There can be problems with audio recording equipment, as voices sometimes break up on cell phones or over Skype or other computer mediated venues, which can cause frustration for both the interviewer and interviewee. Finally, there is always the chance of confidentiality being compromised when one uses CMC tools over the Internet. While this may be unlikely, it is always a consideration for researchers and institutional review boards in dealing with ethical issues in doing research. In sum, all of the strengths and weaknesses of CMC tools in relationship to qualitative interviewing need to be considered when undertaking a qualitative research study.

ASKING GOOD QUESTIONS

The key to getting good data from interviewing is to ask good questions; asking good questions takes practice. Pilot interviews are crucial for trying out your questions. Not only do you get some practice in interviewing, but you also quickly learn which questions are confusing and need rewording, which questions yield useless data, and which questions, suggested by your respondents, you should have thought to include in the first place.

Different types of questions will yield different information. The questions you ask depend upon the focus of your study. Using the example of mentoring in the career development of master teachers, if you wanted to know the role mentoring played in career development, you would ask questions about teachers' personal experience with mentoring and probably get a descriptive history. Follow-up questions about how they *felt* about a certain mentoring experience would elicit information that is more affective in nature. You might also want to know their opinion as to how much influence mentoring generally has in a teacher's career.

The way in which questions are worded is a crucial consideration in extracting the type of information desired. An obvious place to begin is by making certain that what is being asked is clear to the person being interviewed. Questions need to be couched in familiar language. "Using words that make sense to the interviewee, words that reflect the respondent's world view, will improve the quality of data obtained during the interview. Without sensitivity to the impact of particular words on the person being interviewed, the answer may make no sense at all—or there may be no answer" (Patton, 2015, p. 454). Avoiding technical jargon and terms and concepts from your particular disciplinary orientation is a good place to begin. In a study of HIV-positive young adults, for example, participants were asked *how they made sense of or came to terms with their diagnosis*, not *how they constructed meaning in the process of perspective transformation* (the theoretical framework of the study) (Courtenay, Merriam, & Reeves, 1998).

Types of Questions, Good Questions, and Questions to Avoid

An interviewer can ask several types of questions to stimulate responses from an interviewee. Patton (2015) suggests six types of questions:

1. *Experience and behavior questions*—This type of question gets at the things a person does or did, his or her behaviors, actions, and activities. For example, in a study of leadership exhibited by administrators, one could ask, "Tell me about a typical day at work; what are you likely to do first thing in the morning?"
2. *Opinion and values questions*—Here the researcher is interested in a person's beliefs or opinions, what he or she thinks about something. Following the preceding example of a study of administrators and leadership, one could ask, "What is your opinion as to whether administrators should also be leaders?"
3. *Feeling questions*—These questions "tap the affective dimension of human life. In asking feeling questions—'how do you feel about that?'—the interviewer is looking for adjective responses: anxious, happy, afraid, intimidated, confident, and so on" (p. 444).
4. *Knowledge questions*—These questions elicit a participant's actual factual knowledge about a situation.
5. *Sensory questions*—These are similar to experience and behavior questions but try to elicit more specific data about what is or was seen, heard, touched, and so forth.
6. *Background/demographic questions*—All interviews contain questions that refer to the particular demographics (age, income, education, number of years on the job, and so on) of the person being interviewed as relevant to the research study. For example, the age of the respondent may or may not be relevant.

Interestingly, Patton (2015) recommends against asking "why" questions because they tend to lead to speculation about causal relationships and they can lead to dead-end responses. Patton recounts an amusing interview with a child in a study of open class-rooms. When a first grader responded that her "favorite time in school" was recess, Patton asked her why she liked recess. Her answer was because she could go outside and play on the swings. When he asked, "why" she went outside, the child responded, "Because that's where the swings are!" (p. 456). Although "why" questions can put an end to a line of questioning, it has been our experience that an occasional "why" question can uncover insights that might be speculative but that might also suggest a new line of questioning.

Another typology of different types of questions that we have found particularly useful in eliciting information, especially from reticent interviewees, is Strauss, Schatzman, Bucher, and Sabshin's (1981) four major categories of questions: hypothetical, devil's advocate, ideal position, and interpretive questions. Each is defined in Table 5.2 and illustrated with examples from a case study of displaced workers participating in a job training and partnership (JTPA) program.

Hypothetical questions ask respondents to speculate as to what something might be like or what someone might do in a particular situation. Hypothetical questions begin with "What if" or "Suppose." Responses are usually descriptions of the person's actual experience. In the JTPA study, for example, the hypothetical question, "Suppose it were my first day in this training pro-gram—what would it be like?" elicited descriptions of what it was *actually* like for the participants.

Devil's advocate questions are particularly good to use when the topic is controversial and you want respondents' opinions and feelings. This type of question also avoids embarrassing or antago-nizing respondents if they happen to be sensitive about the issue. The wording begins, "Some people would say," which in effect depersonalizes the issue. The response, however, is almost always the respondent's personal opinion or feeling about the matter. In the JTPA example, the question, "Some people would say that employees who lost their job did something to bring it about. What would you say to them?" usually revealed how the respondent came to be unemployed and thus involved in the training program.

TABLE 5.2. FOUR TYPES OF QUESTIONS WITH EXAMPLES FROM
A JTPA TRAINING PROGRAM CASE STUDY.

Type of Question	Example
1. Hypothetical questions—Ask what the respondent might do, or what it might be like in a particular situation; these usually begin with "what if" or "suppose."	Suppose it were my first day in this training program. What would it be like?
2. Devil's advocate questions—The respondent is challenged to consider an opposing view or explanation to a situation.	Some people would say that employees who lost their job did something to bring about being fired. What would you tell them?
3. Ideal position questions—Ask the respondent to describe an ideal situation.	Would you describe what you think the ideal training program would be like?
4. Interpretive questions—The researcher advances tentative explanations or interpretations of what the respondent has been saying and asks for a reaction.	Are you finding returning to school as an adult a different experience from what you expected?

Ideal position questions elicit both information and opinion; these can be used with virtually any phenomenon under study. They are good to use in evaluation studies because they reveal both the positives and the negatives or shortcomings of a program. Asking what the ideal training program would be like in the JTPA example revealed things participants liked and would not want changed, as well as things that could have made it a better program.

Interpretive questions provide a check on what you think you are understanding, as well as offer an opportunity for yet more information, opinions, and feelings to be revealed. In the JTPA example, the interpretive question, "Would you say that returning to school as an adult is different from what you expected?" allowed the investigator to confirm the tentative interpretation of what had been said in the interview.

Overall, *good* interview questions are those that are open-ended and yield descriptive data, even stories about the phenomenon.

The more detailed and descriptive the data, the better. The following questions work well to yield this type of data:

Tell me about a time when . . .

Give me an example of . . .

Tell me more about that . . .

What was it like for you when . . .

Some types of questions should be avoided in an interview. Table 5.3 outlines three types of questions to avoid and illustrates each from the JTPA study. First, avoid multiple questions—either one question that is actually a multiple question or a series of single questions that does not allow the respondent to answer one by one. An example of a multiple question is, "How do you feel about the instructors, the assignments, and the schedule of classes in the JTPA training program?" A series of questions might be, "What's it like going back to school as an adult? How do instructors respond to you? What kind of assignments do you have?" In both cases the respondent is likely to ask you to repeat the question(s), ask for clarification, or give a response covering only one part of the question—and that response may be uninterpretable. If, for example, an interviewee responded to the question, "How do you feel about the instructors, the assignments, and the schedule of classes?" with "They're OK—some I like, some I don't," you would not know whether instructors or assignments or the schedule was being referred to.

Leading questions should also be avoided. Leading questions reveal a bias or an assumption that the researcher is making, which

TABLE 5.3. QUESTIONS TO AVOID.

Type of Question	Example
Multiple questions	How do you feel about the instructors, the assignments, and the schedule of classes?
Leading questions	What emotional problems have you had since losing your job?
Yes-or-no questions	Do you like the program? Has returning to school been difficult?

may not be held by the participant. These set the respondent up to accept the researcher's point of view. The question, "What emotional problems have you had since losing your job?" reflects an assumption that anyone losing a job will have emotional problems.

Finally, all researchers warn against asking yes-or-no questions. Any question that can be answered with a simple yes or no may in fact be answered just that way. Yes-or-no responses give you almost no information. For the reluctant, shy, or less verbal respondent, they offer an easy way out; they can also shut down or at least slow the flow of information from the interviewee. In the JTPA example, questions phrased in a yes-or-no manner, although at their core they are seeking good information, can yield nothing. Thus asking, "Do you like the program?" may be answered yes or no; rephrasing it to, "What do you like about the program?" necessitates more of a response. The same is true of the question "Has returning to school been difficult?" Asking, "How have you found the experience of returning to school?" mandates a fuller response.

A ruthless review of your questions to weed out poor ones before you actually conduct an interview is highly recommended. Ask the questions of yourself, challenging yourself to answer as minimally as possible. Also note whether you would feel uncomfortable honestly answering any of the questions. This review, followed by a pilot interview, will go a long way to ensure that you are asking good questions.

Probes

Probes are also questions or comments that follow up on something already asked. It is virtually impossible to specify these ahead of time because they are dependent on how the participant answers the lead question. This is where being the primary instrument of data collection has its advantages, especially if you are a highly sensitive instrument. You make adjustments in your interviewing as you go along. You sense that the respondent is onto something significant or that there is more to be learned. Probing can come in the form of asking for more details, for clarification, for examples. Glesne and Peshkin (1992) point out that "probes may take numerous forms; they range from silence, to sounds, to a single word, to complete sentences" (p. 85). Silence, "used judiciously

. . . is a useful and easy probe—as is the bunched utterance, '*uh huh, uh huh,*' sometimes combined with a nodding head. 'Yes, yes' is a good alternative; variety is useful" (p. 86, emphasis in original). As with all questions, not just probes, the interviewer should avoid pressing too hard and too fast. After all, the participant is being interviewed, not interrogated.

Probes or follow-up questions—or as Seidman (2013) prefers to call it, "exploration"—can be as simple as seeking more information or clarity about what the person has just said. These are typically who, what, when, and where questions, such as Who else was there? What did you do then? When did this happen? or Where were you when this happened? Other probes seek more details or elaboration, such as What do you mean? Tell me more about that. Give me an example of that. "Walk" me through the experience. Would you explain that? and so on.

The following is a short excerpt (Weeks, n.d.) from an interview with a man in midlife who had been retained (held back a grade) in grammar school. The investigator was interested in how being retained had affected the person's life. Note the follow-up questions or probes used to garner a better understanding of his initial reaction to being retained.

Interviewer: How did you feel about yourself the second time
you were in first grade?

Respondent: I really don't remember, but I think I didn't like it.
It was probably embarrassing to me. I think I may
have even had a hard time explaining it to my
friends. I probably got teased. I was probably
defensive about it. I may even have rebelled in
some childlike way. I do know I got more aggressive
at this point in my life. But I don't know if being
retained had anything to do with it.

Interviewer: How did you feel about your new first grade
teacher?

Respondent: She was nice. I was very quiet for a while, until I got
to know her.

Interviewer: How did you feel about yourself during this second
year?

Respondent: I have to look at it as a follow-up to a period when I was not successful. Strictly speaking, I was not very successful in the first grade—the first time.

Interviewer: Your voice sometimes changes when you talk about that.

Respondent: Well, I guess I'm still a little angry.

Interviewer: Do you feel the retention was justified?

Respondent: (long pause) I don't know how to answer that.

Interviewer: Do you want to think about it for a while?

Respondent: Well, I did *not* learn anything in the first grade the first time, but the lady was nice. She was my Mom's best friend. So she didn't teach me anything, and she made me repeat. I had to be retained, they said, because I did not learn the material, but (shaking his finger), I could have. I could have learned it well. I was smart.

The best way to increase your skill at probing is to practice. The more you interview, especially on the same topic, the more relaxed you become and the better you can pursue potentially fruitful lines of inquiry. Another good strategy is to scrutinize a verbatim transcript of one of your interviews. Look for places where you could have followed up but did not, and compare them with places where you got a lot of good data. The difference will most likely be from having maximized an opportunity to gain more information through gentle probing.

THE INTERVIEW GUIDE

The interview guide, or schedule as it is sometimes called, is nothing more than a list of questions you intend to ask in an interview. Depending on how structured the interview will be, the guide may contain dozens of very specific questions listed in a particular order (highly structured) or a few topical areas jotted down in no particular order (unstructured) or something in between. As we noted earlier, most interviews in qualitative research are semistructured; thus the interview guide will probably contain several specific questions that you want to ask everyone, some more open-ended questions that could be followed up with probes, and perhaps a list of some areas, topics, and issues that you want to know more about but do not have enough information about at the outset of your study to form specific questions.

An investigator new to collecting data through interviews will feel more confident with a structured interview format in which most, if not all, questions are written out ahead of time in the interview guide. Working from an interview schedule allows the new researcher to gain the experience and confidence needed to conduct more open-ended questioning. Most researchers find that they are highly dependent upon the interview guide for the first few interviews but soon can unhook themselves from constant reference to the questions and go with the natural flow of the interview. At that point, an occasional check to see whether all areas or topics are being covered may be all that is needed.

New researchers are often concerned about the order of questions in an interview. No rules determine what should go first and what should come later. Much depends upon the study's objectives, the time allotted for the interview, the person being interviewed, and how sensitive some of the questions are. Factual, sociodemographic-type questions can be asked to get the interview started, but if there are a lot of these, or if some of them are sensitive (for example, if they ask about income, age, or sexual orientation), it might be better to ask them at the end of the interview. By then the respondent has become invested in the interview and is more likely to see it through by answering these questions.

Generally it is a good idea to ask for relatively neutral, descriptive information at the beginning of an interview. Respondents can be asked to provide basic descriptive information about the phenomenon of interest, be it a program, activity, or experience, or to chronicle their history with the phenomenon of interest. This information lays the foundation for questions that access the interviewee's perceptions, opinions, values, emotions, and so on.

Of course, it is not always possible to separate factual information from more subjective, value-laden responses. And again, the best way to tell whether the order of your questions works or not is to try it out in a pilot interview.

In summary, then, questions are at the heart of interviewing, and to collect meaningful data a researcher must ask good questions. In our years of experience doing and supervising qualitative research, the fewer, more open-ended your questions are, the better. Having fewer broader questions unhooks you from the interview guide and enables you to really *listen* to what your participant has to share, which in turn enables you to better follow avenues of inquiry that will yield potentially rich contributions. Exhibit 5.1 is an interview guide for a study of how older adults become self-directed in their health care (Valente, 2005). These open-ended questions, followed up by the skillful use of probes, yielded substantive information about the topic.

EXHIBIT 5.1. INTERVIEW GUIDE.

1. I understand that you are concerned about your health. Tell me about your health.
2. What motivated you to learn about your health?
3. Tell me, in detail, about the kinds of things you have done to learn more about your health. (What did you do first?)
4. Where do you find information about your health?
5. Tell me about a time when something you learned had a positive impact on your health care.
6. What kinds of things have you changed in your life because of your learning?
7. Whom do you talk to about your health?
8. Tell me about your current interactions with your health care provider.
9. Tell me about what you do to keep track of your health.
10. What other things do you do to manage your health?
11. What kinds of challenges (barriers) do you experience when managing your health care?
12. What else would you like to share about your health-related learning?

Source: Valente (2005). Reprinted with permission.

BEGINNING THE INTERVIEW

Collecting data through interviews involves, first of all, determining whom to interview. That depends on what the investigator wants to know and from whose perspective the information is desired. Selecting respondents on the basis of what they can contribute to the researcher's understanding of the phenomenon under study means engaging in purposive or theoretical sampling (discussed in Chapter Four). In a qualitative case study of a community school program, for example, a holistic picture of the program would involve the experiences and perceptions of people having different associations with the program—administrators, teachers, students, community residents. Unlike survey research, in which the number and representativeness of the sample are major considerations, in this type of research the crucial factor is not the number of respondents but the potential of each person to contribute to the development of insight and understanding of the phenomenon.

How can such people be identified? One way is through initial on-site observation of the program, activity, or phenomenon under study. On-site observations often involve informal discussions with participants to discover those who should be interviewed in depth. A second means of locating contacts is to begin with a key person who is considered knowledgeable by others and then ask that person for referrals. Initial informants can be found through the investigator's own personal contacts, community and private organizations, advertisements on bulletin boards, or on the Internet. In some studies a preliminary interview is necessary to determine whether the person meets the criteria for participating in the study. For example, in Moon's (2011) study of the transformational potential of grieving in older adulthood, he first had to determine if prospective participants could identify some change in their sense of self or view of the world as a result of grieving the loss of a loved one.

Taylor and Bogdan (1984) list five issues that should be addressed at the outset of every interview:

1. The investigator's motives and intentions and the inquiry's purpose
2. The protection of respondents through the use of pseudonyms
3. Deciding who has final say over the study's content

4. Payment (if any)
5. Logistics with regard to time, place, and number of interviews to be scheduled (pp. 87–88)

Besides being careful to word questions in language clear to the respondent, the interviewer must be aware of his or her stance toward the interviewee. Since the respondent has been selected by the investigator on purpose, it can be assumed that the participant has something to contribute, has had an experience worth talking about, and has an opinion of interest to the researcher. This stance will go a long way in making the respondent comfortable and forthcoming with what he or she has to offer.

An interviewer should also assume neutrality with regard to the respondent's knowledge; that is, regardless of how antithetical to the interviewer's beliefs or values the respondent's position might be, it is crucial for the success of the interview to avoid arguing, debating, or otherwise letting personal views be known. Patton (2015) distinguishes between neutrality and rapport. "At the same time that I am neutral with regard to the content of what is being said to me, I care very much that that person is willing to share with me what they are saying. *Rapport is a stance vis-à-vis the person being interviewed. Neutrality is a stance vis-à-vis the content of what that person says*" (p. 457, emphasis in original).

There are several ways of maximizing the time spent getting an informant to share information. A slow-starting interview, for example, can be moved along by asking respondents for basic descriptive information about themselves, the event, or the phenomenon under study. Interviews aimed at constructing life histories can be augmented by written narratives, personal documents, and daily activity logs that informants are asked to submit ahead of time. The value of an interview, of course, depends on the interviewer's knowing enough about the topic to ask meaningful questions in language easily understood by the informant.

Interviewer and Respondent Interaction

The interaction between interviewer and respondent can be looked at from the perspective of either party or from the interaction itself. Skilled interviewers can do much to bring about positive interaction. Being respectful, nonjudgmental, and non-threatening is a beginning. Obviously, becoming skilled takes practice; practice combined with feedback on performance is the best way to develop the needed skills. Role playing, peer critiquing, videotaping, and observing experienced interviewers at work are all ways novice researchers can improve their perform-ance in this regard.

What makes a good respondent? Anthropologists and sociolo-gists speak of a good respondent as an "informant"—one who understands the culture but is also able to reflect on it and articulate for the researcher what is going on. Key informants are able, to some extent, to adopt the stance of the investigator, thus becoming a valuable guide in unfamiliar territory. But not all good respondents can be considered key informants in the sense that anthropologists use the term. Good respondents are those who can express thoughts, feelings, opinions—that is, offer a perspective—on the topic being studied. Participants usually enjoy sharing their expertise with an interested and sympathetic listener. For some, it is also an opportunity to clarify their own thoughts and experiences.

Dexter (1970) says there are three variables in every interview situation that determine the nature of the interaction: "(1) the personality and skill of the interviewer, (2) the attitudes and orientation of the interviewee, and (3) the definition of both (and often by significant others) of the situation" (p. 24). These factors also determine the type of information obtained from an interview. Let us suppose, for example, that two researchers are studying an innovative curriculum for first-year college stu-dents. One interviewer is predisposed to innovative practices in general, while the other favors traditional educational practices. One student informant is assigned to the program, while another student requests the curriculum and is eager to be interviewed. The particular combination of interviewer and student that evolves will determine, to some extent, the type of data obtained.

There has been much attention in recent literature to the subjectivity and complexity inherent in the interview encounter. Critical theory, feminist theory, critical race theory, queer theory, and postmodernism have been brought to bear on analyzing the intricacies of the interview encounter. Although each of these perspectives challenges us to think about what we are doing when interviewing, what they have in common is a concern for the participants and their voices, the power dynamics inherent in the interview, the construction of the "story," and forms of representation to other audiences.

Some of this discussion is framed in terms of insider-outsider status, especially with regard to visible social identities, most notably gender, race, age, and socioeconomic class. Seidman (2013, p. 101) discusses how "our experience with issues of class, race, and gender . . . interact with the sense of power in our lives." And, in turn, "the interviewing relationship is fraught with issues of power—who controls the direction of the interview, who controls the results, who benefits." Foster (1994), for example, explores the ambiguities and complexities of the interviewer-respondent relationship in her study of attitudes toward law and order among two generations. She analyzes her stance with regard to interactions with women versus men, the younger generation versus the older, middle class versus the working class.

Does a researcher need to be a member of the group being investigated to do a credible study? Is it preferable for women to interview women or for Hispanics to interview Hispanics? What about the intersection of race, gender, and class? Are people more likely to reveal information to insiders or outsiders? There are of course no single right answers to any of these questions, only the pluses and minuses involved in any combination of interviewer and respondent. Seidman (2013) suggests that along with being highly sensitive to these issues and taking them into account throughout the study, "interviewing requires interviewers to have enough distance to enable them to ask real questions and to explore, not to share, assumptions" (p. 102).

Thus the interviewer-respondent interaction is a complex phenomenon. Both parties bring biases, predispositions, attitudes, and physical characteristics that affect the interaction and the data elicited. A skilled interviewer accounts for these factors in order to evaluate the data being obtained. Taking a stance that is non-judgmental, sensitive, and respectful of the respondent is but a beginning point in the process.

RECORDING AND TRANSCRIBING INTERVIEW DATA

Of the three basic ways to record interview data, the most common by far is to audio record the interview. This practice ensures that everything said is preserved for analysis. The interviewer can also listen for ways to improve his or her questioning technique. The potential drawbacks are malfunctioning equipment and a respondent's uneasiness with being recorded. Most researchers find, however, that after some initial wariness respondents tend to forget they are being recorded, especially if one uses an unobtrusive digital recorder. Occasionally interviews are videotaped. This practice allows for recording of nonverbal behavior, but it is also more cumbersome and intrusive than audio recording the interview.

A second way to record interview data is to take notes during the interview. Since not everything said can be written down, and since at the outset of a study a researcher is not certain what is important enough to write down, this method is recommended only when mechanical recording is not feasible or when a participant does not want to be recorded. Some investigators like to take written notes in addition to recording the session. The interviewer may want to record his or her reactions to something the informant says, to signal the informant of the importance of what is being said, or to pace the interview.

The third—and least desirable—way to record interview data is to write down as much as can be remembered as soon after the interview as possible. The problems with this method are obvious, but at times, writing or recording during an interview might be intrusive (when interviewing terminally ill patients, for example). In any case, researchers must write their reflections immediately following the interview. These reflections might contain insights suggested by the interview; descriptive notes on the behavior, verbal and nonverbal, of the informant; parenthetical thoughts of the researcher; and so on. Postinterview notes allow the investigator to monitor the process of data collection as well as begin to analyze the information itself.

Ideally, verbatim transcription of recorded interviews provides the best database for analysis. Be forewarned, however, that this is a time-consuming prospect; you can either transcribe the interview yourself or have someone do it for you. Hiring a transcriber can be expensive, and there are trade-offs in doing so. You do not get the intimate familiarity with your data that doing your own transcribing affords. Also, a transcriber is likely to be unfamiliar with terminology and, not having conducted the interview, will not be able to fill in places where the recording is of poor quality. If someone else has transcribed your interview, it is a good idea to read through the transcript while listening to it in order to correct errors and fill in blanks. However, hiring someone to transcribe allows you to spend time analyzing your data instead of transcribing. We recommend that new and inexperienced researchers transcribe at least the first few interviews of any study, if at all possible.

There are great benefits to transcribing the interview yourself, not the least of which is increasing your familiarity with your data. If you do it yourself, you can write yourself analytic memos along the way. But even with good keyboarding skills, transcribing interviews is a tedious process, though many of our students have found some voice recognition software extremely helpful to this task, cutting down the time it takes. The one that is mentioned most often and appears to be the most economical in terms of time and money is Dragon NaturallySpeaking. However, it generally recognizes only the voice of the trained speaker. One of our students described her procedure for using it for transcription much the same way as is described on their website: using what they call the "parroting" function, which means to respeak the interview. She found this extremely helpful and relatively quick; further, using it provided her the opportunity to become very familiar with her data in the process. The procedure she used is described on their website (www.nuance.com/dragon/transcription-solutions/index.htm):

> Listen to the recording through the headphones of your Dragon headset and activate your Dragon microphone and repeat the recorded text as you hear it.
>
> Speaking the text aloud in your own voice enables Dragon to accu-rately transcribe the audio using the Dragon profile tuned to your voice.

Dragon turns your voice into text as quickly as you can speak the words—so there's no need to constantly rewind the audio while you try to type out the corresponding text.

This of course is not the only transcription software available, but it is one that she found very helpful and strongly recommends to others. These technological aids are always being developed, so one can either use this method or keep an eye out for new developments.

The format of the interview transcript should be set up to enable analysis. At the top of the first page, list identifying information as to when, where, and with whom the interview was conducted. A crucial factor to enable analysis is to add *line numbering* down the left-hand side of the page. Begin with the first page and number sequentially to the end of the interview. Another format consideration is whether to use single or double spacing. It's been our experience that single spacing works best, but *double space between speakers*. You can also put the interviewer questions in bold or italics, which further enables ease of reading. Finally, leave a wide enough margin on the right-hand side of the pages for you to add notes or codes as you analyze the transcript.

Exhibit 5.2 presents an excerpt from a transcribed interview that was conducted for a study of the role of culture in the health-

---

Exhibit 5.2. Interview Transcript.

(Excerpted from interview with Deepak, March 22, 2008)

1. *Swathi:* Could you tell me a little more about the check-up that you had,
2. you said it is for older people. Where was that?
3.
4. *Deepak:* Lyla Shoals, hospital, they, every year like they have prostate week or
5. something like that. At that time they all the doctors come and give free check-up
6. for 50 or old people, you know. So I just heard that and I said ok let me go and
7. get check-up because I'm 50 and it's free.
8.
9. *Swathi:* It's for the whole community.
10.
11. *Deepak:* Yeah, whole community. Anybody over 50 can go and have a check-up.
12. And there I think 4 or 5 doctors were checking over there.
13.
14. *Swathi:* And how did you find out about that?

(continued)

(*Continued*)

15.

16. *Deepak:* They were advertising on the radio and local newspaper and so I said
17. let's go. So after work I stopped by over there.

18.

19. *Swathi:* But you said they didn't do the blood test at that time.

20.

21. *Deepak:* No, they recommend. Because, you see, I lied on the questions. And you
22. know they take finger test and they checked it. They might have realized that I
23. might have little bit enlarged prostate at that time, but then they weren't sure so
24. that's why they recommend, PSA, take that test, blood test, positively it tell you
25. um that you have enlarged prostate or not. But then I didn't go. I thought it was
26. going to go away.

27.

28. *Swathi:* So, you mentioned that up until this point you hadn't gone to the
29. doctor at all. Why do you think that is?

30.

31. *Deepak:* Not yearly check-up, but also I wasn't that sick at all. Every year I knew
32. that I was getting cold, especially when I was living in New York, but then
33. Contac and those other kind of common cold medicines, I take it and I'm alright.
34. So I never was that seriously sick that I needed to go to the doctor or something
35. for anything, you know. That's why I've never been. At that time, it wasn't like,
36. we didn't know, that actually it's nice to go, even if you're not feeling good, it's
37. ok to go doctor and have physical check-up or something, it would be nice.
38. That's why I just didn't go, until it got worse. And then Sumie, my wife, says go
39. doctor go doctor check it out. And then I knew I had prostate problem so I
40. wanted to take care of that anyway. And lot of time I don't I didn't go because I
41. didn't have insurance you know. Sometimes you work on your own and then you
42. don't have insurance you don't want to go. And for what? I say, for what, nothing
43. wrong, what they going to check up? So 25, 30 years, I never had to go to doctor
44. over here. Only time you go to doctor for check-up if you have some problem,
45. you know. It's not like now, you should go every year and have physical check-up.
46. That concept wasn't there. I mean wasn't there means for me, yeah, nothing, you
47. don't have to go to the doctor.

48.

49. *Swathi:* Had you been to the doctor in India?

50.

51. *Deepak:* Only time if I got hurt or something. Yeah India, when I was small boy,
52. I used to get stay sick lots of time. So every month or two months I go to the
53. doctor, we have family doctor you know over there. So you go over there and say
54. doctor uncle this is what happens so doctor gives you couple of shot. I was sick, I
55. mean not sick but skinny, so always wanted to go and get fat. So I always tell
56. doctor uncle, give me something for fat. He said there is no such thing. You take
57. uh like some vitamins, not vitamins I'm sorry, you drink cod liver oil it's going to
58. be fine, those kind of things. So drink and it will be alright. And after we grew
59. up, and then high school we say we eat meat, eggs, or something like that then we
60. can get fat too. So even though we are Brahmin we are not supposed to, we,
61. friends we go to the Muslim, always the Muslim restaurants you know they serve
62. that and we eat that meat. But no, we didn't get fat (laughs). But otherwise, so
63. that's the only reason I used to go to the doctor. Couple of time I got, one time I

64. got, uh, not influenza, what they call it, then I was sick for a few days. When I
65. was in 11th grade I got small pox, when I was grown up. So, but then doctor,
66. usually then doctor comes to your home you know and check and nothing I can do,
67. just three or four days. You know, there is no cure. Otherwise no, after, like until
68. 3rd or 4th grade I used to get sick, but after 6th grade I never got sick even in India
69. so no need to go to doctor.
70.
71. *Swathi:* How did your experience with the doctor compare in India to here?
72.
73. *Deepak:* Well in India you have lot of friendly doctor because doctor is part of our
74. family you know. We call them Uncle rather than doctor you know. Don't feel
75. any scare or strange or something and um when we're kids, I mean I don't know
76. after that, when you go to doctor you have to go with your bottle you know your
77. own bottle and they give some medications in there. Every doctor over there you
78. go with the bottle and they give you some medication and then you have to take 3
79. times a day or 4 times a day, drink it. This doctor is very nice and I say give me
80. something sweet so medications are most of them not good. I don't know what
81. they mix it but he say ok and we go home and it's so tasty. So you take 3 times a
82. day and then next day you go again and they refill that same medication, 3, 4 days
83. you go there. So over there it was fine. Over here when you came and I went
84. there or when I saw other people you do doctor they don't have any. ... in India
85. they have doctor has whole lot of bottles and whole lot of medications right in
86. their dispensary, what they call it, in their office or they mix it and they give it to
87. you or they give you shot right there. When I came here doctor's office is like a
88. living room you know and then they prescribe you medicine and say go there. So
89. that was the big difference for me that I saw over here. And uh, over there you can
90. talk to doctor as long as you want or something. It is not just time and don't feel
91. that expensive either because it's on monthly account so you even don't know
92. how much you pay. Over here, that was the difference.

Source: Thaker (n.d.). Reprinted with permission.

related behaviors of older Asian Indian immigrants (Thaker, 2008). Notice that identifying information is at the top, there is consecutive line numbering, and the content is single spaced but double spaced between speakers.

In addition to recording interview data for analysis, it is important to assess, as best you can, the quality of the data obtained. Several factors may influence an informant's responses, factors that may be difficult for the researcher to discern. The informant's health, mood at the time of interview, and so on may affect the quality of data obtained, as might an informant's ulterior motives for participating in the project. Furthermore, all information obtained from an informant has been selected, either consciously or unconsciously, from all that he or she knows. What you get in an interview is simply the informant's perception of the phenomenon of interest at that particular point in time. Although this personal perspective is, of course, what is sought in qualitative research, the information in any single interview needs to be considered in light of other interviews and other sources of data such as observations and documents (see Chapter Nine for a discussion of validity and reliability).

SUMMARY

In qualitative research, interviewing is often the major source of the qualitative data needed for understanding the phenomenon under study. Interviews can range in structure from those in which questions and the order in which they are asked are predetermined to totally unstructured interviews in which nothing is set ahead of time. Most common is the semistructured interview that is guided by a set of questions and issues to be explored, but neither the exact wording nor the order of questions is predetermined.

Asking good questions is key to getting meaningful data. Interview questions can ask for experiences, opinions, feelings, knowledge, sensory, or demographic data. Hypothetical, devil's advocate, ideal position, and interpretive questions can also be used to elicit good data; multiple and leading questions, as well as questions yielding yes or no answers, should be avoided. Follow-up questions or probes are an important part of the process. An interview guide contains the questions the researcher intends to ask.

Considering how to begin the interview and accounting for some of the complexities in the interaction between interviewer and respondent will result in a more informed analysis of the interview data. This chapter addressed these issues, along with some of the mechanics of recording interview data.

CHAPTER SIX

BEING A CAREFUL OBSERVER

Interviews are a primary source of data in qualitative research; so too are observations. Observations are common in many types of qualitative research, such as in case studies, ethnographies, and qualitative action research studies. Observations are especially important in ethnographic studies.

Observations can be distinguished from interviews in two ways. First, observations take place in the setting where the phenomenon of interest naturally occurs rather than a location designated for the purpose of interviewing; second, observational data represent a firsthand encounter with the phenomenon of interest rather than a secondhand account of the world obtained in an interview. In the real world of collecting data, however, informal interviews and conversations are often interwoven with observation. The terms *fieldwork* and *field study* usually connote both activities (observation and informal interviews) and may also include the study of documents and artifacts. That caveat notwithstanding, the primary focus of this chapter is on the activity of observation—the use of observation as a research tool, the problem of what to observe, the relationship between observer and observed, and the means for recording observations. We also discuss the whole phenomenon of online observation, given that we now have the ability to observe at a distance through online and various virtual technologies.

OBSERVATION IN RESEARCH

Being alive renders us natural observers of our everyday world and our behavior in it. What we learn helps us make sense of our world and guides our future actions. Most of this observation is routine—largely unconscious and unsystematic. It is part of living, part of our commonsense interaction with the world. But just as casually conversing with someone differs from interviewing, so too does this routine observation differ from research observation. Observation is a research tool when it is systematic, when it addresses a specific research question, and when it is subject to the checks and balances in producing trustworthy results.

Critics of participant observation as a data-gathering technique point to the highly subjective and therefore unreliable nature of human perception. Human perception is also very selective. Consider a traffic accident at a busy intersection. From each different witness to the accident there will be a different, perhaps even contradictory, account of what happened. However, the witnesses were not planning to systematically observe the accident, nor were they trained in observational techniques. These factors differentiate everyday observation from research-related observation. Patton (2015) contends that comparing untrained observers with researchers is like comparing what "an amateur community talent show" can do compared with "professional performers" (p. 331). Training and mental preparation is as important in becoming a good observer as it is in becoming a good interviewer. Wolcott (1992) also notes that the difference between "mere mortals" and qualitative researchers is that "qualitative researchers, like others whose roles demand selective attentiveness—artists and novelists, detectives and spies, guards and thieves, to name a few—pay special attention to a few things to which others ordinarily give only passing attention. Observers of any ilk do no more: We all attend to certain things, and nobody attends to them all" (pp. 22–23).

Just as you can learn to be a skilled interviewer, you can also learn to be a careful, systematic observer. Training to be a skilled observer includes "learning to pay attention," learning how to write "descriptively," practicing the disciplined recording of field notes, "knowing how to separate detail from trivia . . . and using systematic methods to validate and triangulate observations" (Patton, 2015, p. 331). You can practice observing in any number of ways—by being a complete observer in a public place, by being a participant observer in your work or social settings, or by watching films or videotapes. You can also apprentice yourself to an experienced field researcher, comparing his or her observations with yours. You might also read other people's accounts of the experience.

An investigator might want to gather data through observation for many reasons. As an outsider an observer will notice things that have become routine to the participants themselves, things that may lead to understanding the context. Observations are also conducted to triangulate emerging findings; that is, they are used in conjunction with interviewing and document analysis to substantiate the findings (see Chapter Nine). The participant observer sees things firsthand and uses his or her own knowledge and expertise in interpreting what is observed rather than relying on once-removed accounts from interviews. Observation makes it possible to record behavior as it is happening.

Another reason to conduct observations is to provide some knowledge of the context or to provide specific incidents, behaviors, and so on that can be used as reference points for subsequent interviews. This is a particularly helpful strategy for understanding ill-defined phenomena. For example, in a study of respiratory therapists' critical thinking, Mishoe (1995) observed therapists as they worked in the clinical setting, and shortly thereafter she interviewed them. She was thus able to ask them what they were thinking with regard to specific behaviors she had witnessed on site. As an aside, this type of interview is sometimes called "anchored interviewing," as the interview questions are "anchored" to what was observed.

Finally, people may not feel free to talk about or may not want to discuss all topics. In studying a small educational unit, for example, the researcher might observe dissension and strife among certain staff members that an interview would not reveal. Observation is the best technique to use when an activity, event, or situation can be observed firsthand, when a fresh perspective is desired, or when participants are not able or willing to discuss the topic under study.

WHAT TO OBSERVE

What to observe is determined by several factors. The most important is the researcher's purpose in conducting the study in the first place. In other words, the theoretical framework, the problem, and the questions of interest determine what is to be observed. As we noted in Chapter Four, a researcher's disciplinary orientation often determines how a problem is defined. An educator might observe a school because of an interest in how students learn, whereas a sociologist might visit the same school because of an interest in social institutions. Practical considerations also play a part in determining what to observe. Certain behavior is difficult to observe; further, a researcher must have the time, money, and energy to devote to observation and must be allowed to observe by those in the situation of interest. Observers need to be open to early impressions and feelings about what is going on in a setting because it is these early impressions that help determine subsequent patterns of observation. Schensul and LeCompte (2013) write that researchers' curiosity will drive what they initially observe, and that over time "with repeated observation and questioning, the meanings of items, articles, patterns of behavior, and social relationships and events will become clearer" (p. 91).

What to observe is partly a function of how structured the observer wants to be. Just as there is a range of structure in interviewing, there is also a range of structure in observation. The researcher can decide ahead of time to concentrate on observing certain events, behaviors, or persons. A code sheet might be used to record instances of specified behavior. Less-structured observations can be compared to a television camera scanning the area. Where to begin looking depends on the research question, but where to focus or stop action cannot be determined ahead of time. The focus must be allowed to emerge and in fact may change over the course of the study.

Nevertheless, no one can observe everything, and the researcher must start somewhere. Several writers present lists of things to observe, at least to get started in the activity. Here is a checklist of elements likely to be present in any setting:

1. *The physical setting:* What is the physical environment like? What is the context? What kinds of behavior is the setting designed for? How is space allocated? What objects, resources, technologies are in the setting? The principal's office, the school bus, the cafeteria, and the classroom vary in physical attributes as well as in the anticipated behaviors.

2. *The participants:* Describe who is in the scene, how many people, and their roles. What brings these people together? Who is allowed here? Who is not here that you would expect to be here? What are the relevant characteristics of the participants? Further, what are the ways in which the people in this setting organize themselves? "Patterns and frequency of interactions, the direction of communication patterns . . . and changes in these patterns tell us things about the social environment" (Patton, 2015, p. 367).

3. *Activities and interactions:* What is going on? Is there a definable sequence of activities? How do the people interact with the activity and with one another? How are people and activities connected? What norms or rules structure the activities and interactions? When did the activity begin? How long does it last? Is it a typical activity, or unusual?

4. *Conversation:* What is the content of conversations in this setting? Who speaks to whom? Who listens? Quote directly, paraphrase, and summarize conversations. If possible, use a tape recorder to back up your note-taking. Note silences and nonverbal behavior that add meaning to the exchange.

5. *Subtle factors:* Less obvious but perhaps as important to the observation are
   - Informal and unplanned activities
   - Symbolic and connotative meanings of words
   - Nonverbal communication such as dress and physical space
   - Unobtrusive measures such as physical clues
   - "What does *not* happen" . . . especially if "certain things ought to happen or are expected to happen" (Patton, 2015, p. 379, emphasis in original)

6. *Your own behavior:* You are as much a part of the scene as participants. How is your role, whether as an observer or an intimate participant, affecting the scene you are observing? What do you say and do? In addition, what thoughts are you having

about what is going on? These become "observer comments," an important part of field notes.

Each participant observation experience has its own rhythm and flow. The duration of a single observation or the total amount of time spent collecting data in this way is a function of the problem being investigated. There is no ideal amount of time to spend observing, nor is there one preferred pattern of observation. For some situations, observation over an extended period may be most appropriate; for others, shorter periodic observations make the most sense, given the purpose of the study and practical constraints. Most writers do recommend that when learning to do field work, sessions of an hour or less are recommended. Observations take enormous energy and concentration. Further, it is recommended that you allow for writing up your field notes as soon after the observation as possible.

The process of collecting data through observations can be broken into the three stages: entry, data collection, and exit. Gaining entry into a site begins with gaining the confidence and permission of those who can approve the activity. This step is more easily accomplished through a mutual contact who can recommend the researcher to the "gatekeepers" involved. Even with an advocate working on your behalf, it may be difficult to gain entry to certain settings. In our experience, it is difficult for an outsider to gain entry to business and industry, some government agencies, and some groups because of the sensitivity or exclusivity of their mission (such as self-help groups, racial and ethnic groups, and so forth). Bogdan and Biklen (2011) point out that most groups will want answers to the following:

- What are you actually going to do?
- Will you be disruptive?
- What are you going to do with your findings?
- Why us? Why have "they or their organizations" been "singled out for study"? (p. 88)
- What will we get out of this? (pp. 87–88)

You will increase your chances of gaining entry by being prepared to answer these questions as candidly as possible, being persistent, and being able to adjust to modifications in your original request. Once you have gained entry, the following comments by Bogdan and Biklen (2011) can aid you in your first few days in the field:

- "Do not take what happens in the field personally" (p. 91).
- Have someone on site introduce you.
- Keep the first observations fairly short to avoid becoming overwhelmed with the novelty of the situation.
- Be relatively passive and unobtrusive, put people at ease, learn how to act and dress in the setting.
- Be friendly and honest but not overly technical or detailed in explaining what you are doing.

They also suggest that the researcher establish rapport by fitting into the participants' routines, finding some common ground with them, helping out on occasion, being friendly, and showing interest in the activity.

Once you (the researcher) become familiar with the setting and begin to see what is there to observe, serious data collection can begin. There is little glamour and much hard work in this phase of research. It takes great concentration to observe intently, remember as much as possible, and then record in as much detail as possible what has been observed. Conducting an observation, even a short one, can be exhausting, especially in the beginning of a study. Everyone and everything is new; you do not know what will be important, so you try to observe everything; you are concerned about the effect you will have on the scene; you miss things while taking notes; and so on. It is probably best to do more frequent, shorter observations at first. The more familiar everything feels and the more comfortable you are in the setting, the longer you will be able to observe.

The overall time spent on the site, the number of visits, and the number of observations made per visit cannot be precisely determined ahead of time. At some point, time and money will run out, and new information will be scarce. Ideally, depletion of resources coincides with saturation of information. Leaving the field, however, may be even more difficult than gaining entry. Relationships have been formed, habitual patterns established with regard to the site, and so on. Patton (2015, p. 405) recommends thinking through "an exit or disengagement strategy." Bogdan and Biklen (2011, p. 116) suggest that "rather than abruptly ending this phase of . . . research, . . . ease out of the field by coming less frequently and then eventually stopping altogether." In any case, "all field workers, novices and the more experienced, still worry about whether they got it all and got it right. No one gets it all, of course. But researchers ask themselves whether they have captured the range and the variation of patterns relevant to their topics" (Preissle & Grant, 2004, p. 180).

RELATIONSHIP BETWEEN OBSERVER AND OBSERVED

The researcher can assume one of several stances while collecting information as an observer; stances range from being a full participant—the investigator is a member of the group being observed—to being a spectator. Gold's (1958) classic typology offers a spectrum of four possible stances:

1. *Complete participant:* The researcher is a member of the group being studied and conceals his or her observer role from the group so as not to disrupt the natural activity of the group. The inside information obtainable by using this method must be weighed against the possible disadvantages—loss of perspective on the group, being labeled a spy or traitor when research activities are revealed, and the questionable ethics of deceiving the other participants.
2. *Participant as observer:* The researcher's observer activities, which are known to the group, are subordinate to the researcher's role as a participant. Schensul and LeCompte (2013) refer to this as "a data-collection technique that requires the researcher to be present at, involved in, and actually recording the routine daily activities with people in the field setting" (p. 83), while maintaining an active participant role. The trade-off here is between the depth of the information revealed to the researcher and the level of confidentiality promised to the group in order to obtain this information.
3. *Observer as participant:* The researcher's observer activities are known to the group; participation in the group is definitely

secondary to the role of information gatherer. Using this method, the researcher may have access to many people and a wide range of information, but the level of the information revealed is controlled by the group members being investigated. Adler and Adler (1998) refer to this as a "peripheral membership role," which is different from having an active membership role. Here researchers "observe and interact closely enough with members to establish an insider's identity without participating in those activities constituting the core of group membership" (p. 85).

4. *Complete observer:* The researcher is either hidden from the group (for example, behind a one-way mirror) or in a completely public setting such as an airport or library.

More recent work has defined yet another possible stance of the researcher vis-à-vis participants—that of the *collaborative partner.* This role is closest to being a complete participant on the continuum just detailed, but the investigator's identity is clearly known to everyone involved. Although defined variously within the areas of teacher research, feminist research, or action and participatory research, the defining characteristic of this stance is that the investigator and the participants are equal partners in the research process—including defining the problem to be studied, collecting and analyzing data, and writing and disseminating the findings. (For further discussion of this role see Cranton & Merriam, 2015; Herr & Anderson, 2015.)

Inherent in the full participant–full observer continuum is the extent to which the investigation is overt or covert. Whether the researcher is a complete participant or a complete observer, in some cases the "real" activity (or the details of exactly what the researcher is observing) is not entirely known to those being observed. This situation leads to ethical questions related to the privacy and protection of research subjects—issues discussed more fully in Chapter Nine. Uldam and McCurdy (2013) also discuss issues of covert and overt research in more detail.

In reality, researchers are rarely total participants or total observers. Rather, there is often a mix of roles wherein one might either begin as a full participant and then withdraw into more of a researcher stance or the reverse: begin as a total observer and become more of a participant over time. Although the ideal in qualitative research is to get inside the perspective of the participants, full participation is not always possible. A researcher can never know exactly how it feels to be illiterate or mentally ill, for example. A question can also be raised as to just how much better it is to be an insider. Being born into a group, "going native," or just being a member does not necessarily afford the perspective necessary for studying the phenomenon. Conversely, being a member of the group being studied may be the only way to gain access and obtain reliable information. Patton (2015) underscores the balance needed between insider and outsider in qualitative research. "Experiencing the program as an insider accentuates the participant part of participant observation. At the same time, the inquirer remains aware of being an outsider. The challenge is to combine participation and observation so as to become capable of understanding the setting as an insider while describing it to and for outsiders" (p. 338).

As the researcher gains familiarity with the phenomenon being studied, the mix of participation and observation is likely to change. As Walford (2001) notes, being an observer is a "process of role definition, negotiation and renegotiation" (p. 62). Further, there is only one role *initially* open to researchers, despite the intent of the researcher, and that role is restricted to what those who are being observed "automatically assign . . . to a researcher" (p. 63). The researcher might begin as a spectator and gradually become involved in the activities being observed. In other situations an investigator might decide to join a group to see what it is actually like to be a participant and then gradually withdraw, eventually assuming the role of interested observer. Uldam and McCurdy (2013) provide an interesting discussion of insider and outsider status issues in conducting participant observation; they note how the roles can shift and change in studying involvement in various social movements. They highlight how this has happened in studying the Occupy movement; they also consider how the impact of social media can also change these roles further when one posts comments on media sites that members are a part of.

Participant observation is a schizophrenic activity in that the researcher usually participates but not to the extent of becoming totally absorbed in the activity, at least in the way that conducting observation has been traditionally conceptualized. As Roach (2014) notes (and then deconstructs), in traditional conceptualizations of the participant observer role, the researcher tries to stay sufficiently detached to observe and analyze, while participating. But this is a marginal position and personally difficult to sustain. Gans (1982) captures the distress in being a researcher participant: "The temptation to become involved was ever-present. I had to fight the urge to shed the emotional handcuffs that bind the researcher, and to react spontaneously to the situation, to relate to people as a person and to derive pleasure rather than data from the situation. Often, I carried on an internal tug of war, to decide how much spontaneous participation was possible without missing something as a researcher" (p. 54).

The ambiguity of participant observation can be one source of anxiety for the qualitative researcher. Gans (1982) cites three other sources that make this method of gathering data particularly difficult. There is, he writes, "the constant worry about the flow of research activities." And he goes on to ask, "Is one doing the right thing at the right time, attending the right meeting, or talking to the right people?" (p. 58). Another source of anxiety is "how to make sense out of what one is studying, how not to be upset by the initial inability to understand and how to order the constant influx of data" (p. 59). Finally, the inherent deception in participant observation leads to "a pervasive feeling of guilt" and "a tendency to overidentify with the people being studied" (p. 59).

Another concern is the extent to which the observer investigator affects what is being observed. In traditional models of research, the ideal is to be as objective and detached as possible so as not to "contaminate" the study. Feminist, postmodern, and critical researchers have problematized this position, however, arguing that the presence of anything or anyone in a research environment is going to have some effect (Roach, 2014), and that it is better to own one's positionality and attempt to account for it. Further, in qualitative research in which the researcher is the primary instrument of data collection, subjectivity and interaction are assumed. The interdependency between the observer and the observed may bring about changes in both parties' behaviors. The question, then, is not whether the process of observing affects what is observed, but how the researcher can identify those effects and account for them in interpreting the data. At the very least, participants who know they are being observed will tend to behave in socially acceptable ways and present themselves in a favorable manner. Further, participants will regulate their behavior in reaction to even subtle forms of feedback from the observer—as when notes are taken or behavior is attended to in a particular fashion. Finally, the mere presence of the observer in the setting can affect the climate of the setting, often effecting a more formal atmosphere than is usually the case.

The extent to which an observer changes the situation studied is never entirely clear. Frankenberg (1982, p. 51) points out that in traditional anthropological studies the activities of an ethnographer (researcher) are not likely to change "custom and practice built up over years." It is more likely that the researcher will prove to be "a catalyst for changes that are already taking place." Others have suggested that, over time, the stability of a social setting is rarely disrupted by the presence of an observer. Further, as noted earlier, those researchers coming from feminist, postmodern, critical, or complexity science perspectives will argue that there is always an effect, which isn't necessarily negative, and it's simply best to try to account for the effect. It has been the experience of many field researchers that at first their presence may elicit more polite, formal, or guarded behavior, but this cannot be sustained; the social setting returns to its typical functioning. In any case, the researcher must be sensitive to the possible effects one might be having on the situation and account for those effects. "Observers," Patton (2015, p. 413) writes, "must make an effort to observe themselves observing and record the effects of their observations on the people observed and, no less important, reflect on changes they've experienced from having been in the setting. This means being able to balance observation with reflection and manage the tension between engagement and detachment."

Wolcott (2005) sums up this "tension between engagement and detachment" by acknowledging that all researchers have

> to achieve a workable balance between participating and observing. There is always a question of whether those two processes constitute discrete functions or are hopelessly intertwined in the very act of anyone being anywhere, but it is comforting to have our own special label for what we do to

reassure ourselves that our being there is different from anyone else's. That self-conscious role is what we examine when we discuss participant observation—how we can realize the potential not simply of being there, but of being so agonizingly self-conscious about it. (p. 89)

RECORDING OBSERVATIONS

What is written down or mechanically recorded from a period of observation becomes the raw data from which a study's findings eventually emerge. This written account of the observation constitutes *field notes,* which are analogous to the interview transcript. In both forms of data collection, the more complete the recording, the easier it is to analyze the data. How much can be captured during an observation? The answer depends on the researcher's role and the extent to which he or she is a participant in the activity. On-site recording can thus range from continuous (especially for a total observer) to taking sketchy notes to not recording anything at all during an observation. Unfortunately, "writing field notes is an onerous task, but field notes constitute the basis for data upon which the study is based: no field notes, no data" (Schensul & LeCompte, 2013, p. 20).

Although mechanical devices such as video cameras or laptop computers can be used to record observations, the cost and obtrusiveness of these methods often preclude their use. It is much more likely that a researcher will jot down notes during an observation and wait until afterward to record in detail what has been observed. Thus, unlike an interviewer, who can usually fall back on a tape recording of the session, a participant observer has to rely on memory and notes to recount the session. Of course, a tape recorder can be placed somewhere at the site of the observation, such as in the middle of a classroom or a group meeting; this tape recording can aid in writing up field notes of the observation, as it will surely capture some verbal aspects of the activity.

Even if the researcher has been able to take detailed notes during an observation, it is imperative that full notes in a narrative format be written, typed, or dictated *as soon after* the observation as possible. It takes great self-discipline to sit down and describe something just observed. The observation itself is only half the work, and generally more fun than writing extensive field notes on what has just occurred. It is also highly likely that actually writing field notes will take longer than time spent in observation.

Every researcher devises techniques for remembering and recording the specifics of an observation. It can be an intimidating part of qualitative research, however, and we advise beginning with short periods of observation, followed by practice recalling and recording data. Taylor and Bogdan (1984) offer some suggestions for recalling data. Later recall will be helped if during an observation investigators

- Pay attention
- Shift from a "wide angle" to a "narrow angle" lens—that is, focusing "on a specific person, interaction, or activity, while mentally blocking out all the others" (p. 54)
- Look for key words in people's remarks that will stand out later
- Concentrate on the first and last remarks in each conversation
- Mentally play back remarks and scenes during breaks in the talking or observing

Once the observation is completed, they suggest the following: leave the setting after observing as much as can be remembered; record field notes as soon as possible after observing; in case of a time lag between observing and recording, summarize or outline the observation; draw a diagram of the setting and trace movements through it; and incorporate pieces of data remembered at later times into the original field notes (Taylor & Bogdan, 1984). Many of our students have found it helpful to tape record what they recall from the observation just as soon as they leave the site (on the drive home, for example). Bogdan and Biklen (2011) also advise against talking to anyone about the observation before notes have been recorded, because "talking about it diffuses its importance" (p. 127). They also underscore the urgency of writing field notes as soon as possible: "The more time that passes between observing and recording the notes, the poorer your recall will be and the less likely you will ever get to record your data" (p. 127).

Field notes based on observation need to be in a format that will allow the researcher to find desired information easily. Formats vary, but a set of notes usually begins with the time, place, and purpose of the observation. It is also helpful to list the participants present or at least to indicate how many and what kinds of people are present—described in ways meaningful to the research. If the researcher is observing a continuing professional education seminar for nurses, for example, it would be important to note the number of people present, whether they are supervisors or experienced or novice nurses, and demographic characteristics (such as age and gender), if relevant. A diagram of the setting's physical aspects should also be included, indicating where participants and the researcher are situated. Other hints for setting up field notes are to leave a wide margin on one side of the page or the other for later notes; double space between segments of activity for ease of reading and data analysis; and use quotation marks when someone is directly quoted. You might also include consecutive line numbering down the left side of the page; this enables you to easily locate significant passages when analyzing the observational data.

Field notes should be *highly descriptive*. What is described are the participants, the setting, the activities or behaviors of the participants, and what the observer does. By *highly descriptive* we mean that enough detail should be given that readers feel as if they are there, seeing what the observer sees. For example, instead of saying, "The conference room was neat and orderly," you could write, "The four tables in the conference room were moved together to form a neat square with three chairs per table. Materials for the meeting were in blue notebook covers and placed on the tables, three to a table, one in front of each chair. In the center of each table was a pitcher of water and three glasses."

There is also an important *reflective* component of field notes. This reflective component is captured in observer commentary, indicated by being set apart from the description either in the right or left margins or in brackets in the commentary itself. Reflective comments can include the researcher's feelings, reactions, hunches, initial interpretations, speculations, and working hypotheses. These comments are over and above factual descriptions of what is going on; they are comments on and thoughts about the setting, people, and activities. In raising questions about what is observed or speculating as to what it all means, the researcher is actually engaging in some preliminary data analysis. The joint collection and analysis of data is essential in qualitative research.

The content of field notes usually includes the following:

• Verbal descriptions of the setting, the people, the activities
• Direct quotations or at least the substance of what people said
• Observer's comments—put in the margins or in the running narrative and identified by underlining, italics, or bold and bracketing, and the initials "OC"

Exhibit 6.1 presents field notes written after Sharan observed an exercise class at a senior center in Seoul, South Korea. She was particularly interested in instruction and in the interaction between teacher and senior adult students. Note the diagram of the layout of the classroom, including where she was sitting ("Me" in the lower center to the side of the group) and where the instructor was positioned ("I" at the center right in front of the group); the observer's comments are interwoven throughout the recording. These are in italics and labeled "OC" to set them off from the observations. The field notes are highly descriptive to the point that the reader feels present on site with the researcher. The description should transport the reader to the site. Note, too, the observer comments in Exhibit 6.1. These comments are questions or notes *about* what is being observed; with these comments one is actually moving from description to beginning data analysis. Included in these field notes are descriptions of the artifacts on the wall in front of the room.

Ethnographers often maintain something called a fieldwork journal—an introspective record of the anthropologist's experience in the field. It includes his or her ideas, fears, mistakes, confusion, and reactions to the experience and can include thoughts about the research methodology itself. Walford (2001) reveals that he uses a small pocket tape recorder to capture a range of material "from early formulations of theories to shouts of anger, agony and self-pity. At the end of any traumatic experience I would simply talk all my anxiety into the tape recorder, and I would recommend that every ethnographer do this simply for the

EXHIBIT 6.1. KOREAN SENIOR CENTER FIELD NOTES.

Researcher: Sharan Merriam
Place: Korean Senior Center
Purpose: To become acquainted with adult education for
   older adults in Korea
Date/Time: Friday, March 24, 2006; 3–4:15 P.M.

KOREAN SENIOR CENTER CLASSROOM LAYOUT.

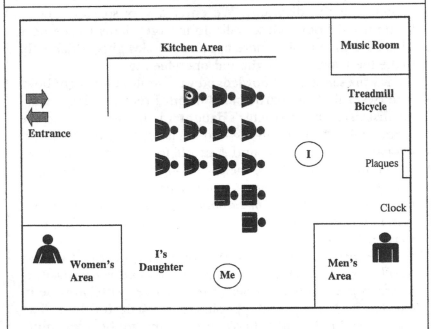

When hearing about my interest in adult education and education for older adults, my neighbor invited me to visit the Senior Center close to our apartments. My neighbor is an exercise instructor three times a week at this center. My first visit I went to see what it was like and actually participated in the exercises. This second visit I went as an observer and did not participate. *The specific focus of my observation was on the instruction and student/teacher interaction.*

(*continued*)

(Continued)

The Senior Center is in a stand-alone building in an apartment complex near my apartment. In addition to the Senior Center, about half of the building houses a preschool day-care center. The building is quite new and the center has been open only about four months.

As we take our shoes off and enter the center, I notice a strong food smell. Apparently someone had done some cooking, perhaps using the kitchen, which is on one wall of the center (see the diagram). We enter a very spacious room, blond wood floors, white walls, four large plants (three near where I decide to sit); there are also two skylights, which help make the room quite light and open-feeling.

My presence is acknowledged with smiles and slight bows from several of the participants whom I recall seeing during my first visit. The instructor's daughter is also with us, and she seems invisible although she told me later it was her first visit. Everyone takes a chair and I sit off to the side. There are eleven women and three men. *(OC—I assume the percentage of older females in Korea is greater than males as in the U.S. While I know these people live in the surrounding apartment buildings, I'm curious if these eleven live alone, with a spouse, or with other family members.)*

The instructor bows and the students applaud. *(OC—they seem happy to see her.)* A boy I guess to be about three years old is wandering around and doesn't seem to be "with" anyone in particular. A couple of people get a chair for him. The instructor holds up a book and seems to be explaining what the overall plan of exercises is. The child runs around, runs out of the room, and returns to sit in the chair. *(OC—I find out later that the child is the grandchild of one of the participants and goes to the day-care center next door—but at no time did I see any adult speak to him directly and although I guessed he might be from the day-care center, I did wonder why he was allowed to wander back and forth—maybe children/family members are OK to be at these classes?)*

The instructor is now showing diagrams of the human body from a book, moving around the room so everyone can see; she is talking all the time. *(OC—seems she is sensitive to poor eyesight of some of the elderly; she also told me that she likes to have them understand what the exercises are trying to do with regard to their circulation, muscles, etc., that it's not enough just to do the exercises— she seems conscious of the holistic nature of learning, mind and body.)*

All but one woman stands for some loose arm/hand exercises. Participants walk around the room swinging their arms. The instructor plays some relaxing instrumental music on a tape player and begins leading the group around the room—with each walk around one or two sit down until most everyone is sitting down. The three-year-old runs in and out of the adjoining room for the men, but no one seems to care or pay attention to him.

The next set of exercises has the participants standing behind their chairs, using the chair for balance for some of the exercises. The instructor occasionally turns with her back to the group so they can see exactly how to do the exercises (and don't have to transpose opposite sides of the body, etc.). The instructor gets the participants to count (I think they are counting) with her, which livens things up. Those who need to sit before the end of the exercises do so, with her encouraging them to do what they can from a sitting position. *(OC—clearly the instructor is aware of their physical limitations and builds it into her instruction, i.e., modifying a standing exercise to fit a sitting position.)* The instructor is constantly talking, making eye contact with individuals in the class, signaling a correction if needed. Her voice is very soothing and inviting; she smiles a lot and she does all the exercises with them.

At about 3:40 P.M. a man I recognize from a previous visit comes in wearing a suit. He goes into the men's area/room and returns minus his suit jacket and joins the exercise group. *(OC— he must be some sort of official, as during my first visit he produced a tape player; he also looks younger than the others—I'll have to ask about him.)*

At 3:45 P.M. the instructor brings out a bag of sponge balls, each about six inches in diameter. She demonstrates squeezing the ball, how to hold one's elbows. She points to different parts of the body, apparently saying what the exercise is designed to do. More exercises with the balls, like reaching from left to right toes and back. At 4 P.M. the group moves into a circle. The instructor collects every other ball and then tries to get the

(continued)

(Continued)

group to raise the ball up and under their leg and pass it on to the next person. There is some confusion here, but all the while people are laughing and joking with each other and with her. The group finally gets the hang of it, the exercise continues, and the balls move to the left. For the first time, the instructor is quiet and she lets them do the exercise, moving the balls to the left. *(OC—another example of how she varies instruction, keeping the attention of the group.)*

Now everyone is given a ball and the instructor places a bag in the center of the circle. She demonstrates how to toss the ball into the bag, exaggerating the arm swing. Everyone tosses at once; her daughter helps collect the balls and the "toss" is repeated several times. The four men in the group seem to be especially enjoying this—smiling, laughing, and clearly eager to toss more balls. At 4:12 P.M. the balls are collected in the bag, everyone claps, and the class ends. *(The instructor tells me later that the class is actually supposed to go 40–45 minutes, but "they seem to want more" and both times I visited, the class was a solid hour in length.)* Some participants leave, two men go into the men's area, several of the women go into the women's area/room off the main entrance. While the instructor is doing some paperwork, I ask her daughter to explain the plaques on the front wall.

Documents/Artifacts

The Senior Center contained a number of "artifacts" that I examined. First were the plants. There is a huge fern under the left front skylight. Near where I was sitting there were three plants in a row—a large green-leaf plant about six feet high, a smaller Japanese-looking plant next to that, and then a purple flowering plant next to that. These plants contributed to the comfortable, welcoming "feel" to the Center. In the left front corner there was a treadmill and a bicycle machine. I didn't see either one being used at the time of my visit, but clearly they were there for use anytime. (I found out later most everything in the center has been donated, including a very sophisticated sound/TV setup for karaoke in a small room off the kitchen.)

The most interesting artifacts for me were a set of six wall plaques and one framed photo hanging on the front wall. Above the plaques was a framed picture of the Korean flag. To the right of these plaques was a wall clock, quite high up. Just below and to the right of the wall clock was what we would call a "grandfather clock"—a large standing clock (this was also donated). It was curious to me that the things on this wall seemed to be just "there," with no particular aesthetic pattern in mind—no balancing of the plaques, and they weren't in the center on the wall, but a bit to the right. The flag and wall clock were quite high. To me it seemed like a hodge-podge of things.

The Plaques and Photo

The instructor's daughter briefly described what each of these plaques said (they were different sizes, but about a foot square on average):

1. The first plaque said "Let's be respectable seniors."
2. The second said something to the effect that "Let's transfer seniors' good experiences and wisdom to young people."
3. This plaque is the Senior Center Registration Certificate.
4. This one was apparently a list of things older people should do:
   Help our country
   Enjoy our life
   Be healthy
   Participate, even if you are old
5. The next was a plaque about the person who is apparently chairman of the Society of Older Adults at this site.
6. The next was a framed photo of eight men, four lined up on each side of the entrance to this new Senior Center building—it apparently is a photo of the opening ceremony.
7. The final plaque was a statement of the purpose of the center—service to society and to help each other.

therapeutic effect alone" (p. 70). In addition to field notes and the fieldwork journal, you might also write analytical memos containing some preliminary analysis and interpretation. Qualitative researchers are more likely to use the integrated format described earlier, although some do keep a separate journal of the experience. That becomes a data source, and the researcher sometimes uses it when writing about the methodology.

ONLINE OBSERVATION

This chapter would not be complete without some discussion of online observation and gathering observational data by making use of new media technologies. As noted earlier, observation (along with in-depth interviews) is an extremely important form of data collection in numerous types of qualitative studies examining or observing how a particular phenomenon unfolds, such as how groups learn, or how communication patterns play out in certain circumstances. It's also a key data collection method in ethnography, which focuses on the examination of culture. There have been numerous discussions of late on digital, virtual, or cyber ethnography (Ardévol & Gómez-Cruz, 2014; Boellstorff, Nardi, Pearce, & Taylor, 2012; Underberg & Zorn, 2013). In their handbook on ethnography and virtual worlds, Boellstorff et al. (2012) argue that ethnographic methods need to be combined with an understanding of virtual worlds, since the online or virtual world is a whole culture in and of itself. Further, online communities are also typically subcultures of larger communities made up of people with a particular interest. For example, Gómez-Cruz conducted an ethnographic study of digital photographic sharing practices of digital photographers (Ardévol & Gómez-Cruz, 2014). In another example, Waldron (2013) conducted a cyber ethnography of music learning and teaching that happens through the online site Banjo Hangout (www.banjohangout.com). This is made up of banjo players and teachers; the site has connections to YouTube and other teaching and learning sites, as well as off-line communities of banjo players who began the site out of their own mutual interest.

Waldron (2013) conducted her cyber ethnography entirely through computer mediated communication (CMC) through Skype interviews and online observations and discussions. Like

Waldron, many ethnographers "observe" and participate in the culture and discussion in online communities while collecting data. But when researchers are collecting ethnographic data in an online observation, the unique medium of the technology must be considered (Boellstorff et al., 2012). Many of the issues of observation are the same as they are when the observer is physically present in the environment, but there are others that are particular to online and virtual environments.

First is the issue of determining what counts as an *observation* and what counts as an *online document*, since in online discussions, blogs, etc., oftentimes the data is exclusively text based and can be printed out. For purposes of the discussion in this chapter on observation, we have opted to consider observation specifically in online, virtual, or cyber communities. However, we will return to further discussion of online documents in the next chapter on documents and artifacts.

A second distinction between online observation through virtual presence and physical presence observations is that it is possible to do virtual or online observations from a completely hidden perspective. This is difficult to do in most situations where one is physically present in conducting an observation, though it is entirely possible in open, public venues like a shopping mall or bus station, or unusual situations, as when one is behind a one-way mirror. One can easily make a choice in most online world environments to conduct an observation from a hidden perspective as a "lurker"; one could also choose to be a participant observer and to ask questions or make comments in the virtual world. As discussed earlier in this chapter, researchers collecting data through observation need to decide the extent to which they will be a participant. However, in the virtual or online world, it is actually quite easy to make observations as a complete observer and to be hidden to participants. The ethics of doing so have been a point of some discussion among digital ethnographers (Boellstorff et al., 2012; James & Busher, 2012); however, collecting data through "lurking" is generally considered acceptable if it is totally public and archived, no password is required for archival data, and the site doesn't prohibit it (Waldron, 2013). However, most cyber researchers want to make themselves known in such sites, because they often need to ask further questions or conduct interviews with particular participants; most are also particularly interested in the topic and have been participating in online communities related to the topic (Ardévol & Gómez-Cruz, 2014).

A third issue in doing ethnographic online observation is related to the many cultural and folklore sites that have been created by museums and digital ethnographers to create access to cultures across the world. Underberg and Zorn (2013) in particular discuss the unique features of conducting ethnographies and observations of such sites. Typically such sites have been created in dialogue with computer specialists to scan images or create video that viewers can access online. Such computer mediated images do raise the question: is an image of a thing really the thing itself? And of course it is not. Nevertheless, such sites give access to images of artifacts and information and online community discussion and virtual tours in ways not available to an earlier generation. Virtual and digital ethnographers explore and conduct online observa-tions of such sites to examine the unique features of these online cultures in digital, virtual, or cyber ethnographies.

A last issue in conducting online observation concerns how one takes field notes. In the preceding example, Sharan developed her field notes from the Korean Senior Center from when she was physically present. Her notes were originally handwritten and then typed up. Cyber ethnographers also take field notes and make obser-vations that they conduct in the field, but this can take a variety of forms. In his study of digital photographers (with both an online and off-line component), Gómez-Cruz wrote his notes in a field diary. However, he also used a smart phone to take both notes and pictures in the field. Hence "[t]he smartphone was, at once, a field data gathering tool and a constant connective device with the group members" (Ardévol & Gómez-Cruz, 2014, p. 512). He later used some of the pictures that he took in the field as a photo elicitation device to pro-voke discussion with participants in online discussion and individual interviews. Thus in conducting observations in online settings, it is as important to carefully document the process and to keep field notes in some form, and to carefully develop a process for doing so.

SUMMARY

Observation is a major means of collecting data in qualitative research. It offers a firsthand account of the situation under study and, when combined with interviewing and document analysis, allows for a holistic interpretation of the phenomenon being investigated. It is the technique of choice when behavior can be observed firsthand or when people cannot or will not discuss the research topic.

Fieldwork, as participant observation is often called, involves going to the site, program, institution, setting—the field—to observe the phenomenon under study. Unless it is public behavior the researcher wants to observe, entry must first be gained from those in authority. While on site, the researcher is absorbed by what to observe, what to remember, what to record. This chapter presents some guidelines for these activities, such as what to observe, but ultimately the success of participant observation rests on the talent and skill of the investigator.

There are several stances an investigator can assume when conducting observations, ranging from being a member of the group and a complete participant—an insider—to being a complete observer, unknown to those being observed; each stance has advantages and drawbacks. Regardless of the stance, an observer cannot help but affect and be affected by the setting, and this interaction may lead to some distortion of the situation as it exists under nonresearch conditions. Being at once a participant and an observer is a corollary of this method of data collection and is a problem not easily dealt with.

Finally, while the area of digital, virtual, or cyber research is a burgeoning area of recent and future inquiry, there are unique features to observation in online and virtual settings that need to be considered in conducting such research. But whether one conducts observation in physical or virtual settings, observation is only half the process. Observations must be recorded in as much detail as possible to form the database for analysis. Field notes can come in many forms, but at the least they include descriptions, direct quotations, and observer comments.

CHAPTER SEVEN

MINING DATA FROM DOCUMENTS AND ARTIFACTS

Interviewing and observing are two data collection strategies designed to gather data that specifically address the research question. Documents and artifacts that are part of the research setting are also sources of data in qualitative research. These are most typically a natural part of the research setting and do not intrude upon or alter the setting in the ways that the presence of the investigator might when conducting interviews or observations. Documents and artifacts are, in fact, a ready-made source of data easily accessible to the imaginative and resourceful investigator. These types of data sources can exist in both a physical setting and an online setting.

This chapter examines the nature of documents and artifacts, their use in qualitative research, and their limitations and strengths. *Document* is often used as an umbrella term to refer to a wide range of written, visual, digital, and physical material relevant to the study (including visual images). *Artifacts* are usually three-dimensional physical "things" or objects in the environment that represent some form of communication that is meaningful to participants and/or the setting. Examples might be art pieces, organizational or school symbols, trophies, awards, or personal gifts, to name a few.

Most documents and artifacts exist *prior* to commencing the research study at hand. Common documents include official records, organizational promotional materials, letters, newspaper accounts, poems, songs, corporate records, government documents, historical accounts, diaries, autobiographies, blogs, and so on. These can be available in the physical environment, on websites, or both. Photographs, film, various forms of video including YouTube, and vlogs (video with blogs) also can be used as data sources (Lee, 2000; Snelson, 2015; Webb, Campbell, Schwartz, & Sechrest, 2000). Some researchers now use the term *visual methods* to refer to the many types of visual documents and images that can be collected and analyzed online and in physical environments in qualitative research (Grady, 2008; Pink, 2013).

This chapter begins by reviewing the different types of documents and artifacts. Although the chapter concentrates a bit more on text-based documents in the physical environment or the virtual online environment, the general discussion applies to all forms of data not gathered through interviews or observations. We discuss various types of online data throughout the discussion on types of documents and also consider some issues specific to the online world later in the chapter.

TYPES OF DOCUMENTS AND ARTIFACTS

Different writers categorize documents and artifacts in different ways. Public records and personal documents are two common types of documents used in qualitative research. A third type to be discussed here is what Bogdan and Biklen (2011) call "popular culture documents," along with a fourth type—visual documents—which include film, video, and photography (Pink, 2012, 2013). Visual documents intersect with popular culture, and even public records and personal documents can be visual in nature, so the same document can be classified in more than one way. Artifacts and physical materials such as objects in the environment or changes in the physical setting are not quite as commonly used as the other types, but nevertheless are a potential source of data for the qualitative researcher. These five types of documents or artifacts/physical material generally occur naturally in the research environment. But we also discuss a sixth type: researcher-generated documents or artifacts, which are less common but are often used in qualitative action research or participatory research designs.

Public Records

Public records are the official, ongoing records of a society's activities. It's safe to assume, especially given today's 24-hour news cycle and Internet coverage, that when an event happens, there will be some record of it somewhere. Public documents include actuarial records of births, deaths, and marriages, the U.S. census, police records, court transcripts, agency records, association manuals, program documents, mass media, government documents, minutes of organizational meetings and so on. Locating public records is limited only by the researcher's imagination and industriousness. Auster (1985), for example, demonstrates how to conduct a study of changing social expectations for family, career, gender roles, and sexual behavior through the sole data source of Girl Scout handbooks. Youth organization handbooks, she points out, "represent the intersection of biography and history" (p. 359), providing an excellent data source for studying changing social mores. Fear (2012) conducted a study of the public record of the minutes of health board meetings in a Welsh organization. He examined how local organizations deal with competing discourses (local, national, and international) and construct and reconstruct their social reality through these public records.

For those interested in educational questions, there are numerous sources of public documents—discussions of educational issues and bills in the *Congressional Record*; federal, state, and private agency reports; individual program records; and the statistical database of the Center for Educational Statistics. Since many case studies are at the program level, it is particularly important to seek out the paper trail for what it can reveal about the program—"things that cannot be observed," things "that have taken place before the study began. They may include private interchanges to which the inquirer would not otherwise be privy. They can reveal aspirations, arrangements, tensions, relationships, and decisions that might be otherwise unknown through direct observation" (Patton, 2015, p. 376). Ideally this paper trail includes "all routine records on clients, all correspondence from and to program staff, financial and budget records, organizational rules, regulations, memoranda, charts, and any other official or unofficial documents generated by or for the program" (p. 376). Such documents are valuable "not only because of what can be learned directly from them but also as stimulus for paths of inquiry that can only be pursued through direct observation and interviewing" (p. 377).

If you were interested in studying the role of parent involvement in a neighborhood school, for example, you could look for public record documents in the form of the following: notices sent home to parents; memos between and among teachers, staff, and the parents' association; formal policy statements regarding parent involvement; school bulletin boards or other displays featuring aspects of parent involvement; newspaper and other media coverage of activities featuring parent involvement; and any official records of parent attendance or presence in the school.

Other sources of public information that are easily accessible but often overlooked include previous studies and data "banks" of information. However, in using these resources the researcher has to rely on someone else's description and interpretation of data rather than use the raw data as a basis for analysis. These meta-analyses, as they are called, are more common in quantitative research, although there has been some recent thinking as to how this strategy might apply to qualitative studies. For large-scale or cross-cultural research, relying on previous studies may be the only realistic way to conduct the investigation.

An example of a data bank that is potentially useful in qualitative research, especially ethnographic studies (see Chapter Two), is the Human Relations Area File (Murdock, Ford, Hudson, Kennedy, Simmons, & Whitney, 2008). This file is a compilation of ethnographic studies of more than 350 societies; data are classified and coded by cultural group and also by more than 700 topics. Education is one broad topic under which subtopics such as elementary education, educational theory and methods, students, and vocational education can be found. The index is organized so that a researcher can retrieve documents related to the educational practices of one particular cultural group, or documents can be retrieved about a specific practice such as "student uprisings" across many cultures. Types of documents found in this file include ethnographer field notes, diary entries, reports to various agencies, books, newspaper articles, works of fiction about the culture, and photographs (for a helpful guide to using this file, see Ember & Ember, 2012).

PERSONAL DOCUMENTS

In contrast to public record sources of data, personal documents "refer to any first-person narrative that describes an individual's actions, experiences, and beliefs" (Bogdan & Biklen, 2011, p. 133). Such documents include diaries, letters, home videos, children's growth records, scrapbooks and photo albums, calendars, autobiographies, travel logs, and personal blogs. In some ways documents are like observations in that documents give us a snapshot into what the author thinks is important, that is, their personal perspective, while observations allow us to see overt behavior. Further, as noted in the last chapter, many authors discuss the ubiquitous material available online from chats, blogs, online discussion groups, various social media sites and vlogs, as online observation or virtual ethnography rather than documents per se (Pink, 2013). Whether one classifies such material as observational data or as documents is not really particularly important. Rather, the point is that such documents, whether online or available only in traditional printed form, can tell the researcher about the inner meaning of everyday events. Such data may yield descriptions of highly unusual or idiosyncratic human experiences, such as can be found in Admiral Byrd's report of his experiences alone at the South Pole, Helen Keller's account of overcoming multiple physical handicaps, or the various travel blogs or illness blogs that are available online.

Personal documents are a good source of data concerning a person's attitudes, beliefs, and view of the world. But because they are personal documents, the material is highly subjective in that the writer is the only one to select what he or she considers important to record. Obviously these documents are not representative or necessarily reliable accounts of what actually may have occurred. They do, however, reflect the participant's perspective, which is what most qualitative research is seeking. In speaking of autobiographies and diaries in particular, Burgess (1991) notes:

> The field researcher needs to consider: Is the material trustworthy? Is the material atypical? Has the material been edited and refined? Does the autobiographical material only contain

highlights of life that are considered interesting? Furthermore, it could be argued that the material is automatically biased as only certain people produce autobiographies and keep diaries; there is self-selectivity involved in the sample of material available; they do not provide a complete historical record. Nevertheless, such material does provide a subjective account of the situation it records; it is a reconstruction of part of life. Furthermore, it provides an account that is based on the author's experience. (p. 132)

An entire study can be based on personal documents. Abramson's (1992) case study of Russian Jewish emigration is based solely on his grandfather's diaries written over a 12-year period. A well-known earlier study of Polish immigrant life relied heavily upon personal letters written between immigrants and relatives in Europe (Thomas & Znaniecki, 1927). Many of these letters were obtained by placing ads in local newspapers asking for them.

In the Internet age, personal accounts are also often available online through blogs and other online material. Hookway (2008) notes that blogs "offer far more extensive opportunities than their 'offline' parallel of qualitative diary research" (p. 92). He goes on to discuss the extent of their availability across the world, which enables researchers to conduct more global analyses from many different theoretical perspectives. The point is that whether online or off-line, personal documents offer a wide array of opportunities to collect data to garner participants' perspective and ways of making meaning from personal experiences.

POPULAR CULTURE DOCUMENTS

In addition to public and personal records, society produces materials designed to entertain, inform, and perhaps persuade the public. These are public in nature and so are sometimes categorized under public records. Popular media forms such as television, film, radio, newspapers, literary works, photography, cartoons, and the Internet are sources of "public" data. Mass communication materials are especially good sources for dealing with questions about some aspect of society at a given time, for comparing groups on a certain dimension, or for tracking cultural change and trends. The changing nature of U.S. presidential political campaigns, for example, could be looked at through the medium of televised debates, with the 2008 campaign incorporating YouTube Internet technology for the first time. Studies have been conducted on the changing role of women and people of color in film and television, the presence of ageism in cartoons, and teenage culture in movies. McLean (2013), Hollenbeck (2005), and Wright and Sandlin (2009) made use of popular culture sources for their studies. McLean asked how informal learning takes place through the reading of self-help books, and Hollenbeck studied contemporary Internet-based social protest groups (anti-McDonald's, anti-Starbucks, and anti-Wal-Mart). Wright and Sandlin (2009) examined how British women who watched the 1960s television show *The Avengers* as young adults constructed their gender identity. The show featured Honor Blackman as the powerful and feminist character Cathy Gale. Wright and Sandlin conducted both a textual analysis of the shows and interviews with the women about their perceptions of how watching it affected their gender consciousness.

Unlike records that are part of a program's history, or personal documents that might augment an interview study, there may be an infinite number of popular cultural documents that might be relevant to a particular study. Bogdan and Biklen (2011) offer some advice when using popular culture as a data source:

> Of all the thousands of hours of commercial videos, films, and popular records as well as the millions upon millions of printed words and pictures that appear each day in the media, how do you ever narrow down the scope to make your task manageable. . . . Think small. Most people who read research do not expect the researcher to cover the universe. Pick a particular program, or a particular event, and work on it intensely rather than spreading yourself too thin. (p. 65)

VISUAL DOCUMENTS

Film, video, photography, and web-based media are visual documents. Of course, these can be found within the categories of documents just discussed. That is, public records, personal documents, and popular cultural materials can all be in visual formats. However, there has been a growing interest in the prevalence and use of visual documents both as a data source and as a means of presenting the findings of a research study. As Pink (2013) wryly observes, "Indeed the camera and the digital image, as an increasingly constant presence in our pockets, our hands and our computers is a part of our contemporary reality" (p. 31). As with other data collection methods, there are now dozens of resources devoted to visual research methods, including a handbook (Margolis & Pauwels, 2011) and a four-volume set (Hughes, 2012).

Although there is burgeoning interest in visual materials in conducting research—thanks to both the Internet and the development of new computer mediated technologies that are relatively easy to use—film, video, and photography have had a long history in anthropology, dating back to the turn of the twentieth century (Pink, 2013). Most famous perhaps were the early 1940s film and photography of Balinese culture by anthropologists Bateson and Mead. However, despite their landmark text, the use of such visual research in anthropology was marginalized until the late twentieth century, when in the 1990s film and photography gained popularity. As a result of their availability, accessibility, and use in inquiry, there are many book-length discussions of various visual materials and methods of their use in research across many disciplines (Margolis & Pauwels, 2011; Pink, 2013).

One can use visual materials that are already available online or in the physical setting that one is studying. One can also use video and photography as a way of collecting data, but doing so has some obvious strengths and limitations. These forms of data collection capture activities and events as they happen, including "nonverbal behavior and communication patterns such as facial expressions, gestures, and emotions" (Marshall & Rossman, 2016, p. 186). What can be captured on video is limited only "by what the mind can imagine and the camera can record" (p. 184), though we are always limited by the camera angle. Video has other, more practical limitations such as the need for the researcher to have some technical expertise, and it can be intrusive (although as "reality" television shows attest, the camera is soon forgotten in many situations).

Unlike video, photography is often less expensive and more easily incorporated into a research study. To begin with, one can make use of what are called "found" photographs (Tinkler, 2013).

These are photos that already exist, either in public archives such as historical societies and libraries or in personal collections such as a participant's photo album of family events. Photos alone can tell the story of what the photographer thought was important to capture, what cultural values might be conveyed by the particular photos, and so on. Photos have recently been used by researchers in postcolonial, African American, and women's studies "to understand how oppressed groups were pictured by those subordinating them" (Bogdan & Biklen, 2011, p. 144).

Photographs can also be generated by the researcher. Such photographs, often taken in conjunction with participant observation, provide "a means of remembering and studying detail that might be overlooked if a photographic image were not available for reflection" (Bogdan & Biklen, 2011, p. 151). Another use of photographs in qualitative research is something called *photo elicitation*, in which participants are shown various photos of the topic of interest in order to stimulate discussion of the topic (Tinkler, 2013). These photos could have been taken by the researcher, found in public or personal records, or taken by participants themselves. They are basically prompts for verbal data. Smith, Gidlow, and Steel (2012), for example, describe making use of photo elicitation in a study of adolescents' experiences in outdoor education programs. They asked the adolescents to take pictures during the program; then the researchers interviewed them about both the pictures and their experiences.

This technique of photo elicitation where participants can be provided disposable cameras and asked to take pictures of the phenomenon of interest, is also sometimes called *photovoice*. Photovoice has been used in participatory action research and in promoting grassroots social action, especially in community development, public health, and education. For example, photovoice was used in a study of the empowerment of 30 African American community health advisors (Mayfield-Johnson, Rachal, & Butler III, 2014), homeless adults (Padgett, Smith, Derejko, Henwood, & Tiderington, 2013), the rural church and women's health promotion (Plunkett, Leipert, Ray, & Olson, 2014), and brain injury survivors (Lorenz, 2010). In all of these studies, photos taken by the participants and interviews asking participants to interpret the photos provided the data for analysis. Harper

(2003, p. 195) reminds us, however, that "in all examples of photo-elicitation research, the photograph loses its claim to objectivity. Indeed, the power of the photo lies in its ability to unlock the subjectivity of those who see the image differently from the researcher."

Physical Material and Artifacts

Artifacts and physical material consist of physical objects found in the study setting; some qualitative researchers collectively refer to such physical objects and artifacts as "material culture" (Lindlof & Taylor, 2011, p. 218). Anthropologists typically refer to these objects as artifacts; they include the tools, implements, utensils, and instruments of everyday living. Archaeologist Hodder (2003) includes artifacts and written texts that have physically endured over time as "mute evidence" in the study of culture. "Such evidence, unlike the spoken word, endures physically and thus can be separated across space and time from its author, producer, or user" (p. 155). One of the more famous studies using physical material is the garbage study conducted over a number of years by researchers at the University of Arizona (Rathje & Murphy, 2001). By sorting through people's garbage, these researchers have been able to tell a lot about the lifestyle choices of various socioeconomic groups. For example, lower-income people tend to buy small containers of name brand products rather than less expensive, large-sized generic brand products. Hawkins (2006) also included garbage in her study of the ethics of "waste" in our lives. In another study of a different kind of garbage, "digital rubbish," Gabrys (2013) studied the emergence and dissolution of electronics as cultural artifacts.

As part of Sharan's observation of an exercise class at a senior center in Korea (see Chapter Six, Exhibit 6.1, for the field notes), she noticed a number of framed plaques on the wall. These "artifacts," which were translated for her, spoke to the Korean view of older adults and their learning. For example, one plaque said "Let's transfer seniors' good experiences and wisdom to young people." Another had a list of things older Koreans should do: "Help our society; enjoy our life; be healthy; and participate, even if you are old." These plaques offered additional evidence of the importance of participation and respect for older adults that she witnessed in observing the class.

Physical trace material is yet another potential source of information. Physical traces consist of changes in the physical setting brought about by the activities of people in that setting. The following are examples of physical evidence used in research studies, as summarized by Webb, Campbell, Schwartz, and Sechrest (2000):

- One investigator wanted to learn the level of whisky consumption in a town that was officially "dry." He did so by counting empty bottles in trash cans.
- The degree of fear induced by a ghost storytelling session was inferred by noting the shrinking diameter of a circle of seated children.
- Library withdrawals were used to demonstrate the effect of the introduction of television into a community. Fiction titles dropped; nonfiction titles were unaffected.
- A child's interest in Christmas was demonstrated by distortions in the size of Santa Claus drawings.
- Racial attitudes in two colleges were compared partly by noting the degree of clustering of blacks and whites in lecture halls. (pp. 2–3)

Two basic means of studying physical traces are to note their erosion, which is the degree of wear, and to note their accretion, which is the degree of accumulation. The wear and tear on floor tiles in front of a museum exhibit as a sign of public interest is a well-known example of erosion (Webb et al., 2000); the accumulation of whisky bottles in the preceding list of examples is a good example of accretion. More commonly, the ebb and flow of physical traces are used as data to document a phenomenon. Moss and McDonald (2004), for example, used school library records to reveal insights into the reading habits of preteen children. And Patton (2015, p. 375) gives an interesting example of how physical traces can be used in evaluation: "In a week-long staff training program for 300 people, I asked the kitchen to systematically record how much coffee was consumed in the morning, afternoon, and evening each day. Those sessions that I judged to be particularly boring had a correspondingly higher level of coffee consumption. Active and involving sessions showed less coffee consumption, regardless of the time of day. (Participants could get up and get coffee whenever they wanted.)"

Because physical traces can usually be measured, they are most often suited for obtaining information on the incidence and frequency of behavior. They are also a good check on information obtained from interviews or surveys. In qualitative research, most physical trace measures are used to supplement data gathered through interviews and observations. For example, a researcher could compare the wear and tear on computers in a school that purports to include computer literacy in its basic curriculum. Rathje (1979, pp. 78–79) highlights other advantages of using trace materials:

- Trace measures record the results of actual behavior, not reported or experimental approximations.
- Trace measures are usually nonreactive and unobtrusive. Since they are applied after behavior has occurred, they do not modify the behavior they seek to study.
- Material traces are ubiquitous and readily available for study.
- Because material traces are applied to inanimate objects, they usually require minimal cooperation and inconvenience from human subjects.
- Because the number of measures of traces depends upon the recorder's interest rather than informant patience, a variety of interrelated behaviors can often be studied at once.
- Because of the minimal inconvenience and expense to informants, trace measures can be used over long time periods as longitudinal monitoring devices.

RESEARCHER-GENERATED DOCUMENTS AND ARTIFACTS

When documents are included in a study, what are commonly referred to as public records, personal documents (online or offline), artifacts, and physical material usually are already present in the research setting. Because they have not been produced for the research purpose, they often contain much that is irrelevant to the study; by the same token, they can provide insights into the phenomenon under study. Most researchers find them well worth the effort to locate and examine.

Researcher-generated documents are documents prepared by the researcher or for the researcher by participants after the study has begun. The specific purpose for generating documents is to learn more about the situation, person, or event being investigated. They are extremely common in action and participatory research studies. Siha (2014), for example, in his action research study of teaching composition at a community college with a critical pedagogy approach, had students fill out critical incident questionnaires every two weeks; he then changed the course according to student recommendations. As part of the course, students also agreed to write reflection papers in relation to some of the issues being discussed in class. These are researcher-generated documents. In other situations, the researcher might request that someone keep a diary or log of activities during the course of the investigation. Or the researcher might solicit a life history of an individual or a historical account of a program to illuminate the present situation. Sometimes researchers ask participants to create an art piece or a collage or to bring an artifact that is representative of their learning or experience. These would be researcher-generated artifacts. Stuckey and Tisdell (2010), for example, discuss the various forms of creative expression, artifacts, and art pieces that participants created in a narrative action research study of the use of creative expression by people with diabetes. As discussed earlier, artifacts that participants create or use to express themselves, or photographs taken by the researcher or the participants all can be a valuable source of data and can provide another avenue of expression that can be captured in symbols as well as words.

Quantitative data produced by the investigator also fall into this category of documents. Projective tests, attitudinal measures, content examinations, statistical data from surveys on any number of topics—all can be treated as documents in support of a qualitative investigation.

In summary, then, documents include a broad range of materials available to the researcher who is creative in seeking them out. Millions of public and private documents, artifacts, and physical traces of human behavior can be used as sources of primary or secondary data. The researcher can also generate documents once the study has begun.

USING DOCUMENTS AND ARTIFACTS IN QUALITATIVE RESEARCH

Using documentary material as data is not much different from using interviews or observations. Glaser and Strauss (1967) compare fieldwork with library research: "When someone stands in the library stacks, he is, metaphorically, surrounded by voices begging to be heard. Every book, every magazine article, represents at least one person who is equivalent to the anthropologist's informant or the sociologist's interviewee. In those publications, people converse, announce positions, argue with a range of eloquence, and describe events or scenes in ways entirely comparable to what is seen and heard during fieldwork" (p. 163).

Whether in fieldwork, library work, or online work, data collection is guided by questions, educated hunches, and emerging findings. Although the search is systematic, these settings also allow for the accidental uncovering of valuable data. Tracking down leads, being open to new insights, and being sensitive to the data are the same whether the researcher is interviewing, observing, or analyzing documents. Since the investigator is the primary instrument for gathering data, he or she relies on skills and intuition to find and interpret data from documents.

Finding relevant materials is the first step in the process. As we mentioned, this is generally a systematic procedure that evolves from the topic of inquiry itself. A qualitative study of classroom instruction would lead to documents in the form of instructors' lesson plans, student assignments, objects in the classroom, official grade reports and school records, teacher evaluations, and so on. Besides the setting itself, the logical places to look are libraries, historical societies, archives, and institutional files. Others have located personal documents like letters and diaries by placing advertisements in newspapers and newsletters or on relevant Internet sites.

Thus the researcher must keep an open mind when it comes to discovering useful documents. Being open to any possibility can lead to serendipitous discoveries. Tobacco company exposés of the late 1990s were buttressed by the discovery of buried memos in which the addictive quality of nicotine is discussed; the famous Watergate tapes came to light during routine questioning of White House staff.

Once documents have been located, their authenticity must be assessed. "The author, the place and the date of writing all need to be established and verified" (McCulloch, 2004, p. 42). In addition, it is important to ascertain, if possible, the conditions under which the document was produced. A news release to the general public serves a quite different purpose than an internal memo on the same issue does. In evaluating an artifact—that is, an object used or produced by a particular cultural group or individual participant—it is important to ask about the artifact's history (how and when was it produced and has it changed over time?) and its use (is it a decorative item? If it is used, by whom is it used, and how is it used?).

Determining the authenticity and accuracy of written documents is part of the research process. It is the investigator's responsibility to determine as much as possible about the document, its origins and reasons for being written, its author, and the context in which it was written. Guba and Lincoln (1981), citing Clark (1967), list the questions a researcher might ask about the authenticity of documents:

- What is the history of the document?
- How did it come into my hands?
- What guarantee is there that it is what it pretends to be?
- Is the document complete, as originally constructed?
- Has it been tampered with or edited?
- If the document is genuine, under what circumstances and for what purposes was it produced?
- Who was/is the author?
- What was he trying to accomplish? For whom was the document intended?
- What were the maker's sources of information? Does the document represent an eyewitness account, a secondhand account, a reconstruction of an event long prior to the writing, an interpretation?
- What was or is the maker's bias?

- To what extent was the writer likely to want to tell the truth?
- Do other documents exist that might shed additional light on the same story, event, project, program, context? If so, are they available, accessible? Who holds them? (pp. 238–239)

While these questions were generated about the use of documents and their authenticity long before the advent of the Internet, many of these questions are still relevant about traditionally printed documents. But the issue of authenticity about dealing with *online* documents and identities is much more complicated, not only from the standpoint of qualitative research, but in everything from online dating to selling items on eBay. Treadwell (2012) conducted a study of men who specifically embraced the opportunities of technology with the intent to trade counterfeit items. Further, there are numerous examples of intentional online misrepresentation with the purpose to exploit. What does this suggest for the qualitative researcher dealing with online documents and observation?

First, we would refer readers to numerous resources that deal more specifically with online data (Paulus, Lester, & Dempster, 2014; Pink, 2012, 2013). Second, it is important to bear in mind that the discrepancy between real and online personalities occurs even when people are trying to be themselves—or at least an idealized version of themselves. However, it is compounded when individuals purposefully create different online personas, which is fairly frequent in some electronic environments, particularly on social simulation sites like Second Life (Fielding, 2014). In fact, numerous researchers specifically study online identities (Bullingham & Vasconcelos, 2013; Gatson, 2011; Parmentier & Roland, 2009). Indeed, online interaction can vary widely, from scholarly communities in which individuals list their real names with their university affiliations and degrees, to fantasy games in which participants intentionally make up names and descriptions that reflect little of their off-line characteristics. Generally researchers who study gaming or simulation sites also study and make note of the "rules" of the game or site; hence they are studying the particulars in light of the context and purpose. So it seems that, on the one hand, judging individuals by the way they choose to present themselves online is a risky business, and verification or triangulation may be far less reliable than in the "real world." On the other hand, Paulus, Lester, and Dempster (2014), who discuss the digital world and its tools for qualitative research, argue that "mobile devices, GIS, online communities and the 'YouTube nation' are making it easier to capture social life as it happens, adding a layer of authenticity to our work" (p. 191). In short, in considering the nuances of the authenticity of documents online, it is important to consult the cited texts that deal with such issues in detail.

An important distinction for historians that qualitative researchers might also attend to is whether documents are primary or secondary sources. Primary sources are those in which the originator of the document is recounting firsthand experience with the phenomenon of interest. The best primary sources are those recorded closest in time and place to the phenomenon by a qualified person. Given this definition, most personal documents and eyewitness accounts of social phenomena could be considered primary resources. Secondary sources are reports of a phenomenon of interest by those who have not directly experienced the phenomenon; these are often compiled at a later date and are "at least one step removed" from the initial account (Altheide & Schneider, 2013, p. 7). Interestingly, the same document could be classified as primary or secondary depending upon the purpose of the study. The diary of a loved one caring for someone with terminal cancer, for example, would be a primary source of data for a study on caretaking; it would be considered a secondary source of data for understanding how patients themselves cope with a terminal disease. Altheide and Schneider (2013) discuss a third category of documents, which they call "auxiliary documents." Auxiliary documents "can supplement a research project . . . but are neither the main focus of investigation nor the primary source of data for understanding the topic. It seems that we are constantly running across new auxiliary documents as new electronic information bases become available. The hundreds of blogs and commentaries on newspaper and news articles that are presented online provide interesting nuggets of emphasis that can be useful in illustrating certain findings obtained from systematic investigation of other documents" (p. 7).

After assessing the authenticity and nature of documents or artifacts, the researcher must adopt some system for coding and cataloging them. If at all possible, written documents should be copied and artifacts photographed or videotaped. By establishing basic descriptive categories early on for coding, the researcher will have easy access to information in the analysis and interpretation stage. In qualitative studies, a form of *content analysis* is most often used to analyze documents. Essentially, content analysis is "an unobtrusive technique that allows researchers to analyze relatively unstructured data in view of the meanings, symbolic qualities, and expressive contents they have and of the communicative roles they play in the lives of the data's sources" (Krippendorff, 2013, p. 49). Historians and literary critics have long used content analysis to analyze historical documents and literary works. Modern content analysis has most often been applied to communications media (newspapers, periodicals, television, film) and has had a strong quantitative focus. For example, Stellefson et al. (2014) did a content analysis of relevant YouTube videos as a form of education about chronic obstructive pulmonary disease, predominantly by counting how many videos dealt with medication, issues of smoking cessation, and the like. As in this case, many content analyses deal with measuring the frequency and variety of messages and confirming hypotheses. Data collection and coding are often carried out by novices using protocols and trained to count units of analysis.

Quantification need not be a component of content analysis, however. Rather, the *nature* of the data can also be assessed. Schreier (2014) describes how qualitative content analysis differs from quantitative content analysis, which traditionally ascribed meaning through counting: "Whereas the focus in quantitative content analysis continues to be on manifest meaning [through counting], qualitative content analysis is also applied to latent and more context dependent meaning" (p. 173). Altheide and Schneider (2013) concur, noting that the major difference between quantitative content analysis and qualitative, or what they call "ethnographic" content analysis, "is the reflexive and highly interactive nature of the investigator, concepts, data collection, and analysis." Unlike in quantitative content analysis, "in which the protocol is the instrument," in qualitative content analysis "the investigator is continually central" (p. 26). Schreier provides a discussion of Shannon's (1954) content analysis of the cartoon *Little Orphan Annie*; Shannon analyzed it for its manifestation of values—in particular, how the newspaper editors used it to transmit "conservative Anti-Roosevelt sentiment and values" (in Schreier, 2014, p. 172). So Shannon focused on five questions in conducting the analysis of how these values were transmitted, such as examining who Annie's friends and enemies are, what goals she approves of and how these goals are attained, what symbols she likes and which ones she feels negative about. Such an analysis gets at the more latent meaning of the cartoon; the evidence is provided in context, and by using words and examples from the text and its pictures, rather than in simple numbers.

LIMITATIONS AND STRENGTHS OF DOCUMENTS AND ARTIFACTS

In judging the value of a data source, a researcher can ask whether it contains information or insights relevant to the research question and whether it can be acquired in a reasonably practical yet systematic manner. If these two questions can be answered in the affirmative, there is no reason not to use a particular source of data. Documents or artifacts have been underused in qualitative research, however. Nearly 50 years ago Glaser and Strauss (1967) listed several reasons for this underuse of documents: researchers prefer to produce their own data, the use of documents is too much like historical research, researchers want "to see the concrete situation and informants in person" (p. 163), and they distrust their own competency in using documentary materials. These barriers seem partially true today. However, given the preponderance of blogging and vlogs in which writers give in-depth thoughts about their experience with a particular phenomenon (Hookway, 2008; Pink, 2013), blogs and online discussion at social media sites are an easy source of data as documents.

Preferences for other sources of data may reflect a researcher's uncertainty about the potential of documents and artifacts for yielding knowledge and insight. But the researcher's caution may also reflect some of the limitations inherent in this data source. Several limitations stem from the basic difference between this source and data gleaned from interviews or observations—that most documentary data have not been developed for research purposes. The materials may therefore be incomplete from a research perspective. In contrast to field notes, available materials may not "afford a continuity of unfolding events in the kind of detail that the theorist requires" (Glaser & Strauss, 1967, p. 182). Whether personal accounts or official documents are involved, the source may provide unrepresentative samples. "Often no one on the project keeps very good notes on processes, few memoranda are generated, and, even more often, the only writing that is done is in response to funders' requests for technical reports or other periodic statements about the progress of the program or project. If no documents exist, however, or if the documents are sparse and seem uninformative, this ought to tell the inquirer something about the context" (Guba & Lincoln, 1981, pp. 234–235).

Because documents generally are not produced for research purposes, the information they offer may not be in a form that is useful (or understandable) to the investigator. Furthermore, such data may be incongruent with emerging findings based on observational or interview data. This is, of course, more of a problem when documents are used as secondary data sources to verify findings based on other data. However, if documents are found to be illuminating to the topic of research and incorporated into the process of inductively building categories and theoretical constructs in the first place, they then become evidence in support of the findings.

Another major problem with documentary materials is determining their authenticity and accuracy. Even public records that purport to be objective and accurate contain built-in biases that a researcher may not be aware of. For example, the incidence and frequency of crimes reported in police records may be a function of how certain crimes are defined and a particular department's procedures for reporting them. Personal documents are subject to purposeful or nonpurposeful deception. There is likely to be, for example, an underestimation of income in a personal income tax report versus an overestimation of expenses in a grant proposal. Distortion in personal documents may be unintentional in that the writer is unaware of his or her biases or simply does not remember accurately. Selltiz, Jahoda, Deutsch, and Cook (1959, p. 325) quote Augustine, who noted this problem of authenticity in his famous personal document *Confessions*: "And when they hear me confessing of myself, how do they know whether I speak the truth?" Concern about authenticity applies to historical documents as well as to anonymous project reports and sources who wish to remain anonymous, such as "Deep Throat" of the 1974 Watergate case (Webb et al., 2000).

Despite these limitations, documents are a good source of data for numerous reasons. To begin with, they may be the best source of data on a particular subject, better than observations or interviews. Many documents are easily accessible and free and contain information that would take an investigator enormous time and effort to gather otherwise. For example, if one were interested in a historical case study of an institution or program, documents would be the best source of data, particularly if persons associated with the institution were not available for interviews. Other situations in which documents are likely to be the best source of data would be studies that rely on technical expertise such as medical reports, and studies of intimate personal relationships that cannot be observed or that people are reluctant to discuss.

The data found in documents can be used in the same manner as data from interviews or observations. The data can furnish descriptive information, verify emerging hypotheses, advance new categories and hypotheses, offer historical understanding, track change and development, and so on. Glaser and Strauss (1967) point to the usefulness of documents for theory building—a process that "begs for comparative analysis. The library offers *a fantastic range* of comparison groups, if only the researcher has the ingenuity to discover them" (p. 179, emphasis in original).

One of the greatest advantages in using documentary material is its stability. Unlike in interviewing and observation, the presence of the investigator does not alter what is being studied. Documentary data are "objective" sources of data compared to other forms. Such data have also been called "unobtrusive." Webb, Campbell, Schwartz, and Sechrest's (1966) classic book on unobtrusive measures, when revised, was titled *Nonreactive Measures in the Social Sciences* (1981) because, they write, "we came to realize over the years that the original title was not the best one since it was the nonreactivity of the measures rather than their unobtrusiveness that was of major concern" (p. ix). In yet another revised edition, the authors use both terms: *Unobtrusive Measures: Nonreactive*

Research in the Social Sciences (2000). Nonreactive measures include physical traces, official records, private documents, and simple observations.

Thus, like any other source of data, documents have their limitations and their advantages. Because they are usually produced for reasons other than research, they may be fragmentary, they may not fit the conceptual framework of the research, and their authenticity may be difficult to determine. However, because they generally exist independent of a research agenda, they are nonreactive—that is, unaffected by the research process. They are a product of the context in which they were produced and therefore grounded in the real world. Finally, many documents or artifacts cost little or nothing and are often easy to obtain.

SPECIAL CONSIDERATIONS IN DEALING WITH ONLINE DATA SOURCES

From its humble beginnings as a communication tool exclusively for university professors and scientists (initially designed to withstand the results of a war), the Internet has become a standard resource for anyone who has a question, or is curious about something, or just wants to randomly explore topics of interest.

In addition to providing a number of reference sources—albeit of uneven quality—the Internet supports interactions among people through various forms of computer mediated communication. E-mail, online discussion groups, newsgroups, chat rooms, wikis, blogs, Facebook, vlogs, YouTube, and various social media sites allow people who have never met to encounter one another and even establish relationships conducted primarily through online contacts. These interactions, still somewhat ill-defined in our society, are of obvious interest to qualitative researchers.

Dealing with such online data sources or virtual data is a burgeoning arena of discussion in qualitative research. We have provided numerous examples of online data sources as documents in the preceding discussion. However, researchers have had the ability to access data online for only about two decades; thus qualitative research in the Internet age is a continually changing landscape, and one that offers infinite research possibilities (Marotzki, Holze, & Verständig, 2014). This can be both exciting and overwhelming, to both novice and more seasoned researchers.

So, what factors must be considered when accessing and analyzing these data sources? In this section we explore some of the issues associated with the use of online data sources. How are these sources similar to more familiar sources, such as documents, interviews, and observations? How are they different? What issues and concerns are raised by the effects of the media on the data-gathering process? What ethical considerations arise in this new research context?

These are not questions easily answered, nor are they the exclusive province of qualitative researchers. Articles in the popular press regularly discuss various effects of the Internet on society at large, ranging from explorations of the "multiple selves" possible online, to mentions of "online affairs" between people who have never seen one another in person, to organizing social protests, to buying and selling consumer goods, and, indeed, to conducting illegal activities. Even standard news magazines highlight issues related to cyberspace—the ambiguous destination to which the information superhighway leads. Since the changing electronic landscape outpaces the publication of specific maps or guides, this discussion merely outlines a general range of concerns. For any particular area of study, the specific application of these considerations will vary.

ONLINE VERSUS OFF-LINE DATA

In qualitative research, the three basic ways to collect data have traditionally been through interviews, observations, and examinations of documents and artifacts. Many of the references and data sources available online reflect characteristics of these familiar data sources. Web pages, papers available through file transfer protocol, and various forms of "electronic paper" can be considered documents that are simply accessed online. Marotzki, Holze, and Verständig (2014) refer to these as "static data," which "(1) are not created with different users interacting with each other and (2) remain basically unchanged while they are continuously accessible" (p. 452). Illustrations and programs—even games—available in static form to be downloaded by the user can be treated as artifacts. These forms of data share most of the same features as documents that are available in the physical environment.

What Marotzki, Holze, and Verständig (2014) refer to as "dynamic data" as a result of the development of the social web are "data that users generate in interactive contexts" (p. 453), such as through social media sites such as Facebook and Twitter. These can be reposted and deleted. Sometimes such data are archived, but they can also be short-lived. Such dynamic data function a bit differently than static data do. Static data is more like a traditional document, whereas dynamic data can be more like an interview, such as those done over e-mail. Or they can function more like an observation, given that the researcher needs to make a decision about both whether or not to join an online community and the extent to which to be a participant or observer.

To some extent, then, online data collection offers an electronic extension of familiar research techniques, widening the scope of data available to the researcher. Certainly, many of the decisions faced in off-line situations emerge in parallel form in online research: whether to join an online community as a complete observer, a complete participant, or something in between; how to select a sample group; how to approach potential participants when initiating a study; how to gain trust; and so on.

However, online data collection has some important differences due to the nature of the medium through which it is conducted. These differences have a profound influence on the study that must not be ignored or trivialized. For example, individuals who do not have access to computers will be automatically excluded from the study. Is this appropriate for the study, or will demographic differences that correlate with computer access distort the findings?

Though the amount of information increases to an overwhelming degree, not all critical interactions are necessarily available for study. Students in an online course may also communicate through private e-mail messages that the researcher never sees. Quantity of information is no guarantee of comprehensiveness.

In addition, each form of computer mediated communication has a unique effect on the information it transmits. For example, an e-mail interview may have the same verbal content as one conducted in person, but it lacks inflection, body language, and the many other nuances that often communicate more vividly than words. Frequent users of e-mail recognize its limitations; new users are regularly warned that jokes and sarcasm do not travel well online, and they are taught "emoticons" that attempt to replicate the emotional richness common in speech. At the same time that some communication characteristics are curtailed or modified, others are artificially enhanced. The asynchronous nature of e-mail can add reflection time to an online interview that would be unavailable in a face-to-face session. Immediate reactions, strong emotional responses, and unguarded expressions are all lost to the researcher unless, after second thought, the participant chooses to make these transient first thoughts available—and is capable of articulating them in writing. These reactions could completely change the interpretation of a response. Conversely, a casual response may have an unexpected and unsettling permanency; e-mail exchanges long forgotten can resurface, sometimes in totally different and even misleading contexts.

Even as they become familiar with the evolving conventions of online expression, researchers need to remain alert to the variables of electronic communication. Participants in online discussion groups and other online communities of various types often have an entire terminology to describe certain types of exchanges.

In terms of group interactions, writing skills and computer literacy strongly influence how individuals are perceived online. Often someone will seem to have an entirely different character: a funny, charming person can seem caustic and sarcastic when the smile accompanying the words disappears. Another individual whose writing is mature and thoughtful may prove to have limited social skills when deprived of reflection time and forced to react spontaneously.

This is new territory, with unfamiliar rules that change as quickly as they are identified. Our best advice for researchers is to recognize that the results of their research are strongly influenced by the characteristics of the data revealed, concealed, or altered because of the nature of the medium through which they are presented. Analyzing, describing, and discussing the potential effects of these characteristics will be an important aspect of research conducted from online data.

EFFECTS OF THE MEDIUM ON DATA GATHERING

In addition to the differences between online and off-line data, differences caused by the manner in which data are gathered must be considered. In qualitative research, the researcher is the primary instrument for data collection and analysis. This factor is usually perceived as an advantage, because humans are both responsive and adaptive. At the same time, it carries the responsibility of assessing and reporting researcher biases that might have an impact on the study.

When collecting data from the Internet, the researcher is no longer the primary instrument for data collection; a variety of software tools must be used to locate, select, and process information. Like the researcher, these tools have inherent biases that may affect the study, but their biases may be very subtle—and often much more difficult for a researcher to detect and describe. For example, in speaking to the benefits and limitations of using webcam technology to conduct focus groups with people in different locations, Tuttas (2015) notes that some participants were not able to participate because either they didn't have access or the technology didn't work properly. Further, despite the many benefits of being able to include participants from different locations, there are limitations in what one can actually see through the technology that could potentially affect how one could analyze data.

The effects of the medium raise critical concerns for qualitative researchers accessing data from the Internet and making use of various communication tools to do so: How are their tools shaping the task? Salmons (2015), in her book on online interviewing, for example, discusses how using technology such as Skype that has a visual component allows the researcher or participant to potentially draw a picture or create a diagram that would easily make sense. One is not likely to do this when conducting an interview over the phone. This is a simple example of how the tools are shaping the task.

ETHICAL ISSUES IN ONLINE ENVIRONMENTS

In any qualitative study, ethical issues relating to protection of the participants are of concern. In an online environment, these issues overlap the public debate about ownership of intellectual property, copyright, and free speech. The ability to read, save, copy, archive, and easily edit huge volumes of material written by faceless masses can lead a researcher to forget that these are the words of individuals. Even when the names are changed, some people are easily identified by the details of their messages. The highly public nature of some of the electronic environments in which people exchange ideas can lull researchers into forgetting the right to privacy that these individuals have, just as the seeming anonymity of electronic communication can lull individuals into revealing highly intimate details of their lives to anyone who happens to be reading their messages.

With the increased use of the Internet for research, more writers are attending to the ethical issues involved in working in this new medium. Hewson, Yule, Laurent, and Vogel (2003) identify four particular issues in Internet research that must be thought through. The first is obtaining informed consent; traditionally, participants sign a statement indicating their willingness to participate and need to be 18 years old or over to give this consent. Creative ways have to be established for giving consent and establishing that the participant is an adult. Ensuring confidentiality and security of information is a second issue; again, mechanisms can be put in place to enable confidentiality, but in this medium they are not as effective as in person-to-person data gathering. A third ethical issue is determining what is public and what is private: "The crucial question is whether the researcher is ethically justified in using publicly available information as data for a research study. Or, more specifically, in which context is this ethically acceptable or not acceptable?" (p. 53). The fourth ethical issue is how to develop debriefing procedures so that participants may make comments or ask questions, and to ensure that no harm has occurred. Some of these issues can be a bit more complicated than they might seem at first blush. Marotzki, Holze, and Verständig (2014) note that even if a pseudonym is used in reference to a person's online remarks to ensure confidentiality, "a direct citation from a newsgroup or discussion board, for example, can easily be back-traced . . ." (p. 461).

The term *participants* is commonly used by qualitative researchers to describe the individuals being studied. It is a carefully chosen identifier, with connotations of inclusion and willing cooperation.

This single word captures a number of attitudes about research from the qualitative paradigm. It also serves as a litmus test concerning ethics. If this term cannot be accurately used—if *subjects* more appropriately describes the inclusion of unwilling or uninformed individuals under the researcher's scrutiny—then the researcher should honestly reevaluate the methods and procedures of the study.

The growing importance of online interaction makes it a natural arena for qualitative research. Three critical areas that the qualitative researcher must consider are the effects of the context on the data, the effects of software functionalities on the data-gathering process, and the effects the medium tends to have on ethical practice. Explicitly considering and describing the impact of these factors is a new responsibility of the qualitative researcher.

Summary

Documents, a third major source of data in qualitative research (in addition to interviews and observation), is broadly defined to include public records, personal papers, popular culture documents, visual documents, and physical material and artifacts. Although some documents might be prepared at the investigator's request (such as a respondent's keeping a diary or writing a life history), most are produced independently of the research study. They are thus nonreactive and grounded in the context under study. Because they are produced for reasons other than the study at hand, some ingenuity is needed in locating documents that bear on the problem and then in analyzing their content. Congruence between documents and the research problem depends on the researcher's flexibility in construing the problem and the related questions. Such a stance is particularly fitting in qualitative studies, which, by their very nature, are emergent in design and inductive in analysis. Documents of all types can help the researcher uncover meaning, develop understanding, and discover insights relevant to the research problem.

Data gathering online is an area of keen interest for qualitative researchers. However, a number of issues must be considered when using data from an online interaction; we reviewed some of these issues in this chapter.

PART THREE

ANALYZING AND REPORTING QUALITATIVE DATA

Choosing a qualitative research design presupposes a certain view of the world that in turn defines how a researcher selects a sample, collects data, analyzes data, and approaches issues of validity, reliability, and ethics. Part Three consists of three chapters that address the later stages of the research process, including one comprehensive chapter on analyzing qualitative data, one chapter on producing valid and reliable knowledge in an ethical manner, and one chapter on writing the qualitative study report.

This book's separate chapters on data analysis and issues of validity, reliability, and ethics may be somewhat misleading; qualitative research is not a linear, step-by-step process. Data collection and analysis are simultaneous activities in qualitative research. Analysis begins with the first interview, the first observation, the first document read. Emerging insights, hunches, and tentative hypotheses direct the next phase of data collection, which in turn leads to the refinement or reformulation of questions, and so on. It is an interactive process throughout that allows the investigator to produce believable and trustworthy findings. Unlike experimental designs in which validity and reliability are accounted for before the investigation, rigor in a qualitative research derives from the researcher's presence, the nature of the interaction between researcher and participants, the triangulation of data, the interpretation of perceptions, and rich, thick description.

It follows, then, that the final report of a qualitative study will look different from the final report of a quantitative research design. While there is no one right way to write up a qualitative study, there are some general guidelines. Some of these include providing detail on how the study was conducted, presenting enough evidence to support the findings, and discussing how the study extends the knowledge base and informs practice.

In these last three chapters of this book, readers will get a sense of the interactive nature of data collection, analysis, and reporting. Chapter Eight, the first chapter in Part Three, discusses the importance of simultaneously analyzing data as they are being collected along with practical guidelines for managing the data set, including a discussion of how computer programs can facilitate both data management and analysis. This chapter is also devoted to exactly *how* to analyze the data you are collecting. Data analysis can result in a write-up that ranges from a descriptive account to theory building. A large segment of the chapter describes the step-by-step process of inductively deriving meaning from the data, especially with regard to the development of categories or themes that cut across the data. The final section of Chapter Eight introduces the reader to a brief overview of data analysis strategies particular to different types of qualitative studies.

Whether one is conducting a study or wants to makes use of someone else's research in their practice, the trustworthiness of the research is paramount. Chapter Nine explores the issues of internal validity, reliability, and external validity—the extent to which the findings of a qualitative study can be applied to other situations. There has probably been more discussion and debate about generalizability than any other single aspect of qualitative research. How to think about these issues, as well as concrete strategies for ensuring the trustworthiness of qualitative research, is the focus of Chapter Nine. Equally important are the ethical concerns that pervade the entire process of qualitative research, from conceptualization of the study to dissemination of findings. These are also discussed.

Chapter Ten, the final chapter in Part Three (and of this book), is devoted to the writing of a qualitative research report. Here we cover the preparation for writing, the content of the report and issues related to that content, and the dissemination of the findings. Also included in this chapter is a brief discussion on writing up the findings in action research and arts based studies.

We present the chapters in this part of the book with the awareness that detailed instructions in analyzing and reporting qualitative research, though helpful, are merely guidelines in need of interpretation and application by the single most important component in qualitative research—the investigator.

CHAPTER EIGHT

QUALITATIVE DATA ANALYSIS

Preceding chapters have explained how to gather data for a qualitative study through interviews, observations, and documents. In this chapter we discuss managing those data and analyzing them. A chapter on data analysis following chapters on collecting qualitative data is a bit misleading because collection and analysis should be a *simultaneous* process in qualitative research. In fact, the timing of analysis and the integration of analysis with other tasks distinguish a qualitative design from traditional, positivistic research. A qualitative design is emergent. The researcher usually does not know ahead of time every person who might be interviewed, all the questions that might be asked, or where to look next unless data are analyzed as they are being collected. Hunches, working hypotheses, and educated guesses direct the investigator's attention to certain data and then to refining or verifying hunches. The process of data collection and analysis is recursive and dynamic. But this is not to say that the analysis is finished when all the data have been collected. Quite the opposite. Analysis becomes more intensive as the study progresses and once all the data are in.

Flick (2014) describes the process of data analysis as "the classification and interpretation of linguistic (or visual) material to make statements about implicit and explicit dimensions and structures of meaning-making in the material and what is represented in it" (p. 5). This chapter covers a range of topics related to data analysis, with an emphasis on how you actually *do* it. First, we talk about the importance of beginning analysis early, as you are collecting data. The organization and management of your data also begins early but must be completed once all the data have been collected to enable intensive analysis. The third section, and the heart of this chapter, focuses on *how* you construct categories or themes that will become your findings. We've also included a discussion of the role of computer software programs for qualitative data analysis. Finally, we review strategies particular to several of the types of qualitative research discussed in Chapter Two.

BEGINNING ANALYSIS DURING DATA COLLECTION

Picture yourself sitting down at the dining room table, ready to begin analyzing data for your modest qualitative study. In one pile to your left are a hundred or so pages of transcripts of interviews. In the middle of the table is a stack of field notes from your on-site observations, and to the right of that is a box of documents you collected, thinking they might be relevant to the study. You review what the purpose of your study is and questions that guided the inquiry. Now what do you do? Where do you start? How do you come up with findings from hundreds of pages of data? You begin by reading a transcript, and then another. You realize you should have asked the second participant something that came up in the first interview. You quickly feel overwhelmed; you begin to feel that you are literally drowning in the data. It is doubtful that you will be able to come up with any findings. You have undermined your entire project by waiting until after all the data are collected before beginning analysis.

In a more enlightened scenario, you sit down at the dining room table with nothing more than the transcript of your first interview, or the field notes from your first observation, or the first document you collected. You review the purpose of your study. You read and reread the data, making notes in the margins, commenting on the data. You write a separate memo to yourself capturing your reflections, tentative themes, hunches, ideas, and things to pursue that are derived from this first set of data. You note things you want to ask, observe, or look for in your next round of data collection. After your second interview, you compare the first set of data with the second. This comparison informs the next data collected, and so on. Months later, as you sit down to analyze and write up your findings, you have a set of tentative categories or themes—answers to your research questions from which to work. You are organizing and refining rather than beginning data analysis.

Data analysis is one of the few aspects of doing qualitative research—perhaps the only one—in which there is a preferred way. As illustrated in the scenario just described, the much-preferred way to analyze data in a qualitative study is to do it simultaneously with data collection. At the outset of a qualitative study, the investigator knows what the problem is and has selected a purposeful sample to collect data in order to address the problem. But the researcher does not know what will be discovered, what or whom to concentrate on, or what the final analysis will be like. The final product is shaped by the data that are collected and the analysis that accompanies the entire process. Without ongoing analysis, the data can be unfocused, repetitious, and overwhelming in the sheer volume of material that needs to be processed. Data that have been analyzed while being collected are both parsimonious and illuminating.

Simultaneous data collection and analysis occurs both in and out of the field. That is, you can be doing some rudimentary analysis while you are in the process of collecting data, as well as between data collection activities, as illustrated in the second scenario. Bogdan and Biklen (2011) offer 10 helpful suggestions for analyzing data as they are being collected:

1. *Force yourself to make decisions that narrow the study.* "You must discipline yourself not to pursue everything . . . or else you are likely to wind up with data too diffuse and inappropriate for what you decide to do. The more data you have on a given topic, setting, or subjects, the easier it will be to think deeply about it and the more productive you are likely to be when you attempt the final analysis" (p. 161).

2. *Force yourself to make decisions concerning the type of study you want to accomplish.* "You should try to make clear in your own mind, for example, whether you want to do a full description of a setting or whether you are interested in generating theory about a particular aspect of it" (p. 161).

3. *Develop analytic questions.* "Some researchers bring general questions to a study. These are important because they give focus to data collection and help organize it as you proceed. We suggest that shortly after you enter the field, you assess which questions you brought with you are relevant and which ones should be reformulated to direct your work" (p. 161).

4. *Plan data collection sessions according to what you find in previous observations.* Review field notes and memos as you go along "and plan to pursue specific leads in your next data-collection session" (p. 163).

5. *Write many "observer's comments" as you go.* "The idea is to stimulate critical thinking about what you see and to become more than a recording machine (p. 163). (See Chapter Six for suggestions on writing observer comments.)

6. *Write memos to yourself about what you are learning.* "These memos can provide a time to reflect on issues raised in the setting and how they relate to larger theoretical, methodological, and substantive issues" (p. 165).

7. *Try out ideas and themes on participants.* As you are interviewing participants you can ask what they think about some pattern or theme you are beginning to detect in the data. "While not everyone should be asked, and while not all you hear may be helpful, key informants, under the appropriate circumstances, can help advance your analysis, especially to fill in the holes of description" (p. 165).

8. *Begin exploring the literature while you are in the field.* "After you have been in the field for a while, going through the substantive literature in the area you are studying will enhance analysis" (p. 169). (Actually, rather than beginning to explore the literature, we recommend *reviewing* the literature that you have consulted in setting up your study [see Chapter Four].)

9. *Play with metaphors, analogies, and concepts.* "Nearsightedness plagues most research. Ask the question, 'What does this remind me of?'" (p. 169).

10. *Use visual devices.* Trying to visualize what you are learning about the phenomenon can bring clarity to your analysis.

Data collection and analysis is indeed an ongoing process that can extend indefinitely. There is almost always another person who could be interviewed, another observation that could be conducted, another document to be reviewed. When should you stop this phase of the investigation and begin intensive data analysis? How do you know when you have collected enough data? The answer depends on some very practical as well as theoretical concerns. Practically, you may have depleted the time and money allocated to the project or run out of mental and physical energy. Ideally, the decision will be based more on the notion of *saturation*. Saturation occurs when continued data collection produces no new information or insights into the phenomenon you are studying. For example, as you continue to interview you begin to realize that you are hearing the same things you've heard earlier; no new information is forthcoming, or some tidbit is relatively minor in comparison to the effort spent collecting the information. Also, the ongoing analysis of your data has produced categories, themes, or findings robust enough to cover what emerges in later data collection.

Managing Your Data

Some system for organizing and managing data needs to be devised early in your study. This involves *coding,* a term that has unfortunately further mystified the already mysterious process of data analysis. *Coding is nothing more than assigning some sort of shorthand designation to various aspects of your data so that you can easily retrieve specific pieces of the data.* The designations can be single words, letters, numbers, phrases, colors, or combinations of these. Most often a code is "a word or short phrase that symbolically assigns a summative, salient, essence-capturing, and/or evocative attribute for a portion of language-based or visual data" (Saldaña, 2013, p. 3).

Each interview, set of field notes, and document needs identifying notations so that you can access them as needed in both the analysis and the write-up of your findings. This basic organization is easy to overlook, because at the time you are collecting data, you will feel there is no way you could ever forget where and when an incident took place or the characteristics of the person you just interviewed. However, 10 interviews later you are quite likely to have forgotten identifying characteristics of your earlier participants. Months later you will have forgotten quite a bit about all of your data. Hence, as you collect your data it is important to code it according to whatever scheme is relevant to your study, and according to the theoretical framework that informs the study. For example, in the study of how traditional healers in Malaysia diagnose and treat cancer (Merriam & Muhamad, 2013), each interview was coded; that is, assigned descriptive notations including a pseudonym, location (rural, urban), age, sex, years in practice, and type of practice (traditional healers were of two general types: those using herbs, roots, and plants, who were called *bomoh*, and those who primarily used verses from the Koran, who were known as Islamic or Koranic healers). This allowed the researchers to access a particular interview transcript or to pull out several transcripts from the total set on any of the coded dimensions or combinations of dimensions—Islamic healers in rural settings, for example.

You also need to keep track of your thoughts, musings, speculations, and hunches as you prepare your data for analysis. This kind of information might be interwoven with your raw data (as in observer comments in field notes; see Chapter Six), or it might be in separate files or memos. Rather than hiring someone, transcribing your own interviews is another means of generating insights and hunches about what is going on in your data. This information, which ideally you capture in your field notes or in the margins of your interview transcript or in a separate memo, is actually rudimentary analysis. These observations or speculations will be quite helpful to you as you move between the emerging analysis and the raw data of interviews, field notes, and documents.

The important task is to create an inventory of your entire data set. You need to know exactly what you have in terms of interviews, field notes, documents, artifacts, memos you wrote while collecting or thinking about your data, and so on. This data set needs to be organized and labeled according to some organizing scheme that makes sense to you, the researcher, and enables you to access any piece of your data at any time. One electronic or hard copy of your entire data set, along with your organizing scheme, should be set aside from the data set that you will actually be working on when you do your analysis. Horror stories abound of lost or damaged memory sticks, computer crashes, stolen briefcases containing hard copies of data, and so on—stories that are better told about someone else! One way of dealing with this and ensuring that data will not be lost is to store data in multiple places, including on a cloud storage site.

You can, of course, do all of this organizing by hand, and some qualitative researchers do. Another option for managing your data is to use a computer software program designed for qualitative research. A third option is a mix of manual and computer management. At the very least, transcripts and field notes will most likely have been transcribed, and the hard copy will have a computer file backup. Several word processing programs are sophisticated enough to be adapted to data management. Indeed, computer software programs designed for qualitative data analysis or word processing programs adapted for qualitative analysis are widely used by both experienced and novice researchers. (See the section later in this chapter on Computers and Qualitative Data Analysis.)

HOW TO ANALYZE QUALITATIVE DATA

The collection of qualitative data through observations, interviews, and documents is something most novice researchers can do and get better at through practice. Analyzing these data is a much more daunting task, especially if faced with a voluminous pile of data that has not had even a preliminary review while it was being collected. In our many years of experience conducting qualitative studies and teaching and advising doctoral students in how to conduct them, data analysis is the most difficult part of the entire process. This is the point at which a tolerance for ambiguity is most critical—and where the novice researcher often will say, "What if I don't find anything?" Again, it is our experience that one can read about data analysis, even take a course in it, but it isn't until you work with your own data in trying to answer your own research questions that you really see how data analysis "works" in qualitative research. Having said that, in this section of the chapter we present a very basic strategy for analyzing your qualitative data. It is our position that qualitative data analysis is primarily *inductive* and *comparative*. We thus draw heavily from the constant comparative method of data analysis first proposed by Glaser and Strauss (1967) as the means for developing grounded theory. However, the constant comparative method of data analysis is inductive and comparative and so has been widely used throughout qualitative research to generate findings (Charmaz, 2014). It is only when the constant comparative method is used to build a substantive theory that the study is considered a grounded theory study (see Chapter Two).

The Goal of Data Analysis

Data analysis is the process of making sense out of the data. And making sense out of data involves consolidating, reducing, and interpreting what people have said and what the researcher has seen and read—it is the process of making meaning. Data analysis is a complex procedure that involves moving back and forth between concrete bits of data and abstract concepts, between inductive and deductive reasoning, between description and interpretation. These meanings or understandings or insights constitute the findings of a study. Findings can be in the form of organized descriptive accounts, themes, or categories that cut across the data, or in the form of models and theories that explain the data. Each of these forms reflects different analytical levels, ranging from dealing with the concrete in simple description to higher-level abstractions in theory construction.

But what does making sense out of the data mean? Basically, data analysis is the process used to *answer your research question(s)*. Chapter Four described how to design a qualitative study and identified the purpose statement and research questions as central to the process. Qualitative purpose statements ask how something happens, what factors are important, and so on. A purpose statement often has subcomponents in the form of research questions. For example, in the purpose statement, "The purpose of this study is to understand how adults cope with a life-threatening illness," you might have several research questions: What is the process? What contextual and personal factors shape the process? How has the illness influenced their sense of self? From your data, then, you would want to inductively: (1) derive a process; (2) identify the factors that shaped the process; and (3) identify how the illness has influenced how they now see themselves. These answers to your research questions are the findings of your study. So the practical goal of data analysis is to find *answers* to your research questions. These answers are also called *categories* or *themes* or *findings*.

The overall process of data analysis begins by identifying segments in your data set that are responsive to your research questions. This segment is a unit of data, which is a potential answer or part of an answer to the question(s) you have asked in this study. A unit of data is any meaningful segment of data (or a potentially meaningful segment; at the beginning of a study the researcher is uncertain about what will ultimately be meaningful). A unit of data can be as small as a word a participant uses to describe a feeling or phenomenon, or as large as several pages of field notes describing a particular incident.

According to Lincoln and Guba (1985), a unit must meet two criteria. First, it should be heuristic—that is, the unit should reveal information relevant to the study and stimulate the reader to think beyond the particular bit of information. Second, the unit should be "the smallest piece of information about something that can stand by itself—that is, it must be interpretable in the absence of any additional information other than a broad understanding of the context in which the inquiry is carried out" (p. 345).

The task is to compare one unit of information with the next, looking for recurring regularities in the data. The process is one of breaking data down into bits of information and then assigning "these bits to categories or classes which bring these bits together again, if in a novel way. In the process we begin to discriminate more clearly between the criteria for allocating data to one category or another. Then some categories may be subdivided, and others subsumed under more abstract categories" (Dey, 1993, p. 44).

For a simple but vivid example of how to take raw data and sort them into categories, consider the task of sorting two hundred food items found in a grocery store. These two hundred food items in a research study would be bits of information or units of data upon which to base an analysis. By comparing one item with another, the two hundred items could be classified into any number of categories. Starting with a box of cereal, for example, you could ask whether the next item, an orange, is like the first. Obviously not. There are now two piles into which the next item may or may not be placed. By this process you can sort all the items into categories of your choice. One scheme might separate the items into the categories of fresh, frozen, canned, or packaged goods. Or you could divide them by color, weight, or price. More likely, you would divide the items into common grocery store categories: meat, dairy, produce, canned goods, and so on. These categories would be fairly comprehensive classes, each of which could be further subdivided. Produce, for example, includes the subcategories of fruits and vegetables. Fruits include citrus and noncitrus, domestic and exotic. Through comparison, all these schemes inductively emerge from the data—the food items. The names of the categories and the scheme you use to sort the data will reflect the focus of your study.

THE STEP-BY-STEP PROCESS OF ANALYSIS

In this section we use the term *category*, which is commonly used in most texts dealing with basic data analysis; however, it should be remembered that in our view a category is the same as a theme, a pattern, a finding, or an answer to a research question. Category construction is data analysis, and all of the caveats about this process that we discussed earlier should be kept in mind, the most important being that data analysis is best done in conjunction with data collection. Once all of the data are in, there is generally a period of intensive analysis in which tentative findings are substantiated, revised, and reconfigured.

Category Construction

The process begins with reading the first interview transcript, the first set of field notes, the first document collected in the study. As you read down through the transcript, for example, you jot down notes, comments, observations, and queries in the margins. These notations are next to bits of data that strike you as interesting, potentially relevant, or important to your study. Think of yourself as having a conversation with the data—asking questions of it, making comments to it, and so on. This process of making notations next to bits of data that strike you as potentially relevant for answering your research questions is also called *coding*. Since you are just beginning the analysis, be as expansive as you want in identifying any segment of data that *might* be useful. Because you are being open to anything possible at this point, this form of coding is often called *open coding*.

What you jot in the margins (or insert in the computer file) can be a repeat of the exact word(s) of the participant, your words, or a concept from the literature. Exhibit 8.1 shows the open coding of a short segment of data from a study of African women who had made a successful transition from being unemployed to being successful businesswomen (Ntseane, 1999). In this segment of the interview, the researcher is exploring how these women

---

EXHIBIT 8.1. LEARNING REQUIRED AND HOW IT WAS BEING OBTAINED.

1. *Researcher:* Now let's talk about training. How did you learn what you do in your
2. business?
3.
4. *Participant:* You see, I did not get far with schooling. So I did not learn anything about
5. businesses in primary school. I just used my experience to start this business. In this   *experience*
6. culture we believe that experience of others can be copied. I think I stole the business   *copy others*
7. management system that I use in this business from the first shop assistance job that I
8. did. They taught me on the job how to treat customers, specifically that I had to be
9. friendly, smile at customers, and treat them with respect. I knew these things before but
10. I did not know then that they were important for the business. Also they showed me
11. how to keep track of what I have sold and things like that. Secondly, I learnt
12. a lot from my sister about how businesswomen in similar businesses like mine in   *sister*
13. Gaborone operate theirs. This learning experience and my common sense were very   *common sense*
14. helpful at the initial stages of this business. Once I was in business, well, you kind of
15. learn from doing things. For example you face problems and what works in what you   *by doing*
16. keep in your head for the next crisis. As the business expanded I learnt a lot from other
17. women. I talk with them about this business, especially those who own similar   *other women*
18. businesses like the ones I travel with to South Africa for our business shopping, those
19. who businesses are next to mine, employees, customers and family. You just have to
20. talk about your business and the sky is the limit with learning from other people.
21.
22. *Researcher:* Very interesting. Do other businesswomen learn from you too?
23.
24. *Participant:* Of course (laughs in disbelief). In this business I would not be where I
25. am without them. You see they made mistakes, suffered, and they do not want those who come
26. after them to go through that painful experience. I have been beaten by South African
27. robbers, humiliated by men who have power in this country over women and I have
28. sworn that I would not like to see any woman go through that experience. This is what
29. keeps me in business, that is to be there for other people either as a role model or a
30. security guard (more laughs). I make an effort to approach new businesswomen to
31. offer help and to let them know that my door is open for them to ask me for anything
32. that will make a difference in their lives and business.

Source: Ntseane (n.d.). Reprinted with permission.

learned about business. Note the codes that appear on the right. These are initial responses to the question of how these women learned to be businesswomen.

Assigning codes to pieces of data is how you begin to construct categories. After working through the entire transcript in this manner, you go back over your marginal notes and comments (codes) and try to group those comments and notes that seem to go together. This is akin to sorting items in the grocery store example. Using the codes at the right in Exhibit 8.1, for example, you might combine "copy others," "sister," and "other women" into a category "Learning from Others." This process of grouping your open codes is sometimes called *axial coding* (Charmaz, 2014; Corbin & Strauss, 2015) or *analytical coding*. Analytical coding goes beyond descriptive coding; it is "coding that comes from interpretation and reflection on meaning" (Richards, 2015, p. 135). Keep a running list of these groupings attached to the transcript or on a separate paper or memo. At the beginning of an inquiry, this list is likely to be fairly long because you do not yet know what will surface across the rest of the data. You also will not yet know which groupings might be subsumed under others.

Moving to your next set of data (transcript, field notes, or document), you scan it in exactly the same way as just outlined, keeping in mind the list of groupings that you extracted from the first transcript and checking to see whether they are also present in this second set. You also make a separate list of comments, terms, and notes from this set and then compare this list with the one derived from the first transcript. These two lists should then be merged into one master list of concepts derived from both sets of data. This master list constitutes a primitive outline or classification system reflecting the recurring regularities or patterns in your study. These patterns and regularities become the categories or themes into which subsequent items are sorted. *Categories* are conceptual elements that "cover" or span many individual examples (or bits or units of the data you previously identified) of the category. This is illustrated in Figure 8.1. The three smaller background boxes represent incidents of the category from which the category was derived. Using the section of the transcript in Exhibit 8.1 of how rural, low-literate women learned to be businesswomen, the segments identified as important in open

FIGURE 8.1. DERIVING CATEGORIES FROM DATA.

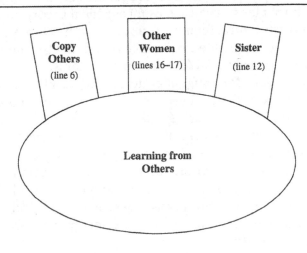

coding, "copy others (1.6)," "sister (1.12)," and "other women (ll.16–17)" are combined into the tentative category "Learning from Others."

The challenge is to construct categories or themes that capture some recurring pattern that cuts across your data. It should be clear that categories are abstractions derived from the data, not the data themselves. To paraphrase Glaser and Strauss (1967), these categories have a life of their own apart from the data from which they came.

Data analysis is a complex process. We sometimes think of it as a dialectic in which you move between seeing the big picture (the "forest"), and the particulars (the "trees"). The following process may help you think about how to analyze your data.

1. First think about **the purpose of your study**. What is it that you are trying to find out, or make happen (if it's an action research study)?
2. Second, **think about the lens of the epistemological framework**, and look through that lens. If you are using a phenomenological theoretical frame—focusing on how people experience a phenomenon, or a constructivist frame focusing

on how people construct knowledge or make meaning—look through that lens. If you are using a critical theory, or structural/poststructural feminist frame, or a critical race theory, think about power/life experience based on class, gender, race (respectively), and/or their intersections.

3. Code your data, focusing on patterns and insights related to your purpose and questions and guided by your theoretical frame. Think "**trees**" here. Read the data set, and just mark in the margins what the main theme is related to this interaction or conversation. This is open coding in which you capture any data with a word or a phrase that seems to be responsive to your research questions. In open coding you most likely will repeat the exact word or phrase used by the respondent. Sometimes you might use a term or concept that captures their exact words.

4. After a while, you have lots of trees (codes of data), and you may forget what the study is about. So here, step back from the data, and think "**forest.**" What are the main themes that emerge when you think about the study? What main insights have you gleaned? What are the answers to your research questions?

5. Go back to the **trees**. Do the trees (the individual data bits) support what you think you see in the forest?

6. Try to develop some categories using the "constant comparative method" (or some other method). Combine the codes from open coding above, into fewer, more comprehensive categories. Some call this axial coding.

Periodically between steps 4 and 5 and steps 5 and 6, think about **your biases** that you brought into the study beyond your epistemological or theoretical framework. What might you be projecting onto the data based on your own beliefs and life experience? How does your "positionality" or "social location" affect what you see? How are you guarding against your biases?

Sorting Categories and Data

At the beginning of your analysis you will most likely generate dozens of tentative categories. As you go along, assigning *codes* or themes or category names to your data, you should be compiling these in a separate memo, retaining those that seem to apply across more than one interview or set of field notes. And as you go along you might rename a category to more precisely reflect what is in the data. Some original categories will probably become subcategories. For example, in the preceding interview data from successful businesswomen, as the analysis and coding proceeded through several interviews, learning from a family member eventually became a subcategory under the category "learning from others." "Family members" and "other businesswomen" were the two subcategories. Once you are satisfied with a preliminary set of categories derived from the data, the categories can be fleshed out and made more robust by searching through the data for more and better units of relevant information. As you do this, your initial set of categories may undergo some revision. This process of refining and revising actually continues through the writing up of your findings.

Once you have derived a tentative scheme of categories or themes or findings, you will need to sort all of the evidence for your scheme into the categories. Marshall and Rossman (2016) visualize these categories as "buckets or baskets into which segments of text are placed" (p. 224). This is done by creating file folders, each labeled with a category name. Each unit of data coded according to this theme is then cut and put into the file folder. This of course can be done by hand (and often is in small-scale studies) or by using a word processing computer program. Each unit of data placed in a category should include original identifying codes such as respondent's name, line numbers of the excerpt, and so on. This will enable you to return to your original transcript, field notes, or document should you want to review the context of the quote.

Numerous computer programs have been developed to store, sort, and retrieve qualitative data. Some researchers have also devised systems using powerful word processing packages or database programs. Interview transcripts, observation notes, and so on are entered verbatim into the computer program. The researcher works on the particular set of data (for example, an interview transcript, field notes, written document) to analyze the data, making notes in the margins and developing themes or categories as illustrated earlier. Files are set up for the categories and their corresponding data are entered. The researcher can then retrieve and print, by category, any set of data desired. Multiple levels of coding are possible for the same unit of information. (For more discussion of computers in qualitative research, see the section in this chapter on Computers and Qualitative Data Analysis.)

The construction of categories is highly inductive. You begin with detailed bits or segments of data, cluster data units that seem to go together, then "name" the cluster. This is a category or theme or finding. As you move through data collection—particularly if you have been analyzing as you go—you will be able to "check out" these tentative categories with subsequent interviews, observations, or documents. At this point there is a subtle shift to a slightly deductive mode of thought—you have a category and you want to see whether it exists in subsequent data. Another way for beginning researchers to think about this is also related to the "forest and the trees" analogy that we outlined above. The "forest" represents the big picture—the initial list of categories that the researcher might come up with inductively from being immersed in the data. Finding the "trees" or bits of data to go with the forest is the shift into the deductive mode of thought. By the time you reach saturation—the point at which you realize no new information, insights, or understandings are forthcoming—you will most likely be thinking in a more deductive rather than inductive mode; that is, you are now largely testing your tentative category scheme against the data. This movement from inductive to deductive is pictured in Figure 8.2.

At the beginning of your study your analysis strategy is totally inductive; you are looking at bits and pieces of data and from them deriving tentative categories. As you collect and analyze more data, you begin to check whether categories derived from earlier data hold up as you analyze subsequent data. As you move further along in the collection and analysis, some categories will remain solid and others will not hold up. As you get toward the end of your study, you are very much operating from a deductive stance in that you are looking for more evidence in support of your final set of categories. By the time you reach a sense of saturation—that is, when nothing new is coming forth—you will be in a deductive mode.

FIGURE 8.2. THE LOGIC OF DATA ANALYSIS.

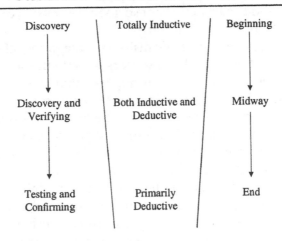

Naming the Categories

Devising categories is largely an intuitive process, but it is also systematic and informed by the study's purpose, the investigator's orientation and knowledge, and the meanings made explicit by the participants themselves. You may recall from Chapter Four that every study has some theoretical framework; that is, every study is situated in some body of literature that gives you the tools to even come up with a purpose statement and research questions. Since the categories or themes or findings are responsive (providing answers) to these research questions, the name of these categories will be congruent with the orientation of the study.

The actual names of your categories/themes/findings can come from at least three sources (or a mix of these sources): (1) yourself, the researcher, (2) the participants' exact words, or (3) sources outside the study, most likely from the literature on your topic. In the most common situation, the investigator comes up with terms, concepts, and categories that reflect what he or she sees in the data. In the second approach, the data can be organized into a scheme suggested by the participants themselves. For example, Bogdan and Biklen (2011) found that in a hospital intensive care unit for infants, the professional staff would classify parents as "good parents," "not-so-good parents," or "trouble-makers" (p. 175).

In addition to the participants' own categories, classification schemes can be borrowed from sources outside the study at hand. Applying someone else's scheme requires that the categories be compatible with the purpose and theoretical framework of the study. The database is scanned to determine the fit of a priori categories, and then the data are sorted into the borrowed categories.

There is some danger in using borrowed classification schemes, however, as it creates a bias in your data analysis (Gray, 2014). As Glaser and Strauss (1967) pointed out in their original discussion of the constant comparative method of data analysis, "Merely selecting data for a category that has been established by another theory tends to hinder the generation of new categories, because the major effort is not generation, but data selection. Also, emergent categories usually prove to be the most relevant and the best fitted to the data" (p. 37).

As can be seen in Exhibit 8.2, the categories constructed during data analysis should meet several criteria:

- Categories should be *responsive to the purpose of the research*. In effect, categories are the answers to your research question(s). One of Kim's (2014) findings (or categories or themes) regarding the career transition process of middle-aged workers to postretirement employment was that participants experienced disequilibrium in a previous career. This category, "experiencing disequilibrium in a previous career" became part of the "answer" to the study's purpose of identifying the steps in the career transition process.
- Categories should be *exhaustive*; that is, you should be able to place all data that you decided were important or relevant to the study in a category or subcategory.
- Categories should generally be *mutually exclusive*. A particular unit of data should fit into only *one* category. If exactly the same unit of data can be placed into more than one category, more conceptual work is needed to refine your categories. That is not to say, however, that part of a sentence could not go into one category or subcategory, and the rest of the sentence into another.

EXHIBIT 8.2. CRITERIA FOR CATEGORIES, THEMES, AND FINDINGS.

Must be responsive to (that is, answer) the research question(s) and . . .

1. Be *exhaustive* (enough categories to encompass all relevant data)
2. Be *mutually exclusive* (a relevant unit of data can be placed in only one category)
3. Be as *sensitive* to the data as possible
4. Be *conceptually congruent* (all categories are at the same level of abstraction)

- Categories should be *sensitizing*. The naming of the category should be as sensitive as possible to what is in the data. An outsider should be able to read the categories and gain some sense of their nature. The more exacting in capturing the meaning of the phenomenon, the better. For example, the category "time" does not reveal as much as the category "time management." In another example, "defiant behavior" is not as sensitizing as "defiance of adult authority figures." "Leadership" is not as sensitizing as "transformational leadership."
- Categories should be *conceptually congruent*. This means that the same level of abstraction should characterize all categories at the same level. In the grocery store example described earlier, the items should not be sorted according to produce, canned goods, and fruit. While produce and canned goods are at the same conceptual level, fruit is a type of produce and should form a subcategory of produce. In Ntseane's (2004) study of women in Botswana who become successful businesswomen, for example, three categories of learning were uncovered: (1) informal pre-business skill training, (2) formal technical training, and (3) business-embedded learning. Each of these categories has subcategories. For example, informal pre-business skill training was acquired from (a) family members, (b) observation on the job, and (c) common sense.

Conceptual congruence is probably the most difficult criterion to apply. Investigators are usually so immersed in their data and their analysis that it is hard for them to see whether or not a set of categories makes sense together. One of the best strategies for checking all the criteria against your category scheme is to display your set of categories in the form of a chart or table. This can be as simple as a list of one-word categories. In a study of the structure of simple reminiscence (Merriam, 1989), for example, the categories or findings were displayed in a list consisting of four terms—selection, immersion, withdrawal, and closure. Data displays can also be quite complex (Miles, Huberman, & Saldaña, 2014). The point is that by laying out the basic structure of your findings in front of you, you can see whether categories are at the same level of abstraction and also how well all of the parts fit together. Finally, by writing out the purpose statement at the top of your display, you can immediately see whether the categories are *answers* to the research question(s).

How Many Categories?

The number of categories a researcher constructs depends on the data and the focus of the research. In any case, the number should be manageable. In our experience, the fewer the categories, the greater the level of abstraction, and the greater the ease with which you can communicate your findings to others. Creswell (2013, p. 184) concurs, saying that in his research he prefers to work with 25 to 30 categories early in data analysis, then strives "to reduce and combine them into the five or six themes that I will use in the end to write my narrative." A large number of categories is likely to reflect an analysis too lodged in concrete description. A number of years ago, Guba and Lincoln (1981) suggested four guidelines for developing categories that are both comprehensive and illuminating for those doing qualitative research in a current context. First, the number of people who mention something or the frequency with which something arises in the data indicates an important dimension. Second, the audience may determine what is important—that is, some categories will appear to various audiences as more or less credible. Third, some categories will stand out because of their uniqueness and should be retained. And fourth, certain categories may reveal "areas of inquiry not otherwise recognized" or that "provide a unique leverage on an otherwise common problem" (p. 95).

Several guidelines can help a researcher determine whether a set of categories is complete. First, there should be a minimum of data that you, the researcher, have determined was illuminating in understanding the phenomenon but are unable to assign to any category or subcategory. Second, the set of categories should seem plausible, given the data from which they emerge, causing independent investigators to agree that the categories make sense in light of the data. This strategy helps ensure reliability or dependability and is discussed further in Chapter Nine.

Becoming More Theoretical

Several levels of data analysis are possible in a qualitative study. At the most basic level, data are organized chronologically or sometimes topically and presented in a narrative that is largely, if not wholly, descriptive. Moving from concrete description of observable data to a somewhat more abstract level involves using concepts to describe phenomena. Rather than just describing a classroom interaction, for example, a researcher might cite it as an instance of "learning" or "confrontation" or "peer support," depending on the research problem. This is the process of systematically classifying data into some sort of scheme consisting of categories, or themes, as discussed previously. The categories describe the data, but to some extent they also interpret the data. A third level of analysis involves making inferences, developing models, or generating theory. It is a process of moving up "from the empirical trenches to a more conceptual overview of the landscape. We're no longer just dealing with observables, but also with unobservables, and are connecting the two with successive layers of inferential glue" (Miles, Huberman, & Saldaña, 2014, p. 292).

Thinking about data—theorizing—is a step toward developing a theory that explains some aspect of practice and allows a researcher to draw inferences about future activity. Theorizing is defined as "the cognitive process of discovering or manipulating abstract categories and the relationships among those categories"

(LeCompte & Preissle, 1993, p. 239). It is fraught with ambiguity. "The riskiness of going beyond the data into a never-never land of inference" (p. 269) is a difficult task for most qualitative researchers because they are too close to the data, unable to articulate how the study is significant, and unable to shift into a speculative mode of thinking. Theorizing about data can also be hindered by thinking that is linear rather than contextual.

Qualitative data analysis is all about identifying themes, categories, patterns, or answers to your research questions. "Since as a qualitative analyst you do not have a statistical test to help tell you when an observation or pattern is significant, you must rely first on your own sense making, understandings, intelligence, experience, and judgment" (Patton, 2015, p. 572). Also important are the responses from participants when you invite them to comment on your interpretation of their experiences (see "member check" in Chapter Nine). As a third check on the meaningfulness of your interpretation, pay attention to the "reactions of those who read and review the results" of your study (p. 572).

Nevertheless, data often seem to beg for continued analysis past the formation of categories. A key circumstance here is when the researcher knows that the category scheme does not tell the whole story—that there is more to be understood about the phenomenon. This often leads to trying to *link* the conceptual elements—the categories—together in some meaningful way. One of the best ways to try this out is to visualize how the categories work together. A model is just that—a visual presentation of how abstract concepts (categories) are related to one another. Even a simple diagram or model using the categories and subcategories of the data analysis can effectively capture the interaction or relatedness of the findings.

The following are two examples of how the categories and properties (the findings) of a study can be linked together in a meaningful way. The first example is from a study of why working adult male students chose to enter a nursing education program and then withdraw before graduation. Blankenship (1991) interviewed male nursing students who had withdrawn as well as those who had completed their degree in order to identify factors that *differentiated* graduates from nongraduates. Exhibit 8.3 presents her findings or categories.

EXHIBIT 8.3. FACTORS INFLUENCING ENTRY AND COMPLETION
OR NONCOMPLETION.

Entry Factors

A. Upward mobility
B. Family support

Completion Factors

A. Goal orientation
   1. Clarity
   2. Proximity
B. Image
   1. Nursing
   2. Self as nurse
C. Salience of student role

Source: Blankenship (1991).

Two factors, upward mobility and family support, characterized the motivation for both groups to enter the nursing program. Three factors—goal orientation, image, and salience of student role—explained why some men completed the nursing program and others did not. Graduates had a much more realistic understanding of what would be gained by acquiring an associate's degree (goal clarity) and how long it would take to complete the degree (goal proximity). Graduates had more realistic images of nursing as a profession as well as themselves in the role of a nurse. Also, for completers the nursing student role was non-negotiable in the face of family or work crises; for nongraduates, the student role was the first commitment to be sacrificed in times of crises. Blankenship felt that these factors as presented didn't completely convey her understanding of the phenomenon. In Figure 8.3 she takes the categories presented in Exhibit 8.3 and maps out the process. As the figure shows, all students entered the nursing program with the belief that becoming a nurse would enable them to be more socially and economically upwardly

FIGURE 8.3. MODEL TO EXPLAIN ENTRY AND PERSISTENCE
IN NURSING EDUCATION.

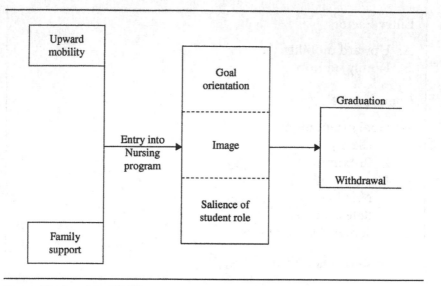

Source: Blankenship (1991).

mobile; they also had family support for this undertaking. Once in
the program, their commitment was filtered through the factors
identified by Blankenship that differentiated between those who
graduated and those who withdrew: "goal orientation, image and
salience of student role interact in such a way as to lead to either
graduation or to withdrawal from the program" (p. 88).

Unlike Blankenship's study, in which her analysis unexpectedly
led to a more theoretical presentation of her findings in the form of
a model, Alston (2014) set out to build a grounded theory about
cross-cultural mentoring relationships. More specifically, her study
explored cross-cultural mentoring relationships between Black
female faculty mentors and their White female doctoral student
mentees. She presents three main categories of findings (pp. 65–66)
in regard to her mentors and mentees: (1) their shared and
unshared cultures of oppression and privilege (around womanhood, motherhood, and race); (2) their ways of negotiating power
within cultures (through age, academic roles, and role reversals);
and (3) their shared culture of intentionality of making their

FIGURE 8.4. CORE DIMENSION: CRITICALITY OF AUTHENTIC CONNECTION.

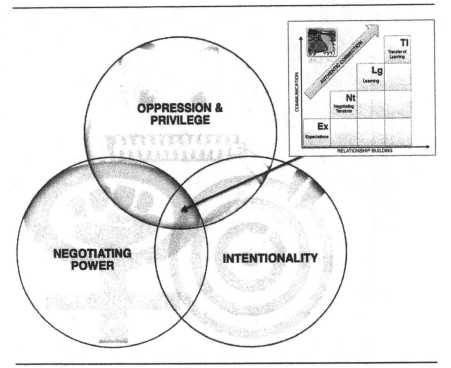

Source: Alston (2014, p. 119). Reprinted with permission.

mentoring relationship work (through trust, communication, and learning). These three categories were the background context of these mentoring relationships, but at their intersection, depicted in the Venn Diagram in Figure 8.4, was what she discusses as the core dimension (recall that grounded theory usually has a core category). This is essentially the further theorizing of the data.

The core dimension that was key to authentic cross-cultural mentoring in Alston's study was what she referred to as the "criticality of authentic connection" (see Figure 8.5). She highlights the importance of communication and relationship building, and the key elements—dealing with expectations, negotiating tensions, moments of learning, and transfer of learning—as what results in authentic connection for both parties. These components are central to mutually beneficial cross-cultural

FIGURE 8.5. CORE DIMENSION DETAIL.

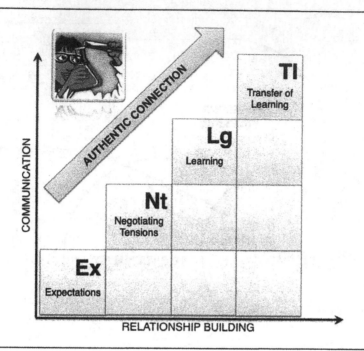

Source: Alston (2014, p. 121). Reprinted with permission.

mentorships. This core dimension—in light of the background context of cultures of dealing with oppression and privilege, negotiating power, and intentionality—is essentially her further theorizing and the grounded theory of her study.

The point here is that thinking about your categories and subcategories and speculating as to how they may be interrelated may lead you to develop a model of these interrelationships or even a theory. When categories and their properties are reduced and refined and then linked together, the analysis is moving toward the development of a model or theory to explain the data's meaning. This level of analysis transcends the formation of categories, for a theory seeks to explain a large number of phenomena and tell how they are related. You may recall that the constant comparative method of data analysis was developed by Glaser and Strauss (1967) to build grounded theory. This is taken up again later in this chapter, in the section on grounded theory.

In summary, data analysis is a process of making sense out of your data. It can be limited to determining how best to arrange the material into a narrative account of the findings. More commonly, researchers extend analysis to developing categories, themes, or other taxonomic classes that interpret the meaning of the data. The categories become the findings of the study. In a nice summary of the process, Dey (1993) compares qualitative data analysis to climbing a mountain to see the view.

> First of all, we must insist that our mountain rises above the plain world of common sense to afford a more "scientific" perspective. . . . We can allow our mountain to be of any size and shape; the small hill of a short undergraduate project, or the precipitous peak of a large-scale research project. . . . For the most part, much the same tasks are required of both. The mountain is climbed bit by bit, and while we are climbing, we focus on one step at a time. But the view we obtain is more than the sum of the sequence of steps we take along the way. Every so often, we can turn and look to the horizon, and in doing so we see the surrounding country from a fresh vantage point. . . . This climb, with its circuitous paths, its tangents and apparent reversals, and its fresh vistas, reflects the creative and non-sequential character of the analytic process. Progress may be slow and laborious, but it can be rewarded with some breath-taking revelations. (pp. 53–54)

COMPUTERS AND QUALITATIVE DATA ANALYSIS

The computer has a great capacity for organizing massive amounts of data, facilitating analysis, and assisting communication among members of a research team. The use of computers has evolved into something of a subfield labeled CAQDAS (or, less frequently, just QDAS), an acronym for *computer assisted qualitative data analysis software*. Bogdan and Biklen (2011) point out that "assisted" is the operative word here, because "the computer program only helps as an organizing or categorizing tool, and does not do the analysis for the researcher" (p. 187). Gibbs (2013), in his recent review of CAQDAS, concurs, pointing out that "CAQDAS is not a distinct method or approach to analysis [and] the software does not 'do' the analysis. On the contrary, a major function of the software is to help organize the analysis. The software no more 'does' the analysis than the word processor I am using now writes this chapter for me" (p. 1).

With this caveat in mind, the researcher can choose among several software programs specifically designed to deal with qualitative data or use basic word processing software such as Microsoft Word or Excel and adapt it to use with qualitative data. Ruona (2005) and Hahn (2008) both feel that these word processing and spreadsheet programs are quite adequate for most qualitative data analysis. They describe in detail how to adapt a word processing program to manage and analyze qualitative data. This section provides a general overview of how computer programs are being used in qualitative research, their advantages and disadvantages, and resources readers can pursue for more information on these programs.

Whether a researcher is adapting a standard commercial program to qualitative research or using a program developed specifically for that purpose, data management is likely to be the major use. Data management can be divided into three phases: data preparation, data identification, and data manipulation. Data preparation involves typing notes, transcribing interviews, and otherwise entering the data from which the researcher will be working. In addition, it might include minor editing or formatting. Its purpose is merely to create a clean record from which to work. A standard word processor is usually the software of choice for this phase, even if the data are later to be used in conjunction with a CAQDAS program.

Data identification, the second phase, is the process of assigning codes to segments of your interviews, field notes, documents, and audio or video files as explained earlier in this chapter. Again, we emphasize that the CAQDAS computer program does not determine these codes—you, as the researcher, determine them. Gibbs (2013) humorously writes that the "software remains agnostic. . . . The software does not care about the analyst's motivation for this act of tagging and it certainly does not understand any interpretation given to it" (p. 7). During data manipulation, these segments may be searched for, sorted, retrieved, and rearranged.

Data management is no small aspect of analysis. First, it is difficult to cleanly separate "data management" from "data analysis" in qualitative research. For example, code-and-retrieve is a commonly used approach (both with and without computer assistance). *Coding* involves labeling passages of text according to content, and *retrieving* entails providing a means to collect similarly labeled passages. As Richards and Richards (1998) point out, "the generation of categories, even the simplest descriptors . . . is a contribution to theory" (p. 215). Furthermore,

> Decisions are being made about what is a category of significance to the study . . . and whether these categories should be altered, redefined, or deleted during analysis. Second, decisions about what text segments are relevant to a category are never merely clerical decisions; they always involve some theoretical consideration.
> Third, the viewing of segments from many documents on one topic or selected topics always offers a new way of seeing data. (p. 215)

Simply making coding and retrieval less tedious provides new avenues for analysis. Automating tedious aspects of qualitative analysis no doubt enables the researcher to creatively observe the possible links and connections among the different aspects of the data. However, it is the researcher, not the computer program, who assigns codes (or names categories) and it is the researcher who determines which units of data go with the codes. This is why we say analysis is "assisted" by these computer programs.

Computer programs enable researchers to assign codes to pieces of data and then retrieve all the data assigned under a particular code. The same segment of data can be coded at multiple levels, which is what happens when you "sort" codes into more abstract categories, or break down categories into subcategories. Software programs have become quite sophisticated in their capacity to enable linkages between and among codes. "These linkages can also be used to display the logical relations between codes and the structure of an emerging theory" (Kelle, 2004, p. 482). Although most programs are limited to a "hierarchical tree structure," some, like ATLAS.ti, "support the construction of complex networks . . . and structures in the developing category scheme" (p. 483). More sophisticated search and retrieval patterns are also allowing users to retrieve data that co-occur in the text. These co-occurring pieces of data or codes could "be used as a *heuristic device*" if not a tentative hypothesis-building activity (Kelle, 2004, p. 485, emphasis in original).

Clearly, there are a number of advantages to using CAQDAS. First, these programs offer an organized filing system for your data and your analysis. Data are sorted into categories, filed, and easily retrieved. "This saves time and effort which might otherwise be expended on boring clerical work, perhaps involving mounds of photocopied paper, color coded, sorted into piles on the floor, cut up, pasted and so on. In turn, this gives the data analyst more time to think about the meaning of the data" (Seale, 2008, p. 235). Second, these programs encourage a close examination of the data, enhancing what Seale calls the "rigor" of the study (p. 236). Third, "the concept mapping feature of computer programs enables the researcher to visualize the relationship among codes and themes by drawing a visual model" (Creswell, 2013, p. 202). Further, some CAQDAS programs now have the ability to import web resources such as blogs, social media such as Facebook and Twitter, and quantitative data so that CAQDAS can be used in mixed methods studies. Davidson and diGregorio (2013) write that we are entering a QDAS 2.0 phase, which includes an expansion "from better tools for visualization, geospatial work, and multiple media modalities to the capacity for greater collaboration and teamwork and integration of quantitative data" (p. 499). Indeed, all writers acknowledge the value of CAQDAS for multimedia data and large data sets and for team research projects. (For a comprehensive list of QDAS and Web 2.0 research tools, see http://digitalresearchtools.pbworks.com.)

The advantages of using CAQDAS are clear, but researchers need to also consider other factors. First is cost, although many universities have site licenses, meaning students and faculty have access to these programs. Two CAQDAS programs, HyperRESEARCH and QDA Miner, offer free versions available for basic analysis (see Table 8.1). Second, CAQDAS may be too powerful—overkill—for your needs. Ask yourself whether you really need a computer program to manage your data. Small-scale qualitative studies probably do not need the capacity of these programs. Further, the time it would take you to learn to operate the program could be spent analyzing your data. We advise our students that only if they are particularly adept at learning computer programs might they want to give it a try. An option is to adapt whatever word processing program you currently use to this

TABLE 8.1. COMPUTER ASSISTED QUALITATIVE DATA ANALYSIS
SOFTWARE (CAQDAS).

	Programs	Web Address	Features
General information	Computer Assisted Qualitative Data Analysis Software (CAQDAS)	www.surrey.ac.uk /sociology/research /researchcentres /caqdas/support /choosing/index.htm	Practical information; discussions and reviews of 10 different CAQDAS packages, with links to other qualitative sites
	Qualitative Data Analysis	https:// digitalresearchtools .pbworks.com/w/page /17801694/Perform% 20Qualitative%20Data% 20Analysis	Digital research tools wiki that provides links for several qualitative software packages
Popular commercial CAQDAS programs	Atlas.ti	http://ATLASti.com/	Free trial and training; for Windows or Mac
	NVivo	www.qsrinternational .com/products_nvivo .aspx	Free trial and tutorials; for Windows only
	MAXQDA	www.maxqda.com/	Free trial and tutorials; for Windows or Mac
	HyperRESEARCH	www.researchware.com/	Free version available with limited features for basic analysis; free tutorials; for Windows or Mac
	QDA Miner	http://provalisresearch .com/products /qualitative-data -analysis-software/	Free version available with limited features for basic analysis; free tutorials; for Windows or Mac
	Qualrus	www.ideaworks.com /qualrus/index.html	Free trial; best used on Windows, but can be used on Mac and Linux OS with Windows virtual machine
	Transana	www.transana.org /index.htm	For analyzing video, auditory, and still image data; free demo; for Windows or Mac

purpose (Ruona, 2005; Hahn, 2008). Another consideration is how much you like to directly handle your data. As Creswell (2013, p. 202) points out, "A computer program may, to some individuals, put a machine between the researcher and the actual data. This may cause an uncomfortable distance between the researcher and his or her information." Finally, it will take time to decide which program is best suited to your type of study and the type of data you have. For example, does the program handle visual data? Further, Seale (2008) feels that "CAQDAS packages are of little help in examining small data extracts, of the sort often examined by conversation analysts and some discourse analysis" (p. 242).

Selecting the right CAQDAS program can take some time. A good beginning would be to access reviews of these programs. Fortunately, these are becoming readily available, and they usually address the methodological roots of a program as well as detailing its functional strengths and weaknesses. Since each of these programs is designed by someone who has experience doing qualitative research, each program reflects his or her particular analysis preferences and strategies. An up-to-date website that includes reviews and information about 10 different CAQDAS programs is http://www.surrey.ac.uk/sociology/research/researchcentres /caqdas/support/choosing/index.htm. It is important for you to find the program that feels comfortable to you, which is why we highly recommend you try several. In addition to consulting resources such as these, you might also contact the software developers for updated information and demos (if available) and interview colleagues about their reactions to these products. Most of the more popular programs have websites where you can download a demonstration. Table 8.1 presents a sampling of some of these sites. The first two contain general information about the programs; the next seven are program-specific.

DATA ANALYSIS AND TYPES OF QUALITATIVE RESEARCH

The data analysis process presented in this chapter is a basic inductive and comparative analysis strategy suitable for analyzing data in most interpretive qualitative studies. There are approaches to analyzing data—such as conversation or discourse analysis or postmodern analysis, even something called *poetic analysis* (Grbich, 2013)—that are beyond the scope of this book to review. In keeping with the types of interpretive qualitative research presented in Chapter Two, this section on data analysis briefly addresses particular analysis strategies found in a phenomenological study, grounded theory, ethnography, narrative analysis, case study research, and action research (which was discussed in Chapter Three). However, for all of these types of qualitative research, the basic strategy is still inductive and comparative.

PHENOMENOLOGICAL ANALYSIS

Lodged as it is in the philosophy of phenomenology (see Chapter Two), this type of analysis attends to ferreting out the essence or basic structure of a phenomenon. Several specific techniques—such as epoche, bracketing, phenomenological reduction, horizontalization, imaginative variation, and so on—are used to analyze experience. *Epoche*, for example, as Van Manen (2014) explains it, is the process through which the researcher brackets or isolates biases in order to be open to the experience itself. The purpose of phenomenological reduction is to lead the researcher back to the experience of the participants and to reflect on it, in order to try to suspend judgment, so that one can stay with the lived experience of the phenomenon in order to get at its essence. Imaginative variation has to do with trying to see the object of study—the phenomenon—from several different angles or perspectives. As Moustakas (1994) explains, "the task of Imaginative Variation is to seek possible meanings through the utilization of imagination . . . approaching the phenomenon from divergent perspectives, different positions, roles, or functions. The aim is to arrive at structural descriptions of an experience, the underlying and precipitating factors that account for what is being experienced. How did the experience of the phenomenon come to be what it is?" (pp. 97–98). A version of phenomenological analysis is called *heuristic inquiry* (Moustakas, 1990). Heuristic inquiry is even more personalized than phenomenological inquiry in that the researcher includes an analysis of his or her own experience as part of the data. Moustakas (1994) presents a step-by-step method for analyzing data in a phenomenological or heuristic study.

GROUNDED THEORY

The constant comparative method of data analysis was developed by Glaser and Strauss (1967) as the means of evolving grounded theory. A grounded theory consists of categories, properties, and hypotheses that are the conceptual links between and among the categories and properties. Because the basic strategy of the constant comparative method is compatible with the inductive, concept-building orientation of all qualitative research, the constant comparative method of data analysis has been adopted by many researchers who are not seeking to build substantive theory or grounded theory.

The basic strategy of the method is to do just what its name implies—constantly compare. The researcher begins with a particular incident from an interview, field notes, or document and compares it with another incident in the same set of data or in another set. These comparisons lead to tentative categories that are then compared to each other and to other instances. Comparisons are constantly made within and between levels of conceptualization until a theory can be formulated. The type of theory is called *substantive theory*—theory that applies to a specific aspect of practice. Since the theory is grounded in the data and emerges from them, the methodology is called *grounded theory*.

A grounded theory begins with *categories*, as in the Alston (2014) study discussed earlier. In addition to categories, a theory consists of three other elements—properties, a core category, and hypotheses. *Properties* are also concepts, but ones that describe a category; properties are not examples of a category but dimensions of it. For example, in the Alston (2014) study of cross-cultural mentoring relationships of Black women faculty mentors and their White women doctoral student mentees, one of the categories was their shared and unshared cultures of oppression and privilege. The properties or dimensions of the category were womanhood, motherhood, and race. As another example, the category "career malaise" could be defined by the properties of "boredom," "inertia," and "trapped." The *core category* is like the hub of a wheel; it is the central defining aspect of the phenomenon to which all other categories and hypotheses are related or interconnect. *Hypotheses* are the suggested links between categories and properties. For example, in a grounded theory study of how nurses deal with workplace bullying (Gaffney, DeMarco, Hofmeyer, Vessey, & Budin, 2012), the researchers identified a core category, "making things right" and four other categories, all of which explained the process the nurses engaged in. Of their data analysis, they wrote, "We developed categories by clustering similar codes, and from those categories we generated hypotheses about how the categories were related" (p. 3). Such hypotheses emerge simultaneously with the collection and analysis of data. The researcher tries to support tentative hypotheses while remaining open to the emergence of new hypotheses. "Generating hypotheses requires evidence enough only to establish a suggestion—not an excessive piling up of evidence to establish a proof" (Glaser & Strauss, 1967, pp. 39–40).

To enable the development of a grounded theory, Corbin and Strauss (2015) suggest three phases of coding—open, axial, and selective. *Open coding* is what one does at the beginning of data analysis, as described earlier in this chapter; it is tagging any unit of data that might be relevant to the study. *Axial coding* is the process of relating categories and properties to each other, refining the category scheme. In *selective coding*, a core category, propositions, or hypotheses are developed. Similar to Corbin and Strauss's three phases of coding, Charmaz (2014) also discusses three phases of coding, which she labels *focused coding*, *axial coding*, and *theoretical coding*.

ETHNOGRAPHIC ANALYSIS

An ethnographic study focuses on the culture and social regularities of everyday life. Rich, thick description is a defining characteristic of ethnographic studies. Wolcott (1994), in a book devoted to ethnographic data analysis presents analysis as description, analysis, and interpretation, terms he admits, "are often combined (such as *descriptive analysis, interpretive data*) or used interchangeably" (p. 11, emphasis in original). He does differentiate them as follows: *description* is just that—description—of "What is going on here?" (p. 12); *analysis* involves "the identification of essential features and the systematic description of interrelationships among them" (p. 12); and *interpretation* speaks to meanings; in other words, what "does it all mean?" (p. 12).

Anthropologists sometimes make use of preexisting category schemes to organize and analyze their data. The Outline of Cultural Materials developed by Murdock (Murdock, Ford, Hudson, Kennedy, Simmons, & Whitney, 2008) lists nearly 80 descriptive categories, each with up to nine subcategories by which readers can code data. This is a particularly useful scheme for comparing different cultures. Lofland and Lofland (1995) also suggest categories and subcategories for organizing aspects of society. Their four broad categories deal with (1) the economy; (2) demographics such as social class, sex, ethnicity, and race; (3) "basic situations of human life" (p. 104), including family, education, and health care; and (4) the environment, both "natural" and "built" (p. 104).

Although educational ethnographies may make use of these category schemes, more often a classification scheme is derived from the data themselves. The scheme can employ terms commonly found in the culture (an emic perspective) or terms constructed by the ethnographer (an etic perspective). If the topics or variables within the scheme are seen to be interrelated, a typology may be created. Typologizing is defined by Lofland, Snow, Anderson, and Lofland (2006) as "the process of charting the possibilities that result from the conjunction of two or more variables" (p. 148). Tesch (1990) elaborates on how relationships in the data can be displayed: "These relationships are often depicted in diagrams, such as grids or other structured boxes, outline- or tree-shaped taxonomies, . . . flow charts, decision tables, overlapping circles, starburst charts (with one term in the center and the related terms around the periphery), causal chains or networks, or anything else the researcher can invent" (p. 82). In an ethnographic study, these classification systems or *cognitive maps* are used to order data regarding sociocultural patterns. Comparing elements within a classification system can lead to tentative hypotheses and explanations.

With the emergence of online communities, there have been numerous virtual ethnographies analyzing online cultures through social media from an ethnographic perspective. Kozinets, Dolbec, and Earley (2014) refer to analysis of these forms of data as "netnographic" analysis. They have four primary recommendations for conducting such an analysis. First, given that the amount of data available on social networking sites can be overwhelming, they recommend that the researcher should begin with one site first, to understand from a deep cultural perspective "what is going on in that social space" (p. 269). Second, they recommend appropriate cultural engagement as a participant observer, and third, that their communications are "experienced, processed, and understood exactly as cultural members experience them" (p. 269). They further highlight the importance of doing the analysis in light of the medium itself, at least initially. Finally, they emphasize analyzing the contents, posts, and so on in reference to the timing at which they unfolded.

The actual data analysis itself of an online ethnographic study using social media is similar to other forms of analysis in terms of coding and categorizing, but the medium, and the fact that there can be pictures, vlogs, and other material, can affect how data are coded. For example, in their study of Black female natural hair care vloggers, who used videos to facilitate adult learning about hair care, Alston and Ellis-Hervey (2014) note how the medium influenced their coding procedures. In particular, they explain how they "used the timestamps within the videos to assist with the coding process (e.g., HUMILITY-2:42)" and how "this system of organization allowed us to easily refer back to specific data components" (p. 5). Hence, although the process of data analysis in using social media is not much different, the medium itself does affect how one will do the analysis.

NARRATIVE INQUIRY

At the heart of narrative inquiry is "the ways humans experience the world" (Connelly & Clandinin, 1990, p. 2). As a research technique, the study of experience is done through stories. Emphasis is on the stories people tell and on how these stories are communicated—on the language used to tell the stories. Some forms of narrative analysis focus more on a holistic analysis where "each story is viewed as a whole and the parts within it interpreted in relation to other parts of the story" (Beale, 2013, p. 694). The write-up tends to keep each story intact, rather than analyzing categories across the stories. Other forms of narrative analysis focus more on conducting a categorical analysis whereby "units are abstracted from the completed stories" (p. 694) in much the same way we have described earlier.

First-person accounts of experience form the narrative "text" of this research approach. Whether the account is in the form of autobiography, life history, interview, journal, letters, or other materials that we collect "as we compose our lives" (Clandinin & Connelly, 1998, p. 165), the text is analyzed using the techniques of a particular discipline or perspective. Sociological and socio-linguistic models of narrative analysis emphasize the structure of the narrative and its relationship to the social context. "The processes of understanding, recalling and summarizing stories" (Cortazzi, 1993, p. 100)—in short, memory—characterize the psychological approach. Anthropologists would be interested in how story narratives vary across cultures, as well as in "the cultural patterning of customs, beliefs, values, performance and social contexts of narration" (Cortazzi, 1993, p. 100). Literary models emphasize grammar, syntax, narration, and plot structure. In addition, ideological perspectives such as those embodied in femi-nist theory, critical theory, and postmodernism can be used to interpret life history narratives. Riessman's (2007) book on narra-tive methods focuses on four analytic methods for analyzing stories—thematic, structural, dialogic performance, and visual. Holstein and Gubrium's (2012) book *Varieties of Narrative Analysis* presents several ways to analyze narratives, via psychological themes, rhetorical analysis, an ethnographic approach to stories, and so on. As Coffey and Atkinson (1996) observe, "there are no formulae or recipes for the 'best' way to analyze the stories we elicit and collect. Indeed, one of the strengths of thinking about our data as narrative is that this opens up the possibilities for a variety of analytic strategies" (p. 80).

CASE STUDIES

Although the basic strategy for analyzing data outlined earlier in this chapter applies to all types of qualitative research, some features of case studies affect data analysis. First, a case study is an intensive, holistic description and analysis of a single, bounded unit. Conveying an understanding of the case is the paramount consideration in analyzing the data. Data have usually been derived from interviews, field observations, and documents. In addition to a tremendous amount of data, this range of data sources may present disparate, incompatible, even apparently contradictory information. The case study researcher can be seriously challenged in trying to make sense out of the data. Attention to data management is particularly important under these circumstances.

To begin the more intensive phase of data analysis in a case study, all the information about the case should be brought together—interview logs or transcripts, field notes, reports, records, the investigator's own documents, physical traces, and reflective memos. All this material needs to be organized in some fashion so that data are easily retrievable. Yin (2014) calls this organized material the case study database—a "systematic archive of all the data . . . from a case study" (p. 238) that he differentiates from the case study report. In a similar fashion, Patton (2015) differentiates the case record from the final case study: "The case record pulls together and organizes the voluminous case data into a comprehensive, primary resource package. The case record includes all the major information that will be used in doing the case analysis and case study. Information is edited, redundancies are sorted out, parts are fitted together, and the case record is organized for ready access either chronologically and/or topically. The case record must be complete but manageable" (p. 537). The *case study database* (or record), then, is the data of the study organized so the researcher can locate specific data during intensive analysis.

The various procedures for deriving meaning from qualitative data described in this chapter apply to the single case study. Although the final write-up or case report may have a greater proportion of description than other forms of qualitative research in order to convey a holistic understanding of the case, the level of interpretation may also extend to the presentation of categories, themes, models, or theory.

Multiple or comparative case studies involve collecting and analyzing data from several cases. Lightfoot (1983), for example, did not study just one good high school; she studied six. Her findings are presented first as six individual case studies (or "portraits" as she calls them); she then offers a cross-case analysis leading to generalizations about what constitutes a good high school. Lopez (2013) conducted a multiple case study of long-term outcomes of early intensive behavior treatment for children with autism. She first presents write-ups for each of the five students in her study, followed by a cross-case synthesis addressing each of her research questions.

In a multiple case study, there are two stages of analysis—the *within-case analysis* and the *cross-case analysis*. For the within-case analysis, each case is first treated as a comprehensive case in and of itself. Data are gathered so the researcher can learn as much as possible about the contextual variables that might have a bearing on the case. Once the analysis of each case is completed, cross-case analysis begins. A qualitative, inductive, multicase study seeks to build abstractions across cases. Although the particular details of specific cases may vary, the researcher attempts to build a general explanation that fits all the individual cases (Yin, 2014).

As with the single case study, one of the challenges in a multicase study is the management of the data; the researcher probably has considerably more raw information and must find ways to handle it without becoming overwhelmed. Ultimately, cross-case analysis differs little from analysis of data in a single qualitative case study. The level of analysis can result in a unified description across cases; it can lead to categories, themes, or typologies that conceptualize the data from all the cases; or it can result in building substantive theory offering an integrated framework covering multiple cases. Thus data analysis in case studies must account for some of the identifying features of this particular type of qualitative research, including the focus on understanding and the typically broad range of data available for analysis. In a multiple case study, a within-case analysis is followed by a cross-case analysis.

ACTION RESEARCH STUDIES

The purpose of action research is to make something happen. It is typically aimed at solving a problem in practice, or developing an intervention and to research not only its overall effects, but also how the process itself unfolds (Herr &

Anderson, 2015). As such, the data analysis in qualitative action research studies is going to focus not only on what happens but also *how* it happens over the course of the ongoing action research cycle of plan, act, observe, reflect. So while the mechanisms of data analysis as described in other types of studies—in terms of coding data and gathering it into themes—is the same, the analysis would also focus on how this unfolded in various stages. For example, in the planning stage, researchers usually conduct individual or focus group interviews to find out participants' initial views or experiences of the subject under study, and to make plans with them about the research process. They typically code the data and present these initial themes from the beginning of the study. They also present themes of findings at various stages of the study to show how the process unfolded. And of course, most action researchers interview their participants at the end of the study, and present the final themes of findings. Hence they capture the process as well as the final findings.

Typically, in journal-length discussions of studies, the author(s) deal with only some aspects of describing these phases. Stuckey (2009), for example, in discussing her action research study of using creative expression to help participants make further meaning of their diabetes, briefly describes the planning phase and then focuses more on an analysis of how their use of creative expression unfolded and was manifested in the second and final phases of the process. Ramaswamy (2014), in her action research study of using Natya yoga therapy with patients with schizophrenia, focuses most of her analysis on the types of knowledge that were created at each one of the therapy sessions, and its overall effects. The point here is that the process of data analysis isn't necessarily different from the process in other types of studies; rather, the focus in the analysis is on the unfolding of the findings in stages and phases over time.

SUMMARY

This chapter on data analysis in qualitative research has covered a lot of ground in an attempt to give readers an overview of this most important and, for many, most challenging part of the qualitative research process. Data analysis is not easy, but it can be made manageable if you are able to analyze along with data collection. To wait until all data are collected is to lose the opportunity to gather more reliable and valid data; to wait until the end is also to court disaster, as many a qualitative researcher has been overwhelmed and rendered helpless by the sheer amount of data in a qualitative study.

In preparation for a period of more intensive data analysis once most of your data has been collected, you must set up some system for organizing your data, a system that will make it easy to retrieve any segment of your data as needed. Once your data set is inventoried, organized, and coded for easy retrieval and manipulation, you can begin intensive analysis. Drawing from the constant comparative method of data analysis, we have presented a step-by-step process of basic data analysis that is inductive and comparative and will result in findings. These findings are commonly called categories or themes; they are, in effect, answers to your research questions; it is these questions that guide your analysis and coding of the raw data. The step-by-step process includes naming the categories, determining the number of categories, and figuring out systems for placing data into categories. Using categories as the basic conceptual element, we have discussed how analysis can be extended to theory building.

Although there are a number of factors to be considered in whether or not to use a computer software program for qualitative data analysis, such programs are certainly an option that enables quick retrieval of data, and they are especially good for large data sets or teams of researchers. A short section on these programs discussed the advantages and limitations of CAQDAS and listed resources for further information.

In the last section of the chapter we presented particular data analysis strategies in phenomenology, grounded theory, ethnography, narrative analysis, case study research, and qualitative action research. Although the overall approach in these types of qualitative research is still inductive and comparative, each has strategies unique to the genre.

CHAPTER NINE

DEALING WITH VALIDITY, RELIABILITY, AND ETHICS

All research is concerned with producing valid and reliable knowledge in an ethical manner. Being able to trust research results is especially important to professionals in applied fields because practitioners intervene in people's lives. No classroom teacher, for example, will want to experiment with a new way of teaching reading, nor will a counselor want to implement a new technique to engage with a bereaved family without some confidence in its probable success. But how can you know when research results are trustworthy? They are trustworthy to the extent that there has been some rigor in carrying out the study. Because qualitative research is based on assumptions about reality different from those of quantitative research (see Chapter One), the standards for rigor in qualitative research necessarily differ from those of quantitative research. However, since both the criteria and the terminology for discussing and assessing rigor in qualitative research are in flux (Denzin & Lincoln, 2011; Lichtman, 2013), we have chosen to discuss trustworthiness and rigor in interpretive qualitative research with reference to the traditional terminology of validity and reliability, though we recognize these are contested terms.

Ensuring validity and reliability in qualitative research involves conducting the investigation in an ethical manner. Although well-established guidelines for the ethical conduct of research date back to the late 1940s, only within the last few decades has attention been given to the ethical concerns unique to qualitative research. We conclude the chapter by considering how ethical practices are also important in establishing the trustworthiness of your study.

VALIDITY AND RELIABILITY

To have any effect on either the practice or the theory of a field, research studies must be rigorously conducted; they need to present insights and conclusions that ring true to readers, practitioners, and other researchers. The applied nature of most social science inquiry thus makes it imperative that researchers and others have confidence in the conduct of the investigation and in the results of any particular study. Lincoln, Lynham, and Guba (2011, p. 120) underscore this point by asking whether a study's findings are "sufficiently authentic . . . that I may trust myself in acting on their implications? More to the point, would I feel sufficiently secure about these findings to construct social policy or legislation based on them?"

Regardless of the type of research, validity and reliability are concerns that can be approached through careful attention to a study's conceptualization and the way in which the data are collected, analyzed, and interpreted, and the way in which the findings are presented. Firestone (1987) explores how the quantitative and qualitative paradigms employ different rhetoric to persuade consumers of their trustworthiness. "The quantitative study must convince the reader that procedures have been followed faithfully because very little concrete description of what anyone does is provided. The qualitative study provides the reader with a depiction in enough detail to show that the author's conclusion 'makes sense'" (p. 19). Further, "the quantitative study portrays a world of variables and static states. By contrast the qualitative study describes people acting in events" (p. 19). In the more recent mixed methods designs, both qualitative and quantitative criteria are applied to assess the trustworthiness of the study (Creswell, 2015).

Research designs are based on different assumptions about what is being investigated, and they seek to answer different questions. If, as in the case of qualitative research, *understanding* is the primary rationale for the investigation, the criteria for trusting the study are going to be different than if discovery of a law or testing a hypothesis is the study's objective. What makes experimental studies scientific or rigorous or trustworthy is the researcher's careful design of the study, applying standards well developed and accepted by the scientific community. Qualitative research also has strategies for establishing the authenticity and trustworthiness of a study—strategies based on worldviews and questions congruent with the philosophical assumptions underlying this perspective (see Chapter One).

Many writers on the topic argue that qualitative research, which is based on different assumptions about reality and different world-views, should consider validity and reliability from a perspective congruent with the philosophical assumptions underlying the paradigm. This may even result in naming the concepts themselves differently, as Lincoln and Guba (1985) did. *Credibility, transferability, dependability,* and *confirmability*—as substitutes for *internal validity, external validity, reliability,* and *objectivity*—were for a while widely adopted in qualitative research. More recent writing from post-modern, poststructural, constructivist, critical, and action research perspectives (Cho & Trent, 2006; Denzin & Lincoln, 2011; Herr & Anderson, 2015; Patton, 2015; Richardson & St. Pierre, 2005) calls for the careful thinking through of totally different conceptualizations of validity and reliability. Denzin and Lincoln (2000), for example, consider the postmodern turn in qualitative research as problematic for evaluating qualitative research. "This is the legitimation crisis. It involves a serious rethinking of such terms as *validity, generalizability,* and *reliability,* terms already retheorized" in other types of qualitative research (p. 17, emphasis in original). More recently, Lincoln, Lynham, and Guba (2011) proposed two forms of rigor—methodological, related to the application of methods, and interpretive, related to judging outcomes, that is, "Can our co-created constructions be trusted to provide some purchase on some important human interpretation?" (p. 121).

Lichtman (2013) uses a continuum to capture this fluidity in changing notions of defining and assessing trustworthiness in qualitative research. Prior to 1990 the concepts of objectivity, reliability, and internal validity were used to assess qualitative research. In the next decade, 1990–2000, the concepts of *credibility, transferability, dependability,* and *confirmability* (Guba & Lincoln, 1981; Lincoln & Guba, 1985) were thought to be more suitable criteria. Beginning in 2000 she identifies both "a resurgence of interest" in traditional criteria and criteria that represent "differing points of view. These criteria tend to emphasize the role of the researcher, for example," and they are "very much influenced by some of the newer ideas of post-structuralism, feminism, and postmodernism. Politics and power also play a critical role here" (p. 292).

Furthermore, with the wide variety of types of qualitative research (see Chapters Two and Three), there are bound to be differences in criteria for validity and reliability. Creswell (2013), for example, applies somewhat different criteria for evaluating how "good" a narrative study is compared to phenomenological research, grounded theory research, ethnographic research, or case study research. In a narrative study he suggests that good narrative tells an engaging story versus one criterion of a good ethnography being "a detailed description of the cultural group" (p. 263). Lichtman (2013) offers her own "personal criteria" for "a good piece of qualitative research" (p. 294). These include being explicit about the researcher's role and his or her relationship to those studied, making a case that the topic of the study is important, being clear about how the study was done, and making a convincing presentation of the findings of the study.

Similar to Lichtman's "personal criteria" is Tracy's (2013) "big-tent" criteria for conducting "excellent" qualitative research. Her eight criteria are that the research (1) be on a worthy topic; that it be conducted with (2) rich rigor and (3) sincerity—that is, transparency of methods—and (4) credibility; that the research (5) resonates with a variety of audiences and (6) makes a significant contribution; (7) that it attends to ethical considerations; and finally, (8) that the study have meaningful coherence; that is, "meaningfully interconnects literature, research, questions/foci, findings, and interpretations with each other" (p. 230). Wolcott (1994) takes yet another direction, arguing "the absurdity of validity" (p. 364). Instead of validity, what he seeks "is something else, a quality that points more to identifying critical elements and wringing plausible interpretations from them, something one can pursue without becoming obsessed with finding the right or ultimate answer, the correct version, the Truth" (pp. 366–367). For Wolcott that "something else" is understanding.

To further underscore the complexity of addressing the issue of validity and reliability in a world of burgeoning qualitative research designs, Patton (2015) offers *seven* "alternative sets of criteria for judging the quality and credibility of qualitative inquiry" (p. 680). Depending upon the type of research, he suggests criteria for (1) traditional scientific, (2) constructivist, (3) artistic, (4) systems/complexity, (5) participatory, (6) critical, and (7) pragmatic/utilization focused research.

Those conducting qualitative investigations do not want to wait for the research community to develop a consensus as to the appropriate criteria for assessing validity and reliability, if indeed that is even possible. While the theoretical debate goes on, there are immediate needs to be met in the field. As Stake (2005) notes, knowledge gained in an investigation "faces hazardous passage from writing to reading. The writer seeks ways of safeguarding the trip" (p. 455). Further, qualitative researchers need to respond to the concerns of outsiders, many of whom may be unfamiliar with or blatantly challenging of the credibility of qualitative research. Exhibit 9.1, for example, is a list of sample questions often asked of qualitative researchers. Each question asks something about the validity or reliability of qualitative research.

Exhibit 9.1. Challenging the Trustworthiness of Qualitative Research.

1. What can you possibly tell from an n of 1 (3, 15, 29, and so on)?
2. What is it worth just to get the researcher's interpretation of the participant's interpretation of what is going on?
3. How can you generalize from a small, nonrandom sample?
4. If the researcher is the primary instrument for data collection and analysis, how can we be sure the researcher is a valid and reliable instrument?
5. How will you know when to stop collecting data?
6. Isn't the researcher biased and just finding out what he or she expects to find?
7. Without hypotheses, how will you know what you're looking for?
8. Doesn't the researcher's presence result in a change in participants' normal behavior, thus contaminating the data?
9. Don't people often lie to field researchers?
10. If somebody else did this study, would they get the same results?

Fortunately, several strategies can be used to enhance the validity and reliability of qualitative studies. In keeping with our goal of introducing qualitative research to our readers based upon a constructivist worldview, we have chosen to focus on methodological rigor; that is, what you, as a researcher can do to ensure trustworthiness in your study. The following sections address the specific concerns in constructivist qualitative research with respect to internal validity, reliability, and external validity—or what Lincoln and Guba (1985) call credibility, consistency/dependability, and transferability—and suggest appropriate strategies for dealing with each of these issues.

Internal Validity or Credibility

Internal validity deals with the question of how research findings match reality. How congruent are the findings with reality? Do the findings capture what is really there? Are investigators observing or measuring what they think they are measuring? Internal validity in all research thus hinges on the meaning of reality. Becker (1993) humorously points out that "reality is what we choose not to question at the moment," and "the leading cause of stress amongst those in touch with it" (p. 220). On a more serious note, Ratcliffe (1983) offers an interesting perspective on assessing validity in every kind of research. It should be remembered, he suggests, that (1) "data do not speak for themselves; there is always an interpreter, or a translator" (p. 149); (2) that "one cannot observe or measure a phenomenon/event without changing it, even in physics where reality is no longer considered to be single-faceted"; and (3) that numbers, equations, and words "are all abstract, symbolic representations of reality, but not reality itself" (p. 150). Validity, then, must be assessed in terms of something other than reality itself (which can never be grasped). That "something other than reality itself" is Lincoln and Guba's (1985) notion of credibility; that is, are the findings *credible*, given the data presented?

One of the assumptions underlying qualitative research is that reality is holistic, multidimensional, and ever-changing; it is not a single, fixed, objective phenomenon waiting to be discovered, observed, and measured as in quantitative research. Assessing the isomorphism between data collected and the "reality" from which they were derived is thus an inappropriate determinant of validity. In writing about his scientific journey to the Sea of Cortez more than seventy years ago, Steinbeck (1941) eloquently contrasted the two views of reality:

> The Mexican sierra has "XVII–15–1X" spines in the dorsal fin. These can easily be counted. But if the sierra strikes hard on the line so that our hands are burned, if the fish sounds and nearly escapes and finally comes in over the rail, his colors pulsing and his tail beating the air, a whole new relational externality has come into being—an entity which is more than the sum of the fish plus the fisherman. The only way to count the spines of the sierra unaffected by this second relational reality is to sit in a laboratory, open an evil smelling jar, remove a stiff colorless fish from formalin solution, count the spines, and write the truth "D. XVII–15–1X." There you have recorded a reality which cannot be assailed—probably the least important reality concerning either the fish or yourself. The man with his pickled fish has set down one truth and has recorded in his experience many lies. The fish is not that color, that texture, that dead, nor does he smell that way. (p. 2)

Maxwell (2013) concurs that one can never really capture reality. "Validity is never something that can be proved or taken for granted. Validity is also relative: It has to be assessed in relationship to the purposes and circumstances of the research, rather than being a context-independent property of methods or conclusions" (p. 121).

Then what *is* being studied in qualitative research, and how does a researcher assess the validity of those observations? What is being investigated are people's constructions of reality—how they understand the world. And just as there will be multiple accounts of eyewitnesses to a crime, so too there will be multiple constructions of how people have experienced a particular phenomenon, how they have made meaning of their lives, or how they have come to understand certain processes.

Because human beings are the primary instrument of data collection and analysis in qualitative research, interpretations of reality are accessed directly through their observations and interviews. We are thus "closer" to reality than if a data collection instrument had been interjected between us and the participants. Most agree that when rigor is viewed in this manner, internal validity is a definite strength of qualitative research. In this type of research it is important to understand the perspectives of those involved in the phenomenon of interest, to uncover the complexity of human behavior in a contextual framework, and to present a holistic interpretation of what is happening.

LeCompte and Preissle (1993) list four factors that lend support to the claim of high internal validity of ethnographic research:

> First, the ethnographer's common practice of living among participants and collecting data for long periods provides opportunities for continual data analysis and comparison to refine constructs; it ensures a match between researcher categories and participant realities. Second, informant interviews, a major ethnographic data source, are phrased in the empirical categories of participants; they are less abstract than many instruments used in other research designs. Third, participant observation—the ethnographer's second key source of data—is conducted in natural settings reflecting the life experiences of participants more accurately than do more contrived or laboratory settings. Finally, ethnographic analysis incorporates researcher reflection, introspection, and self-monitoring that Erickson (1973) calls disciplined subjectivity, and these expose all phases of the research to continual questioning and reevaluation. (p. 342)

Though qualitative researchers can never capture an objective "truth" or "reality," there are a number of strategies that you as a qualitative researcher can use to increase the "credibility" of your findings, or as Wolcott (2005, p. 160) writes, increase "the correspondence between research and the real world." Probably the best-known strategy to shore up the internal validity of a study is what is known as *triangulation*. Usually associated with navigation or land surveying, wherein two or three measurement points enable convergence on a site, the best-known discussion of triangulation is Denzin's (1978), in which he proposes four types: the use of multiple methods, multiple sources of data, multiple investigators, or multiple theories to confirm emerging findings. The use of multiple theories such as approaching "data with several hypotheses in mind, to see how each fares in relation to the data" (Seale, 1999, p. 54) is less common in qualitative research than are the other three forms.

With regard to the use of multiple *methods* of data collection, for example, what someone tells you in an interview can be checked against what you observe on site or what you read about in documents relevant to the phenomenon of interest. You have thus employed triangulation by using three methods of data collection—interviews, observations, and documents.

Triangulation using multiple sources of *data* means comparing and cross-checking data collected through observations at different times or in different places, or interview data collected from people with different perspectives or from follow-up interviews with the same people. *Investigator* triangulation occurs when there are multiple investigators collecting and analyzing data. Patton (2015, p. 665) suggests a related strategy, that of "*triangulating analysts*—that is, having two or more persons independently analyze the same qualitative data and compare their findings" (emphasis in original). This notion of multiple researchers has also been discussed in other contexts as collaborative or team research. In participatory research, where the goal of the research is political empowerment, the participants along with the researcher collectively define the problem to be addressed, conduct the study, and engage in collective action to bring about change.

Thus, *triangulation*—whether you make use of more than one data collection method, multiple sources of data, multiple investigators, or multiple theories—is a powerful strategy for increasing the credibility or internal validity of your research. As Patton (2015) explains, "triangulation, in whatever form, increases credibility and quality by countering the concern (or accusation) that a study's findings are simply an artifact of a single method, a single source, or a single investigator's blinders" (p. 674).

It might be noted that as with other strategies for ensuring trustworthiness in qualitative research, triangulation is being revisited in the literature from a postmodern perspective. Richardson (2000; see also Richardson & St. Pierre, 2005) points out that triangulation assumes a "'fixed point' or 'object' that can be triangulated." But in postmodern research, "we do not triangulate; we *crystallize*. We recognize that there are far more than three sides from which to approach the world" (Richardson, 2000, p. 934). Crystals exhibit "an infinite variety of shapes, substances, trans-mutations, multidimensionalities, and angles of approach. Crystals are prisms that reflect externalities and refract within themselves, creating different colors, patterns, and arrays casting off in different directions. What we see depends on our angle of response—not triangulation but rather crystallization" (Richardson, in Richardson & St. Pierre, 2005, p. 963). However, from an interpretive-constructivist perspective, which is the basis of this book, triangulation remains a principal strategy to ensure validity and reliability.

A second common strategy for ensuring internal validity or credibility is *member checks*. Also called *respondent validation*, the idea here is that you solicit feedback on your preliminary or emerging *findings* from some of the people that you interviewed. "This is the single most important way of ruling out the possibility of mis-interpreting the meaning of what participants say and do and the perspective they have on what is going on, as well as being an important way of identifying your own biases and misunderstanding of what you observed" (Maxwell, 2013, pp. 126–127). The process involved in member checks is to take your preliminary analysis back to some of the participants and ask whether your interpretation "rings true." Although you may have used different words (it is *your* interpretation, after all, but derived directly from their experience), participants should be able to recognize their experience in your interpretation or suggest some fine-tuning to better capture their perspectives. Some writers suggest doing member checks through-out the course of the study. Table 9.1 is a sample of the results from a member check. In this study, Crosby (2004) was interested in how learning experiences foster commitment to a career in teaching English as a foreign language. He asked several of his participants to comment on his findings regarding their experiences teaching English in a cross-cultural setting.

Adequate engagement in data collection is a third strategy that makes sense when you are trying to get as close as possible to participants' understanding of a phenomenon. How long one needs to observe or how many people need to be interviewed are always difficult questions to answer, since the answers are always dependent on the particular study itself. The best rule of thumb is that the data and emerging findings must feel saturated; that is, you

Table 9.1. Member Check Comments.

Name	Comments	Action Taken
Holly	"I think your statements are an accurate reflection of what I said and what my experience has been."	Write back and explain about meaning of "disorientating dilemma"
	The category you term "disorientating dilemma" puzzles me. That as a category doesn't quite ring true for me. Perhaps it came across that way, although I should also say that I'm not sure what you mean with that term and how it fits into learning experiences. Do you mean my challenges in teaching have encouraged/discouraged my commitment to teaching EFL?	No action needed to change research results
Kate	"It was kind of fun to see a bunch of my own thoughts already categorized into a graphic!"	Spelling corrected; phrases need not be adjusted
	Change spelling of Bombera to Bambara.	
	Clarification of two phrases used as coding: Getting a Masters in TESOL, and looking for more teaching experiences.	
Grace	"I would agree with your categorization of comments."	No action needed
	"I'd definitely agree with your conclusions." Charts gave "me greater insight into my own thinking."	
Mary	"Everything is right on! I have reviewed attachments and agree with what is written. The themes are accurate."	No action needed

(*continued*)

TABLE 9.1   (*Continued*)

Name	Comments	Action Taken
	"I really like the table; it was exciting to see my progression through your eyes."	
Ann	"I'd say it's pretty accurate. I can't think of anything I would add, change, etc."	No action needed
Shauna	"I do believe that the analysis rings true."	Note comment of commitment first to God then profession
	"It was definitely an enlightening read. . . . It reminded me of certain convictions the Lord had placed on my heart to enter the field in the first place, and I feel encouraged as I look ahead towards my next step in the profession."	
	"My commitment is first to God and His will for my life more so that [*sic*] my profession."	
Bob	"Both documents look great."	No action needed
Oliver	"When I left my interview with you I didn't feel like I expressed myself well, but after looking at your documents I think what you have is fine and rings true."	No action needed

Source: Crosby (2004). Reprinted with permission.

begin to see or hear the same things over and over again, and no new information surfaces as you collect more data.

Adequate time spent collecting data should also be coupled with purposefully looking for variation in the understanding of the phenomenon. Patton (2015) argues that credibility hinges partially on the integrity of the researcher, and one approach to dealing with this issue is for the researcher to "*look for data that support alternative explanations*" (p. 653, emphasis in original). He goes on to point out that "failure to find strong supporting evidence for alternative ways of presenting the data or contrary explanations helps increase confidence in the initial, principal explanation you generated" (p. 654). Patton also reminds readers that there is often no clear-cut "yes" or "no" answer to whether data support an alternative explanation. Rather, "you're searching for *the best fit*, the preponderance of evidence. This requires assessing the weight of evidence and looking for those patterns and conclusions that fit the preponderance of data" (p. 654, emphasis in original). Some writers even suggest that you should purposefully seek data that might disconfirm or challenge your expectations or emerging findings. This strategy has been labeled *negative* or *discrepant case analysis*.

Related to the integrity of the qualitative researcher is a fourth strategy sometimes labeled *researcher's position*, or *reflexivity*, which is how the researcher affects and is affected by the research process (Probst & Berenson, 2014). Investigators need to explain their biases, dispositions, and assumptions regarding the research to be undertaken. Even in journal articles, authors are being called upon to articulate and clarify their assumptions, experiences, worldview, and theoretical orientation to the study at hand. Such a clarification allows the reader to better understand how the individual researcher might have arrived at the particular interpretation of the data. As Maxwell (2013, p. 124) explains, the reason for making your perspective, biases, and assumptions clear to the reader is not to eliminate "the researcher's theories, beliefs, and perceptual lens. Instead, qualitative research is concerned with understanding how a *particular* researcher's values and expectations influenced the conduct and conclusions of the study" (emphasis in original).

Yet another strategy is called *peer examination* or *peer review*. Certainly there's a sense in which all graduate students have this process built into their thesis or dissertation committee, since each member of the committee reads and comments on the findings. A similar process takes place when an article is sent in to a peer-reviewed journal for publication; "peers" knowledgeable about the topic and the methodology review the manuscript and recommend publication (or do not). But such an examination or review can also be conducted by either a colleague familiar with the research or one new to the topic. There are advantages to both, but either way, a thorough peer examination would involve asking a colleague to scan some of the raw data and assess whether the findings are plausible, based on the data.

Reliability or Consistency

Reliability refers to the extent to which research findings can be replicated. In other words, if the study is repeated, will it yield the same results? Reliability is problematic in the social sciences simply because human behavior is never static. Even those in the hard sciences are asking similar questions about the constancy of phenomena. Reliability in a research design is based on the assumption that there is a single reality and that studying it repeatedly will yield the same results. This is a central concept of traditional experimental research, which focuses on discovering causal relationships among variables and uncovering laws to explain phenomena.

Qualitative research, however, is not conducted so that the laws of human behavior can be isolated. Rather, researchers seek to describe and explain the world as those in the world experience it. Since there are many interpretations of what is happening, there is no benchmark by which to take repeated measures and establish reliability in the traditional sense. Wolcott (2005) underscores the inappropriateness of considering reliability in studying human behavior: "In order to achieve reliability in that technical sense, a researcher has to manipulate conditions so that replicability can be assessed. Ordinarily, fieldworkers do not try to make things happen at all, but whatever the circumstances, we most certainly cannot make them happen twice. And if something does happen more than once, we never for a minute insist that the repetition be exact" (p. 159).

Traditionally, reliability is the extent to which research findings can be replicated. In other words, if the study were repeated, would it yield the same results? Reliability is problematic in the social sciences simply because human behavior is never static, nor is what many experience necessarily more reliable than what one person experiences. All reports of personal experience are not necessarily unreliable, any more than all reports of events witnessed by a large number of people are reliable. Consider the magician who can fool the audience of hundreds but not the stagehand watching from the wings. Replication of a qualitative study will not yield the same results, but this does not discredit the results of any particular study; there can be numerous interpretations of the same data. The more important question for qualitative research is *whether the results are consistent with the data collected*. Lincoln and Guba (1985) were the first to conceptualize reliability in qualitative research as "dependability" or "consistency." That is, rather than demanding that outsiders get the same results, a researcher wishes outsiders to concur that, given the data collected, the results make sense—they are consistent and dependable. The question then is not whether findings will be found again but whether the results are consistent with the data collected.

The connection between reliability and internal validity from a traditional perspective rests for some on the assumption that a study is more valid if repeated observations in the same study or replications of the entire study produce the same results. This logic relies on repetition for the establishment of truth, but as everyone knows, measurements, observation, and people can be repeatedly wrong. A thermometer may repeatedly record boiling water at 85 degrees Fahrenheit; it is very reliable, since the measurement is consistent, but not at all valid. And in the social sciences, simply because a number of people have experienced the same phenomenon does not make the observations more reliable.

It is interesting, however, that the notion of reliability with regard to instrumentation can be applied to qualitative research in a sense similar to its meaning in traditional research. Just as a quantitative researcher refines instruments and uses statistical techniques to ensure reliability, so too the human instrument can become more reliable through training and practice. Furthermore, the reliability of documents and personal accounts can be assessed through various techniques of analysis and triangulation.

Because what is being studied in the social world is assumed to be in flux, multifaceted, and highly contextual; because information gathered is a function of who gives it and how skilled the researcher is at getting it; and because the emergent design of a qualitative study precludes a priori controls, achieving reliability in the traditional sense is not only fanciful but impossible. Wolcott (2005) wonders whether we need "address reliability at all" other than to say why it is an inappropriate measure for assessing the rigor of a qualitative study. His objection is that "similarity of responses is taken to be the same as accuracy of responses," and we know that is a problematic assumption (p. 159).

Thus, for the reasons discussed, replication of a qualitative study will not yield the same results. As Tracy (2013) points out, "because socially constructed understandings are always in process and necessarily partial, even if the study were repeated (by the same researcher, in the same manner, in the same context, and with the same participants), the context and participants would have necessarily transformed over time—through aging, learning, or moving on" (p. 229). That fact, however, does not discredit the results of the original or subsequent studies. Several interpretations of the same data can be made, and all stand until directly contradicted by new evidence. So if the findings of a study are consistent with the data presented, the study can be considered dependable.

Strategies that a qualitative researcher can use to ensure consistency and dependability or reliability are triangulation, peer examination, investigator's position, and the audit trail. The first three have been discussed already under Internal Validity or Credibility. The use of multiple methods of collecting data (methods triangulation), for example, can be seen as a strategy for obtaining consistent and dependable data, as well as data that are most congruent with reality as understood by the participants. The audit trail is a method suggested by Lincoln and Guba (1985). Just as an auditor authenticates the accounts of a business, independent readers can authenticate the findings of a study by following the trail of the researcher. While "we cannot expect others to replicate our account," Dey (1993, p. 251) writes, "the best we can do is explain how we arrived at our results." Calling the audit trail a "log," as in what a captain might keep in detailing a ship's journey, Richards (2015) writes that "good qualitative research gets much of its claim to validity from the researcher's ability to show convincingly how they got there, and how they built confidence that this was the best account possible. This is why qualitative research has a special need for project history, in the form of a diary or log of processes" (p. 143).

An audit trail in a qualitative study describes in detail how data were collected, how categories were derived, and how decisions were made throughout the inquiry. In order to construct this trail, you as the researcher keep a research journal or records memos on the process of conducting the research as it is being undertaken. What exactly do you write in your journal or your memos? You write your reflections, your questions, and the decisions you make with regard to problems, issues, or ideas you encounter in collecting data. A running record of your interaction with the data as you engage in analysis and interpretation is also recommended. In a book-length or thesis-length report of the research, the audit trail is found in the methodology chapter (often with supporting appendixes). Essentially, it is a detailed account of how the study was conducted and how the data were analyzed. Due to space limitations, journal articles tend to have a very abbreviated audit trail or methodology section.

EXTERNAL VALIDITY OR TRANSFERABILITY

External validity is concerned with the extent to which the findings of one study can be applied to other situations. That is, how generalizable are the results of a research study? Guba and Lincoln (1981) point out that even to discuss the issue, the study must be internally valid, for "there is no point in asking whether meaningless information has any general applicability" (p. 115). Yet an investigator can go too far in controlling for factors that might influence outcomes, with the result that findings can be generalized only to other highly controlled, largely artificial situations.

The question of generalizability has plagued qualitative investigators for some time. Part of the difficulty lies in thinking of generalizability in the same way as do investigators using experimental or correlational designs. In these situations, the ability to generalize to other settings or people is ensured through a priori conditions such as assumptions of equivalency between the sample and population from which it was drawn, control of sample size, random sampling, and so on. Of course, even in these circumstances, generalizations are made within specified levels of confidence.

It has also been argued that applying generalizations from the aggregated data of enormous, random samples to individuals is hardly useful. A study might reveal, for example, that absenteeism is highly correlated with poor academic performance—that 80 percent of students with failing grades are found to be absent more than half the time. If student Alice has been absent more than half the time, does it also mean that she is failing? There is no way to know without looking at her record. Actually, an individual case study of Alice would allow for a much better prediction of her academic performance, for then the particulars that are important to her situation could be discovered. The best that research from large random samples can do vis-à-vis an individual is to "make teachers and other clinicians more informed gamblers" (Donmoyer, 1990, p. 181). In qualitative research, a single case or a small, nonrandom, purposeful sample is selected precisely because the researcher wishes to understand the particular in depth, not to find out what is generally true of the many.

Although generalizability in the statistical sense (from a random sample to the population) cannot occur in qualitative research, that's not to say that nothing can be learned from a qualitative study. As Eisner (1998, pp. 103–104) points out, "generalization is a ubiquitous aspect" of our lives. However, "no one leads life by randomly selecting events in order to establish formal generalizations. We live and learn. We try to make sense out of the situations in and through which we live and to use what we learn to guide us in the future." As with internal validity and reliability, we need to think of generalizability in ways appropriate to the philosophical underpinnings of qualitative research.

Lincoln and Guba (1985) suggest the notion of *transferability*, in which "the burden of proof lies less with the original investigator than with the person seeking to make an application elsewhere. The original inquirer cannot know the sites to which transferability might be sought, but the appliers can and do." The investigator needs to provide "sufficient descriptive data" to make transferability possible (p. 298).

There are a number of understandings of generalizability that are more congruent with the worldview of qualitative research. Some argue that empirical generalizations are too lofty a goal for social science; instead, they say, we should think in terms of what Cronbach (1975) calls working hypotheses—hypotheses that reflect situation-specific conditions in a particular context. Working hypotheses that take account of local conditions can offer practitioners some guidance in making choices—the results of which can be monitored and evaluated in order to make better decisions in the future. Thus "when we give proper weight to local conditions, any generalization is a working hypothesis, not a conclusion" (p. 125). Patton (2015) also promotes the notion of extrapolating rather than making generalizations: "Unlike the usual meaning of the term *generalization*, an *extrapolation* clearly connotes that one has gone beyond the narrow confines of the data to *think about other applications of the findings*. Extrapolations are modest speculations on the likely applicability of findings to other situations under similar, but not identical, conditions. Extrapolations are logical, thoughtful, case derived and problem oriented rather than statistical and probabilistic" (p. 713, emphasis in original).

Modest extrapolations or working hypotheses are not the only way to think about generalizability in qualitative research. Erickson (1986) suggests the notion of "concrete universals" in which "the search is not for abstract universals arrived at by statistical generalizations from a sample to a population, but for concrete universals arrived at by studying a specific case in great detail and then comparing it with other cases studied in equally great detail" (p. 130). Every study, every case, every situation is theoretically an example of something else. The general lies in the particular; that is, what we learn in a particular situation we can transfer or generalize to similar situations subsequently encountered. This is, in fact, how most people cope with everyday life. You get one speeding ticket from a trooper pulling out from behind a billboard; subsequently, you slow down whenever you come upon a billboard on any road. You have taken a particular incident and formed a concrete universal. Erickson makes this same point with regard to teaching.

> When we see a particular instance of a teacher teaching, some aspects of what occurs are absolutely generic, that is, they apply cross-culturally and across human history to all teaching situations. This would be true despite tremendous variation in those situations—teaching that occurs outside school, teaching in other societies, teaching in which the teacher is much younger than the learners, teaching in Urdu, in Finnish, or in a mathematical language, teaching narrowly construed cognitive skills, or broadly construed social attitudes and beliefs.

> Each instance of a classroom is seen as its own unique system, which nonetheless displays universal properties of teaching. These properties are manifested in the concrete, however, not in the abstract. (p. 130)

The idea that the general resides in the particular, that we can extract a universal from a particular, is also what renders great literature and other art forms enduring. Although we may never live at the South Pole, we can understand loneliness by reading Byrd's account; and although we are not likely to be president, we can come up with concrete generalizations about power and corruption by listening to the Watergate tapes.

Probably the most common understanding of generalizability in qualitative research is to think in terms of the reader or user of the study. *Reader or user generalizability* involves leaving the extent to which a study's findings apply to other situations up to the people in those situations. The person who reads the study decides whether the findings can apply to his or her particular situation. This is a common practice in law and medicine, where the applicability of one case to another is determined by the practitioner. Nevertheless, the researcher has an obligation to provide enough detailed description of the study's context to enable readers to compare the "fit" with their situations.

Finally, Eisner (1998) argues that one of the stumbling blocks to our thinking about generalizability in the social sciences is the erroneous assumption that individual, nongeneralizable studies are limited in contributing to the accumulation of knowledge. However, knowledge is not inert material that "accumulates." Rather, he asserts, in qualitative research, accumulation is not vertical, but horizontal: "It is an expansion of our kit of conceptual tools" (p. 211). Connections between qualitative studies and one's world "have to be built by readers, who must . . . make generalizations by analogy and extrapolation, not by a watertight logic" (p. 211). "Human beings," Eisner writes, "have the spectacular capacity to go beyond the information given, to fill in gaps, to generate interpretations, to extrapolate, and to make inferences in order to construe meaning. Through this process knowledge is accumulated, perception refined, and meaning deepened" (p. 211).

To enhance the possibility of the results of a qualitative study "transferring" to another setting several strategies can be employed. The most commonly mentioned is the use of *rich, thick description*. Although *thick description*, "a phrase coined by the philosopher Gilbert Ryle (1949) and applied to ethnographic research by Geertz (1973)" originally meant an emic or insider's account (Maxwell, 2013, p. 138), it has come to be used to refer to a highly descriptive, detailed presentation of the setting and in particular, the findings of a study. Today, when rich, thick description is used as a strategy to enable transferability, it refers to a description of the setting and participants of the study, as well as a detailed description of the findings with adequate evidence presented in the form of quotes from participant interviews, field notes, and documents. As Lincoln and Guba (1985, p. 125) state, the best way to ensure the possibility of transferability is to create a "thick description of the sending context so that someone in a potential receiving context may assess the similarity between them and . . . the study."

Another strategy for enhancing transferability is to give careful attention to selecting the study sample. *Maximum variation* in the sample, whether it be the sites selected for a study or the participants interviewed, allows for the possibility of a greater range of application by readers or consumers of the research. As Patton (2015) notes, maximum variation sampling involves "purposefully picking a wide range of cases to get variation on dimensions of interest." There are two reasons for selecting a wide range of cases: "(1) to document diversity and (2) to identify important common patterns that are common across the diversity (cut through the noise of variation) on dimensions of interest" (p. 267). We would also add that including a variety of participants and/or sites in your study will enable more readers to apply your findings to their situation. Let's assume, for example, that you are a school principal interested in research on factors that promote community involvement in the school. The chances of your finding some helpful research are going to be increased if there's been a study that included a school in a community similar to yours. As another example, a qualitative study of the process and factors related to compliance with diabetes treatment will have more possibility of generalizing to more people if there was some variation in the characteristics of the participants (such as gender, age, education, length of time diagnosed).

Maximum variation is not the only sampling strategy one could use to enhance transferability. One could purposefully select a typical or modal sample. In typicality or modal category sampling, one describes how typical the program, event, or individual is compared with others in the same class, so that users can make comparisons with their own situations. In Wolcott's (2003) classic case study of an elementary school principal in the early 1970s, for example, he tells how he selected a principal who, "like the majority of elementary school principals" at the time of his study, would be male, responsible for one school, and "regard himself as a career principal" (p. 1).

Although maximum variation or typical sampling can be used to enhance transferability, there are certainly good reasons for studying a particular situation because of its uniqueness. And one would study the particular because there is something that can be learned from it, something that contributes, as Eisner (1998) noted in the quotes cited earlier, to the horizontal accumulation of knowledge. As Wolcott (2005, p. 167) points out, "every case is, in certain aspects, like all other cases, like some other cases, and like no other case."

Table 9.2 is a summary of the strategies discussed in this chapter for enhancing the rigor—indeed, the trustworthiness—of a qualitative study. These strategies are by no means inclusive of all that could be used, but they are some of the most commonly employed to ensure internal validity, reliability, and generalizability in interpretive qualitative research.

Most of the issues already described are appropriate considerations for validity and reliability in qualitative research designs in general. At the same time, some research designs require alternate and/or additional conceptualizations of validity in light of the purposes of the study. This is particularly the case for action research designs. As discussed in Chapter Three, the purpose of action research is to make something happen in order to solve a problem in practice. It is also to study the process of change itself. Hence, in addition to dealing with issues of validity and reliability in the ways described earlier, there are additional validity criteria particular to this form of research, including outcome validity, democratic validity, catalytic validity, and process validity (Herr & Anderson, 2015). Outcome validity is "the extent to which outcomes occur, which leads to a resolution of the problem that led to the study" (p. 67). Democratic validity refers to the extent to which the research is conducted in collaboration with the participants; catalytic validity refers to how the participants and researchers changed their views in the process. Process validity focuses on the

TABLE 9.2. STRATEGIES FOR PROMOTING VALIDITY AND RELIABILITY.

Strategy	Description
1. Triangulation	Using multiple investigators, sources of data, or data collection methods to confirm emerging findings.
2. Member checks/ Respondent validation	Taking tentative interpretations/findings back to the people from whom they were derived and asking if they are plausible.
3. Adequate engagement in data collection	Adequate time spent collecting data such that the data become "saturated"; this may involve seeking *discrepant* or *negative* cases.
4. Researcher's position or reflexivity	Critical self-reflection by the researcher regarding assumptions, worldview, biases, theoretical orientation, and relationship to the study that may affect the investigation.
5. Peer review/ examination	Discussions with colleagues regarding the process of study, the congruency of emerging findings with the raw data, and tentative interpretations.
6. Audit trail	A detailed account of the methods, procedures, and decision points in carrying out the study.
7. Rich, thick descriptions	Providing enough description to contextualize the study such that readers will be able to determine the extent to which their situations match the research context, and, hence, whether findings can be transferred.
8. Maximum variation	Purposefully seeking variation or diversity in sample selection to allow for a greater range of application of the findings by consumers of the research.

extent to which ongoing learning occurred during the *process* and stages of the research, as well as whether adequate evidence was provided to document the findings at each of those stages. While these additional criteria are important in action research, essentially validity and reliability in any qualitative study are about providing information and rationale for the study's processes and adequate evidence so that readers can determine the results are trustworthy.

HOW ETHICAL CONSIDERATIONS RELATE TO THE TRUSTWORTHINESS OF QUALITATIVE RESEARCH

To a large extent, the validity and reliability of a study depend upon the ethics of the investigator. Patton (2015) identifies the credibility of the researcher along with rigorous methods as essential components to ensure the credibility of qualitative research: "ultimately, for better or worse, the trustworthiness of the data is tied directly to the trustworthiness of those who collect and analyze the data—and their demonstrated competence" (p. 706). It is the training, experience, and "intellectual rigor" of the researcher, then, that determines the credibility of a qualitative research study. "Methods do not ensure rigor. A research design does not ensure rigor. Analytical techniques and procedures do not ensure rigor. Rigor resides in, depends on, and is manifest in *rigorous* thinking—about everything, including methods and analysis" (p. 703). These qualities are essential because as in all research, we have to trust that the study was carried out with integrity and that it involves the ethical stance of the researcher. Suppose, for example, that you are studying an alternative high school reputed to have an unusually high student retention and graduation rate. You interview teachers, administrators, and students and begin to identify the factors that might account for the school's success. In reviewing some of the school records, you find that attendance and graduation rates have been inflated. Your decision as to how to handle this discovery will have a direct impact on the trustworthiness of your entire study. Although some sense of the researchers' values can be inferred from the statement of their assumptions and biases or from the audit trail, readers of course are likely never to know what ethical dilemmas were confronted and how they were dealt with. It is ultimately up to the individual researcher to proceed in as ethical a manner as possible.

Although policies, guidelines, and codes of ethics have been developed by the federal government, institutions, and professional associations, actual ethical practice comes down to the individual researcher's own values and ethics. Tracy (2013) suggests that ethical issues can exist with respect to procedures; that is, those guidelines "prescribed by certain organizational or institutional review boards (IRB) as being universal or necessary" (p. 243), such as "do no harm" and informed consent; they can be situational, such as those that come up in the research context; and they can be relational. "A relational ethic means being aware of one's own role and impact on relationships and treating participants as whole people rather than as just subjects from which to wrench a good story" (p. 245). The protection of subjects from harm, the right to privacy, the notion of informed consent, and the issue of deception all need to be considered ahead of time, but once in the field, issues have to be resolved as they arise. This situational and relational nature of ethical dilemmas depends not upon a set of general preestablished guidelines but upon the investigator's own sensitivity and values.

In qualitative studies, ethical dilemmas are likely to emerge with regard to the collection of data and in the dissemination of findings. Overlaying both these processes is the researcher-participant relationship. For example, this relationship and the research purpose determine how much the researcher reveals about the actual purpose of the study—how informed the consent can actually be—and how much privacy and protection from harm is afforded the participants. Ethical considerations regarding the researcher's relationship to participants are a major source of discussion and debate in qualitative research, especially with the interest in critical, participatory, feminist, and postmodern research. When the research is highly collaborative, participatory, or political, ethical issues become prominent. Lincoln (1995) in particular aligns ethical considerations with the researcher's relationship with research participants and considers validity to be an ethical question. She suggests seven standards for validity, such as the extent to which the research allows all voices to be heard, the extent of reciprocity in the research relationship, and so on.

The standard data collection techniques of interviewing and of observation in qualitative research present their own ethical dilemmas. As Stake (2005) observes, "Qualitative researchers are guests in the private spaces of the world. Their manners should be good and their code of ethics strict" (p. 459). Interviewing—whether it is highly structured with predetermined questions or semistructured and open-ended—carries with it both risks and benefits to the informants. Respondents may feel their privacy has been invaded, they may be embarrassed by certain questions, and they may tell things they had never intended to reveal.

In-depth interviewing may have unanticipated long-term effects. What are the residual effects of an interview with a teacher who articulates, for the first time perhaps, anger and frustration with his choice of career? Or the administrator who becomes aware of her own lack of career options through participation in a study of those options? Or the adult student who is asked to give reasons for failing to learn to read? Painful, debilitating memories may surface in an interview, even if the topic appears routine or benign.

However, an interview may improve the condition of respondents when, for example, they are asked to review their successes or are stimulated to act positively in their own behalf. Most people who agree to be interviewed enjoy sharing their knowledge, opinions, or experiences. Some gain valuable self-knowledge; for others the interview may be therapeutic—which brings up the issue of the researcher's stance. Patton (2015) points out that the interviewer's task "is first and foremost to gather data" (p. 495). The interviewer is neither a judge nor a therapist nor "a cold slab of granite—unresponsive to learning about great suffering and pain that may be reported and even re-experienced during an interview" (p. 495). Patton and others recommend being able to make referrals to resources for assistance in dealing with problems that may surface during an interview.

Observation, a second means of collecting data in a qualitative study, has its own ethical pitfalls, depending on the researcher's involvement in the activity. Observations conducted without the awareness of those being observed raise ethical issues of privacy and informed consent. Webb, Campbell, Schwartz, and Sechrest (1981), in their book on nonreactive measures, suggest that there is a continuum of ethical issues based on how "public" the observed behavior is. At one end, and least susceptible to ethical violations, is the public behavior of public figures. At midposition are public situations that "may be regarded as momentarily private," such as lovers in a park (p. 147). At the other end are situations involving "'spying' on private behavior," in which distinct ethical issues can be raised (p. 148).

Participant observation raises questions for both the researcher and those being studied. On the one hand, the act of observation itself may bring about changes in the activity, rendering it somewhat atypical. On the other, participants may become so accustomed to the researcher's presence that they may engage in activity they will later be embarrassed about, or reveal information they had not intended to disclose. Further, an observer may witness behavior that creates its own ethical dilemmas, especially behavior involving abuse or criminal activity. What if inappropriate physical contact between instructor and participant is witnessed while observing a volunteer CPR training session? Or a helpless teen is attacked by the group under study? Or a researcher witnesses utterly ineffective, perhaps potentially damaging counseling behavior? Knowing when and how to intervene is perhaps the most perplexing ethical dilemma facing qualitative investigators. Taylor and Bogdan (1984) conclude that although "the literature on research ethics generally supports a noninterventionist position in fieldwork," failure to act is itself "an ethical and political choice" (p. 71) that researchers must come to terms with.

Somewhat less problematic are the documents a researcher might use in a study. At least public records are open to anyone's scrutiny, and data are often in aggregated (and hence anonymous) form. But what of documents related to a continuing professional education program, for example, that reveal a misappropriation of funds? Or documents showing that administrative duties are based on certain favors being extended? And personal records pose potential problems unless they are willingly surrendered for research purposes.

Whether you are collecting data via interviews, observations, or documents, these sources of data in the *online* environment present additional ethical considerations such as how to obtain informed consent, assessing the authenticity of the data source, determining what is considered in the public domain and available to the researcher without consent, and so on. (See Chapter Seven for a fuller discussion of issues in online data collection.)

Analyzing data may present other ethical problems. Since the researcher is the primary instrument for data collection, data have been filtered through his or her particular theoretical position and biases. Deciding what is important—what should or should not be attended to when collecting and analyzing data—is almost always up to the investigator. Opportunities thus exist for excluding data contradictory to the investigator's views. Sometimes these biases are not readily apparent to the researcher. Nor are there practical guidelines for all the situations a researcher might face.

Disseminating findings can raise further ethical problems. If the research has been sponsored, the report is made to the sponsoring agency, and the investigator loses control over the data and its subsequent use. The question of anonymity is not particularly problematic in survey or experimental studies, when data are in aggregated form. At the other end of the continuum is a qualitative case study that, by definition, is an intensive investigation of a specific phenomenon of interest. The case may even have been selected because it was unique, unusual, or deviant in some way. At the local level, it is nearly impossible to protect the identity of either the case or the people involved. In addition, "The cloak of anonymity for characters may not work with insiders who can easily locate the individuals concerned or, what is even worse, claim that they can recognize them when they are, in fact, wrong" (Punch, 1994, p. 92).

This discussion on ethics in qualitative research has merely touched upon some of the issues that might arise when conducting this type of study. Readers interested in pursuing ethical considerations in more depth can turn to any number of sources. Patton (2015), for example, has a lengthy discussion and provides an "Ethical Issues Checklist" identifying the following 12 items to be considered when engaging in qualitative research:

1. Explaining the purpose of the inquiry and methods to be used
2. Reciprocity (what's in it for the interviewee and issues of compensation)
3. Promises
4. Risk assessment
5. Confidentiality
6. Informed consent

7. Data access and ownership
8. Interviewer mental health
9. Ethical advice (who will be your counselor on ethical matters)
10. Data collection boundaries
11. Ethical and methodological choices
12. Ethical versus legal (pp. 496–497)

In summary, part of ensuring for the trustworthiness of a study—its credibility—is that the researcher himself or herself is trustworthy in carrying out the study in as ethical a manner as possible.

SUMMARY

As in any research, validity, reliability, and ethics are major concerns. Every researcher wants to contribute knowledge to the field that is believable and trustworthy. Since a qualitative approach to research is based upon different assumptions and a different worldview than traditional research, most writers argue for employing different criteria in assessing qualitative research.

The question of internal validity—the extent to which research findings are credible—is addressed by using triangulation, checking interpretations with individuals interviewed or observed, staying on site over a period of time, asking peers to comment on emerging findings, and clarifying researcher biases and assumptions. Reliability—the extent to which there is consistency in the findings—is enhanced by the investigator explaining the assumptions and theory underlying the study, by triangulating data, and by leaving an audit trail; that is, by describing in detail how the study was conducted and how the findings were derived from the data. Finally, the extent to which the findings of a qualitative study can be generalized or transferred to other situations—external validity—continues to be the object of much debate. Working hypotheses, concrete universals, and user or reader generalizability are discussed in this chapter as alternatives to the statistical notion of external validity. Rich, thick description facilitates transferability.

The trustworthiness of a qualitative study also depends on the credibility of the researcher. Although researchers can turn to guidelines and regulations for help in dealing with some of the ethical concerns likely to emerge in qualitative research, the burden of producing a study that has been conducted and disseminated in an ethical manner lies with the individual investigator.

No regulation can tell a researcher when the questioning of a respondent becomes coercive, when to intervene in abusive or illegal situations, or how to ensure that the study's findings will not be used to the detriment of those involved. The best a researcher can do is to be conscious of the ethical issues that pervade the research process and to examine his or her own philosophical orientation vis-à-vis these issues.

CHAPTER TEN

WRITING UP QUALITATIVE RESEARCH

For most practitioners, doing research means designing a study that addresses some problem arising from practice, collecting and analyzing data relevant to the problem, and finally, interpreting the results. Often neglected—especially by graduate students who do much of the research in applied fields such as education, health care, social work, management, and so on—is the important step of reporting and disseminating results. The research is of little consequence if no one knows about it; other practitioners have no way to benefit from what the researcher learned in doing the study. For qualitative research in particular, being in the field collecting data is engaging and exciting; so is analyzing your data as you try to answer your questions. By contrast, sitting down and writing up your findings is not immediately rewarding, so it requires an incredible amount of discipline.

Several factors contribute to making this stage of the research process particularly daunting. First, because data collection and analysis is continuous and simultaneous in qualitative research, there is no clean cutoff—no time when everything else stops and writing begins. Second, a great amount of qualitative data must be sorted through, selected, and woven into a coherent narrative. Finally, there is no standard format for reporting such data. Over 40 years ago Lofland (1974) commented on the lack of consensus: "Qualitative field research seems distinct in the degree to which its practitioners lack a public, shared, and codified conception of how what they do is done, and how what they report should be formulated" (p. 101). Lofland's observation is even more true today, as postmodernist critiques of traditional qualitative writing practices have resulted in the emergence of an incredible diversity in representation: "autoethnography, fiction, poetry, drama, readers' theater, writing stories, aphorisms, layered texts, conversations, epistles, polyvocal texts, comedy, satire, allegory, visual texts, hypertexts, museum displays, choreographed findings, and performance pieces, to name some" (Richardson, in Richardson & St. Pierre, 2005, p. 962).

Although more advanced researchers may want to experiment with creative and postmodern forms of representing their findings, in this chapter we focus on writing up qualitative research congruent with the constructivist perspective of this book (see Chapter One). First, we offer suggestions as to how you can prepare for the writing of the report. In the second and major portion, we will examine the options available to researchers with regard to the content and dissemination of the report. A final section addresses writing up qualitative action research and arts based research. Although qualitative research reports can take an oral, pictorial, or even dramatic form, the focus of this chapter is on the more common written form.

Preparing to Write

There are few things more frustrating than sitting down to a blank computer screen and not being able to write. Unfortunately, there is no formula to make this an easy task. You can read tips on how to write, talk to those who write a lot, read exemplary accounts—but, like learning to swim, there is no substitute for plunging in and doing it. This is not to say that it is a totally serendipitous or haphazard process. Writing up the results of your study can be greatly facilitated by attending to the following tasks prior to writing: determining the audience, selecting a focus, and outlining the report.

Determining the Audience

The first consideration—and one of the most important—in preparing to write your final report is deciding whom the report is for. Schatzman and Strauss (1973) call this process *audience conjuring*. "Since one can hardly write or say anything without there being some real or imagined audience to receive it, any description necessarily will vary according to the audience to which it is directed. Audiences 'tell' what substances to include, what to emphasize, and the level and complexity of abstractions needed to convey essential facts and ideas" (p. 118). Once it is clear who will be reading the report, you can ask what that audience would want to know about the study. The answer to that question can help structure the content of the report and determine the style of presentation.

The primary audience interested in your results might be the general public, policymakers, the funding source, practitioners, the research community in your field, or members of the site or project studied. Each audience would have a different interest in the research and would require a somewhat different approach. Take, for example, a qualitative study of how older residents in an assisted care facility learn to use computers for study and entertainment. The general public, reading about the study in a popular magazine, would respond to a human interest report that highlighted the experiences of some of the residents. Policymakers, though, are concerned with policy options. Policymakers involved in legislation for the aged or nursing home administration might want to know how the program has affected the management of staff and residents, whether funding should be channeled into the project, and so on. The funding source for the study—a computer company, for example—would have its own questions, such as how the residents fared with their computers or whether this population represents a market.

Practitioners would be most interested in whether the research setting sufficiently resembles their own situation to warrant adopting the same practice. "Practitioners may say they want tips," writes Erickson (1986), "but experienced practitioners understand that the usefulness and appropriateness of any prescriptions for practice must be judged in relation to the specific circumstances of practice in their own setting. Thus the interest in learning by positive and negative example from a case study presupposes that the case is in some ways comparable to one's own situation" (p. 153). With regard to the preceding example, practitioners in recreation and leisure studies, adult education, health education, and gerontology might be particularly interested in how learning to use computers enhanced the residents' quality of life. Thus the implicit comparison would be between the residents and setting of the study and the residents and setting of the practitioner.

Other researchers interested in the problem, including a thesis or dissertation committee, would need to know the theoretical framework and such technical aspects of the study as how the data were collected and analyzed and what was done to ensure reliability and validity. With this information they could judge the study's value and its contribution to knowledge.

Finally, the study's results might be presented to those who participated. The main concern of participants, Erickson (1986) points out, relates to "their personal and institutional reputations" (p. 154). If the findings are to be helpful to the participants, "the reports must be sensitive to the variety of personal and institutional interests that are at stake in the kinds of information that are presented about people's actions and thoughts" (p. 154). Patton (2015) underscores that reports need to be useful to participants, and "if you try to include everything, you risk losing your readers or audience members in the sheer volume of the presentation. To enhance a report's coherence or a presentation's impact, follow the adage that *less is more*. This translates into covering a few key findings or conclusions well, rather than lots of them poorly" (p. 621, emphasis in original).

Determining the audience should help a researcher define the relative emphasis of different components of the research report. It may be even more helpful to address the report to a particular person in the target group, such as your advisor, a particular administrator, a friend who represents a general audience, and so on. By "speaking" to a specific person or group, you are more likely to adopt an appropriate tone (scholarly, academic, popular, personal) and be consistent throughout the report. Yin (2014) suggests not only examining the selected audience closely but also reading reports that have been previously submitted to this audience. A prior report can be used as a template for organizing your report.

Selecting a Focus

The next step is to select a focus for the report. The focus depends on the audience for whom it is being written, the original purpose of the study, and the level of abstraction obtained during analysis of the data (see Chapter Eight).

To illustrate how audience, purpose, and level of data analysis can be taken into consideration in determining the focus of a report, take the earlier example of teaching residents in an assisted care facility how to use computers. A report for a practitioner-oriented journal or magazine could have as its focus the benefits of introducing computers into this environment; or the focus might be on tips for instructing older adults in computer usage. In either case, a full description of the setting would be important; the research study itself would be briefly summarized in jargon-free language; the benefits or tips would be highlighted.

If the write-up of this same study were for a dissertation committee or scholarly research journal, the focus would reflect the purpose of the study—cognitive strategies employed by residents in learning to use computers, for example. If the study had developed a substantive theory, that would be the focus of the write-up. The report or article would emphasize the methodology of the study and the analysis and interpretation of the findings.

Bogdan and Biklen (2011) suggest another type of focus—the thesis. A thesis is a proposition put forth to be argued and defended that often arises out of the discrepancy between what some theory or previous research says should happen in a situation and what actually does happen. Because of its argumentative nature, the thesis is a good attention-getting device and particularly suited to popular accounts of research. In preparing a report of the previously mentioned research for a policy group or funding agency, for example, this more propositional focus might ask whether buying computers for residents in an assisted care facility is a waste of money.

The important thing is that some focus be chosen for the study. The focus "states a purpose and then fulfills the promise. Coming up with a focus means deciding what you want to tell your reader. You should be able to state it in a sentence or two" (Bogdan & Biklen, 2011, p. 199). Thus the focus depends on the audience being addressed and the message the researcher wants to convey. Patton (2015) advises researchers to "FOCUS! FOCUS! FOCUS! The agony of omitting on the part of the qualitative researcher or evaluator is matched only by the readers' or listeners' agony in having to read or hear those things that were not omitted but should have been" (p. 623). In writing up qualitative research, Wolcott (2009) is even more specific. Focus, he explains, is being able to complete "the critical sentence, 'The purpose of this study is . . .' If that is where you are stuck, writing is not your problem. Your problem is conceptual" (pp. 34–35).

OUTLINING THE REPORT

Before writing the report, all relevant data must be gone through, culled for extraneous material, and organized in some manner. Ideally you have been doing this all along. At the very minimum you should have devised some system for keeping track of the voluminous data typical of qualitative investigations, your analysis of that data, and your own reflections on the process (see Chapter Eight). With these resources at hand, and with your audience and focus determined, making an outline is the next step.

Some writers say they just sit down and write with no outline; perhaps they have only a vague notion of what they want to say. Except for these extraordinary and usually highly creative writers, most everyone else can be immeasurably aided in their writing by even a sketchy outline. The mere act of jotting down some of the major points you want to be sure to cover reveals whether you have anything to say or not. Trying to write something—anything—is a good clue as to whether you have done enough background reading, analyzed your data enough, or thought about it enough. As Dey (1993) points out, "What you cannot explain to others, you do not understand yourself. Producing an account of our analysis is not just something we do for an audience. It is also something we do for ourselves" (p. 237).

An easy way to outline is to write down all the topics that might be covered in the report. Next, arrange the topics in some order that will be understood by the intended audience. All research reports need an introduction defining the problem that was studied and, depending on the audience, information about the methodology. The main body of the report contains the findings in the form of topics that have been listed and organized in some way. A conclusion summarizes the study and its findings and offers some commentary on the findings.

A strategy we have used in conjunction with an outline is to estimate the number of pages that will be devoted to each section. If you are writing up the research as a journal article, for example, you would first decide which journal is your target and find out the average number of pages for a manuscript (this information is available at the journal's website and is usually printed on the inside page of each issue under the heading "Guidelines for Authors" or "Submission Guidelines"). For a 5,000-word or 20-page manuscript, you might allot one page for the introduction, four pages for the first topic in your outline, and so on. Of course this gets adjusted as you actually write, but it does give you a sense of how much attention you want to devote to each section of the report.

BEGINNING TO WRITE

From the outline, you can begin to write the first draft of the report. The outline breaks the writing task into manageable units, making the task less overwhelming. However, there is no substitute for actually writing—all the preparation in the world does not save you from having to put words on paper or characters on a screen. The act of writing itself causes something to happen, probably because most composition researchers agree that writing is a form of thinking (Becker, 2007; Wolcott, 2009). It is a "recursive social process that enables writers to develop and clarify ideas and improve their communication through successive stages of idea formulation, feedback, and revision" (Lofland, Snow, Anderson, & Lofland, 2006, p. 222). Lofland et al. (2006) go on to say that "*the physical activity of writing* itself can bring into sharp focus and crystallize what you are trying to say or even produce new insights that layer or elaborate what you have to say about something in ways that you didn't anticipate" (p. 229, emphasis in original). This is why Dey (1993) considers writing "another tool in our analytic tool-kit." It is partially "through the challenge of explaining ourselves to others [that] we can help to clarify and integrate the concepts and relationships we have identified in our analysis" (p. 237).

All writers occasionally experience writer's block, but if writing is a form of thinking, writer's block is probably more accurately termed a "thinking" block. Wolcott (2009) agrees: "Writing is not only a great way to discover what we are thinking, it is also a way to uncover lacunae in our knowledge thinking. Unfortunately, that means we must be prepared to catch ourselves red-handed whenever we seem not to be thinking at all. The fact should not escape us that when the writing is not going well, our still-nebulous thoughts cannot yet be expressed in words" (p. 19).

If writer's block occurs, several tactics may be tried. First, you might go back to your materials, read through them, and then think more about the story in those materials that you want to tell. Second, writing anything is better than not writing. The material may or may not be used later, but forcing yourself to write something may trigger more thinking and writing. Another strategy is to set deadlines for completing a certain number of pages, and meet these deadlines no matter what you have written. Werner and Schoepfle (1987) suggest shifting to a different medium of communication—writing a letter about the research to a friend, for example, or giving a talk, formal or informal, on the topic. A recording of the lecture or conversation can later be used as a stimulus for writing.

There are other subtle barriers to writing. In writing something for others to read, we open ourselves up to scrutiny and criticism. Although in reality it may be our ideas that are being critiqued, we see our ideas as extensions of ourselves. We are afraid we'll be "found out"—that we don't know much, that we are incompetent, that maybe we haven't cited key references, that there's some fatal flaw in our argument, and so on. Becker (2007) captures some of this angst about writing in his discussion of two fears expressed by his students—one, that "they would not be able to organize their thoughts, that writing would be a big, confusing chaos" and two, that "what they wrote would be 'wrong' and that (unspecified) people would laugh at them" (p. 4). Another barrier that Becker discusses is the myth that there is only One Right Way to write something, that there is some "preordained structure" that, if only it were revealed, would make writing easy (p. 43).

For all these reasons, every writer should start out writing a draft. The first draft of the report is just that—a first draft. No matter how rough or disjointed some sections may be, it is infinitely easier to work from something than from nothing. The first draft can be given to colleagues, friends, or participants for comments. Incorporating their suggestions with your own editing will result in a more refined draft that will be getting closer to the final version. In any case, writing the initial draft is the most laborious and time-consuming phase. Successive revisions are much less tedious; gradually the report takes shape, and you can feel a sense of accomplishment as the research process comes to a close.

In summary, the writing up of a research study can be made easier by breaking the task into smaller steps. With a well-thought-out strategy for tackling the report, it becomes a manageable undertaking. One such strategy has been described here:

1. First, assemble all the materials related to the study in an organized fashion.
2. Second, determine the intended audience, since different audiences will be interested in different questions and components of the study.
3. Third, select a focus that meets the interest of the intended audience and addresses the original purpose of the study.
4. Fourth, outline the report once the central message has been determined.
5. Finally, begin writing.

The outline may be refined, adjusted, or revised entirely to coincide with the thoughts and ideas you have while writing. It is also wise to have others read the first draft before undertaking revisions that lead to the final form of the report.

CONTENTS OF A QUALITATIVE STUDY REPORT

In the first part of this chapter we presented a strategy for engaging in the writing process. This section addresses some of the questions qualitative investigators face regarding the content of the report. What are the common components of a report? Where should the methodology, references to other research, data displays, and other such elements be placed? How should description be integrated with analysis? How can some balance be maintained between the two? Also discussed are outlets for disseminating the final report, as well as issues in writing up action research and arts based studies.

There is no standard format for reporting qualitative research. The reporting styles have been characteristically diverse over the years and are even more experimental today. The contents of a qualitative study report depend on the audience's interest as well as the investigator's purpose in doing the research in the first place. Practitioners or the general public, for example, will not be much interested in methodological information, whereas colleagues and other researchers will find such information crucial for assessing the study's contribution to the field. The best that we can offer here is a presentation of the basic components of most qualitative reports and the options available for handling different parts of the report.

COMPONENTS OF THE QUALITATIVE STUDY REPORT

The relative emphasis given each section, as well as the overall form of the report, can vary widely. Nevertheless, all reports discuss the nature of the problem investigated, the way the investigation was conducted, and the findings that resulted. In standard research reports, the problem that gave rise to the study is laid out early in the report. This section usually includes references to the literature, the theoretical framework of the study, a problem statement and the purpose of the study, and research questions that guided the study (see Chapter Four). At the very least, the reader must have some clue as to what this study is all about, even in the more postmodern, experimental write-ups. Tierney's (1993) ethnographic fiction of a university's non-discrimination policy, for example, opens by quoting the policy. This is followed by descriptive portraits of six personalities involved in the policy change. Through his quoting the 27-word policy statement at the opening of his report, we at least know that the study takes place at a university and involves discrimination in some way.

Early in some reports, especially qualitative case studies, is a description of the context of the study or where the inquiry took place. In forms of qualitative research in which interviewing is the major or only source of data, a general description of the sample as a whole is given in the methodology section. Some interview-based studies also include short portraits of each participant.

The methodology section includes, at a minimum, how the sample was selected, how data were collected and analyzed, and what measures were taken to ensure validity and reliability. It is becoming quite common in reports of qualitative research to include an additional section on the investigator—his or her training, experience, philosophical orientation, and biases. For example, in an article reporting the experiences of 18- to 25-year-olds who had left high school and transitioned into adult basic education programs, the author includes a section titled "Positionality" (Davis, 2014). There she reveals her interest in and experience with adult basic education students, as well as her belief that "many adult students operate within societal and systemic structures of inequality because they are adults without a high school diploma" (p. 242). As another example, in a qualitative case study of his Russian immigrant grandfather, Abramson (1992) includes a discussion of the biases inherent in translating his grandfather's Hebrew diaries, as well as his own personal biases, which included a tendency to "pathologize" the man. Of this tendency he writes:

> Though I never knew him, I knew his offspring (my father) well. I did not like my father. He was frequently volatile, impulsive, and out-of-control. He also had a raging temper and was plagued with obsessional fears. . . . He seemed stuck in the role of "master sergeant," his rank in the army. . . . On the positive side, my father was very bright, was a gifted musician, and could occasionally be charming. . . . Since my father did not "spring from the cosmos," I have assumed—whether fair or not—that there was a causal relationship between his behavior and that of my grandfather. Thus, as a consequence, I am predisposed to malign Samuel Abramson. (pp. 12–13)

In addition to some attention to the problem of the study and information as to how it was carried out, every report offers the findings derived from the analysis of the data. Basically, findings are the outcome of the inquiry—what you, the investigator, learned or came to understand about the phenomenon. For this section of the report there are few guidelines. Richardson (2000) reviews a range of creative possibilities for presentation of a study's findings:

Margery Wolf, in *A Thrice-Told Tale* (1992), takes the same event and tells it as fictional story, field notes, and a social scientific paper. John Steward, in *Drinkers, Drummers and Decent Folk* (1989), writes poetry, fiction, ethnographic accounts, and field notes about Village Trinidad. Valerie Walkerdin's *Schoolgirl Fictions* (1990) develops/displays the theme that "masculinity and femininity are fictions which take on the status of fact" (p. xiii) by incorporating into the book journal entries, poems, essays, photographs of herself, drawings, cartoons, and annotated transcripts. Ruth Linden's *Making Stories, Making Selves: Feminist Reflections on the Holocaust* (1992) intertwines autobiography, academic writing, and survivors' stories. (p. 935)

Richardson supports the "blurring of the humanities and the social sciences" in representing one's findings "not because it is 'trendy' but rather because the blurring coheres more truly with the life sense and learning style of so many" (in Richardson & St. Pierre, 2005, pp. 964–965). Further, writing from this multilens perspective "becomes more diverse and author centered, less boring, and humbler" (p. 965). She proposes four criteria for evaluating such writing—substantive contribution, aesthetic merit, reflexivity, and impact. With regard to the first criterion, we can ask, does it make a substantive contribution "to our *understanding* of social life?" Second, "is the text artistically shaped, satisfying, complex, and not boring?" Has reflexivity—that is, the author's self-awareness—been addressed? And what is the impact of this piece? "Does this piece affect me emotionally or intellectually?" (p. 964, emphasis in original).

Although Richardson is proposing some exciting alternatives that experienced researchers might experiment with, the most common way findings are presented in a qualitative report is to organize them according to the categories, themes, or theory derived from the data analysis (see Chapter Eight). Typically, a "findings" section begins with a brief overview of the findings, followed by presentation of each separate finding supported by quotes from interviews or field notes or references to documentary evidence. Exhibit 10.1 is an abbreviated example taken from a study of how consumers with low literacy skills negotiate the marketplace (Ozanne, Adkins, & Sandlin, 2005). Four groups of participants were identified from interviews with 22 learners possessing a range of literacy skills—alienated consumers, conflicted identity managers, identity exchanging and enhancing consumers, and savvy consumers. An overview of these four findings is presented at the beginning of the "Findings" section. This overview functions like a map, so the reader can follow the presentation. The first finding—"Alienated Consumers"—is introduced, explained, and supported by data from interviews with participants (see Exhibit 10.1).

EXHIBIT 10.1. FINDINGS PRESENTATION.

Alienated Consumers

These participants accepted the stigma of low literacy and felt shame . . . They suggested their low literacy skills socially discredited them, which was experienced as embarrassment and shame. This shame ranged in intensity from just "feeling bad" to panic and even "breaking out in tears every time I told someone." Many of the alienated consumers shared stories of their experiences of prejudicial treatment, such as being called names like "stupid," "slow," or "lazy."

> *You know a lot of people on the other side. When you are in a group and you're talking, they'll look at you and think, "What do you know?" especially these people with an education . . . And they really make you feel beneath them. (Sarah)*

Market interactions were filled with uncertainty and the constant fear that their limited literacy skills would be exposed. These participants fit traditional deficit stereotypes of the adult learner as a failed decision maker who lacks power in his or her social encounters. One participant explained that when he was renewing a driver's license,

> *I went in and was told to fill out the paper. I said, "I can't." He wouldn't listen. He said, "Of course you can. Go over to that table, read it, and fill it out." Felt as if every eye in the room was on me. I looked at it and froze. I could read name, address, and phone, but I was so nervous and embarrassed, I couldn't even do that. Left and never went back. (Sarah)*

(continued)

(*Continued*)

Sometimes this negative treatment is unambiguous. Some sales clerks cheated the adults. But often, social interactions are vaguely menacing, and the adult learners are uncertain whether their limited literacy was actually revealed.

> *I know once at the Post Office . . . And I know it was me he was talking about. I wasn't sure of really what I heard all of it, but I know they was saying something about I couldn't read very well. (Olive)*

Source: Ozanne, Adkins, and Sandlin (2005, p. 256). Reprinted with permission.

Knowing how much data to include in support of a category or theme is a judgment call. You need enough to be convincing, but not so much that the reader becomes buried. The findings are also discussed, either along with their presentation or in a separate section, often titled "Discussion," in which you tell the reader what you make of the findings. Were there any surprises? How do they compare with what is already known? What conclusions do you draw overall? What unique contribution does your study make to the knowledge base in this area?

Placement of Component Parts

Where should the methodology section, the references to previous research and literature, and the visual displays be placed? Again, the answers depend on the interest of the target audience. For the general public, practitioners, and funding agencies, the methodology section is likely to be placed in an appendix to the report. Referring to an ethnographic study, Werner and Schoepfle (1987) write, "The average reader is not interested in how the ethnography was obtained as long as he or she retains a feeling for the quality, validity, and reliability of the monograph. On the other hand, for fellow ethnographers a methodological section may be of great importance. Under no circumstances should it be left out, but its placement should be dictated by the anticipated readership" (p. 282).

Qualitative studies in journals or as chapters in a book present a discussion of methodology early in the write-up—often as part of the introduction of the problem or immediately following it. Hyde (2006) tells us how she conducted her multisite case study of the organizational dynamics of mental health teams as follows:

> The research took place within one mental health trust that covered a city and its densely populated suburbs. A case-study design was used whereby each mental health team was treated as a separate case. Following negotiations for access, each case study began with observations of daytime shifts or whole working days, depending on the opening hours of the unit. I recorded these observations in fieldwork diaries. These included records of my own emotional reactions to the environment and initial interpretations for later exploration alongside the usual records of observed events, interactions and details.
>
> In-depth interviews were conducted with mental health service managers and commissioners and with staff, patients and carers. Opportunistic conversations were used throughout the study to explore other staff experiences linked to work processes. These conversations took place any time a participant was free and willing to talk for a short period. The information gleaned from these was compared with the findings from observations and with secondary data sources such as service information leaflets. The purpose of these comparisons was to identify differences between espoused values and daily practice that could indicate defensive processes. (pp. 222–223)

Where should the references to literature that is relevant to the problem being studied be placed? In the write-up of most qualitative research, a review of previous research and writing is part of the introduction and development of the problem. The literature that helped shape the focus of the study will also be referred to in discussing your findings. It's also possible that your framework for analyzing your data has been derived from the literature. For example, if you were to discover, in your inductive analysis of the process of adopting an innovation, that the process mirrors an established framework in the literature, there's no reason why you cannot use that framework. As Patton (2015) notes, "the published literature on the topic being studied focuses the contribution of a particular study. Scholarship involves an ongoing dialogue with colleagues about particular questions of interest within the scholarly community. The analytical focus, therefore, derives in part from what one has learned that will make a contribution to the literature in a field of inquiry. That literature will likely have contributed to the initial design of the study (implicitly or explicitly), so it is appropriate to revisit that literature to help focus the analysis" (p. 526). Thus if a qualitative study is being undertaken as a critique of some theory, principle, or accepted piece of folk wisdom, the investigator should establish that fact with appropriate reference to the literature early in the report. However, if someone else's categorical scheme is being used to interpret the data collected (rather than evolving one from the data), such references should be made just prior to use of the material. Finally, discussion of the study's findings usually incorporates references to other research in pointing out where the study's findings support or deviate from previous work.

Thus references to relevant literature can be placed early in the report when describing the problem, in a section reviewing previous work, and in the section devoted to presentation and interpretation of the study's results. Keep in mind the intended audience and the desired length of the report when making this decision.

What about charts, tables, and figures? Although most reports of qualitative research use words in a narrative text, an occasional chart, table, or figure will enable readers to grasp major findings or ideas central to the study. Displaying qualitative data in the form of a chart, matrix, table, or figure enables readers to more quickly grasp complexities in the analysis that would take an enormous amount of narrative writing to convey. Displays provide something of a shorthand version of the findings. They should be used judiciously, however.

There are three common displays in qualitative reports. Most common is a table listing participants and key bits of information about them, such as can be found in Kim's (2014) study of the postretirement career transition process of Korean middle-aged adults. A table titled "Participant Profiles" lists the pseudonym for each participant, gender, age, educational attainment, primary career, current career, and years in current career. A study that is primarily based on observations might first include an "Observation Grid," as Enomoto and Bair (1999) did in their study of the role of school in the assimilation of Arab immigrant children. A second type of display is a narrative display of findings; that is, a listing of categories and properties, sometimes accompanied by a sample of evidence. A third type of display is a model in the form of a figure that shows the interrelationships and interconnectedness of the findings. For example, Figure 10.1 illustrates the process of self-directed learning of older, rural adults (Roberson & Merriam, 2005). As depicted in the diagram, the process is initiated by either

FIGURE 10.1. THE PROCESS OF SELF-DIRECTED LEARNING.

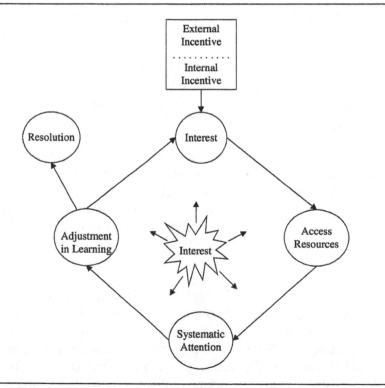

Source: Roberson and Merriam (2005, p. 275). Reprinted with permission.

an external or an internal incentive. If the person has an interest in the topic or activity, he or she then accesses resources relevant to the learning activity. For the process to continue, deliberate and systematic attention is devoted to the project. Adjustments are made through trial and error, and eventually most projects come to a close (resolution). An important dimension of the process is an event or encounter that acts as a catalyst to speed up the process or motivate them to learn on a deeper level. For example, Charlie's wife was diagnosed with Alzheimer's disease, and this became a personal catalyst for his learning; a chance encounter at a town meeting led Hattie to resume her efforts to get sidewalks built on her side of town.

In using visual displays in a study report, the researcher should

- Keep the display simple, including only the information that is necessary in understanding the presentation.
- Keep the number of displays to a minimum; using just a few figures to represent important ideas will draw attention to those ideas.
- Mention the display in the text, placing the display as close to its discussion as possible.
- "Walk" the reader through the display, illustrating how to read or interpret the display.

Displays should be an integrated part of the study narrative; displays accompanied by only a sentence or two leave too much interpretation up to the reader. The researcher must at least explain how the data displayed in the table or figure or chart illustrate some aspect of the study, whether it is descriptive or interpretive information.

Description and Analysis

Two of the most difficult dilemmas to resolve in writing up qualitative research are (1) how much concrete description to include, as opposed to analysis and interpretation and (2) how to integrate one with the other so that the narrative remains interesting and informative. The findings of a qualitative study are inductively derived from the data collected through interviews, observations, or documents. Some of these very same data need to be presented as *evidence* for the findings. It is the quality and quantity of the evidence provided that persuades the reader that the findings are trustworthy. The amount of evidence that can be included depends on the type of report—space is much more limited in a journal article than in a thesis or dissertation, for example. As reviewers for a number of journals that report qualitative research, we have seen the extremes. Most write-ups of qualitative studies present the categories of findings of the research after describing the methodology. Some authors present long, multipage extracts to support minor points in their findings; others become so excited about their findings that they present little evidence to support their conceptual scheme. Our preference and our advice is to, in most cases, avoid lengthy, single-spaced quotes; rather, embed shorter, multiple pieces of evidence in the narrative. Further, do not put multiple pieces of evidence (quotes) in a list; rather, each piece should be woven into the narrative. An obvious exception to these guidelines would be in presenting narrative forms of research. Your purpose here is to present a participant's narrative in depth to illustrate how the phenomenon under study unfolded, or how the participants told their story as part of the findings. An example is Tobin and Tisdell's (2015) recent study of the embodied learning of creative writers.

In descriptive forms of research, in which you are presenting categories of findings, you might ask yourself, how much is enough evidence? There is no answer other than that you should attempt to achieve some balance between description and interpretation, evidence and analysis. Patton (2015) also addresses this concern: "Description precedes and is then balanced by analysis and interpretation. Endless description becomes its own muddle. The purpose of analysis is to organize the description so that it is manageable. Description provides the skeletal frame for analysis that leads into interpretation. An interesting and readable report provides sufficient description to allow the reader to understand the basis for an interpretation, and sufficient interpretation to allow the reader to appreciate the description" (p. 606).

Erickson's (2012) differentiation among particular description, general description, and interpretive commentary may be helpful in determining this balance: the raw data are reported as particular description, patterns discovered in the data are reported as general description, and ever higher levels of abstraction become interpretive commentary. Particular description consists of quotes from people interviewed and quotes from field notes and/or from documents pertinent to the study. General description is needed to tell the reader whether the vignettes and quotes are typical of the data as a whole. "Combinations of general and particular description are much clearer substantively and are also more persuasive to the reader than presenting only general description through which one sees patterns in the forest but learns nothing about the trees, or presenting only particular description, in which a tree might be exquisitely described but the reader has no sense of the forest" (Erickson, 2012, p. 1465). Interpretive commentary, the third element in a qualitative study report, provides a framework for understanding the particular and general descriptions just discussed. This type of commentary "let[s] the reader know where the text is going and where it has just been" (p. 1465). Of the balance between description and commentary, Erickson points out that "whether in a classic book-length monograph or in a journal article-length presentation, alternation of general and particular description and of general and particular orienting commentary is found in the best examples of qualitative research reporting" (p. 1466).

Since there are no set guidelines on how to achieve the right balance between the particular and the general, between description and analysis, the qualitative investigator usually learns how to balance the two through trial and error. Reading published reports or consulting experienced colleagues might also be helpful in learning how to balance description and analysis. The main thing to keep in mind here is that "your task is to convince the reader of the plausibility of your presentation. Quoting your subjects and presenting short sections from the fieldnotes and other data help convince the reader and help him or her get closer to the people you have studied" (Bogdan & Biklen, 2011, p. 206).

DISSEMINATING THE STUDY REPORT

Depending on the study's sponsor, its purpose, and the intended audience, the format used in reporting the results can vary. For certain groups, executive summaries or specialized condensations are effective. Or the narrative could be replaced with a set of open-ended questions and answers drawn from the data. This format is particularly useful for reporting multiple-case studies. A reader "need only examine the answers to the same question or questions within each case study to begin making her or his own cross-case comparisons. Because each reader may be interested in different questions, the entire format facilitates the development of a cross-case analysis tailored to the specific interest of each reader " (Yin, 2014, p. 185). Still another possibility is to prepare analytic summaries with supporting data in appendixes. Certainly oral delivery in the form of conference presentations, debriefings, press conferences, and the like serves the purpose of communicating and disseminating the results of some research. In fact, a study's findings could be presented in the form of film, video disc, or pictorial display.

Most researchers are interested in disseminating the results of their studies beyond a sponsor and participants. Such dissemination is done primarily through conferences or journals in the field. Conferences are organized by professional associations, institutions, and agencies and are usually open to anyone interested in the topic. Any conference is an avenue for disseminating the results of research—depending, of course, on the conference's goals and whether or not you can frame the report in terms of those goals. A qualitative study on teachers' influence on the social studies curriculum, for example, could be presented at a conference on educational research, curriculum issues, teaching, or social studies.

Publishing the study in a professional journal means familiarizing yourself with the journal's format, style, procedures for submission, and focus. There is no point in sending a qualitative study to a journal that publishes only experimental research, even if the topic matches the journal's content. Since there is wide diversity in qualitative reporting, it is a good idea to find examples of qualitative studies in a journal in your field to serve as prototypes. For example, most journals in fields of education—curriculum and supervision, science education, adult education, and so on—will consider qualitative research for publication. Journals in related fields such as anthropology, sociology, and psychology might also publish studies dealing with educational issues. There are also journals devoted solely to reporting qualitative research such as

International Journal of Qualitative Studies in Education, Qualitative Inquiry, Qualitative Social Work, International Journal of Qualitative Methods, Kaleidoscope: A Graduate Journal of Qualitative Communication Research, Narrative Inquiry, The Qualitative Report, Qualitative Research Reports in Communication, Qualitative Health Research, Journal of Contemporary Ethnography, International Review of Qualitative Research, Qualitative Research, and *Qualitative Research in Organizations and Management: An International Journal.*

Other modes of dissemination might be through the in-house publications of professional associations, foundations, social service agencies, and community organizations. And, of course, qualitative studies sometimes get published in book form. Often such books are produced by presses associated with universities or professional organizations, such as Wuthnow's *The God Problem: Expressing Faith and Being Reasonable* (2012). Occasionally a commercial press will publish research results that have wide appeal. Preston's (1995) account in *The Hot Zone* of an outbreak of a strain of Ebola virus among monkeys in Reston, Virginia, is an example, as is Terkel's (2001) book, *Will the Circle Be Unbroken?* about the mysteries of death and the end of life.

ISSUES IN WRITING UP ACTION RESEARCH AND ARTS BASED STUDIES

There is no single correct way to write up any research study; as we have discussed already, the form the write-up takes depends on the audience, the venue of publication, and the realities of space limitations. How one writes for a scholarly journal is different from how one writes for the popular press in terms of language used and the form of presentation. This is a consideration in writing up any form of qualitative research. But there are some issues that are particular to writing up action research and arts based studies.

As noted earlier, a standard dissertation is written in a five-chapter format. This mirrors traditionally written research articles with these five sections: introduction and purpose of the research, background literature review, methodology of the study, presentation of findings, and discussion. While there is now a wide variety in how qualitative studies are written up, the five-section format (or five-chapter format in the case of a thesis or dissertation) doesn't work well for action research studies or for writing up arts based research.

As we discussed in Chapter Three, action research is about solving a problem in practice with participants while developing a process to do so (Herr & Anderson, 2015; Kemmis et al., 2014). So the issue in action research studies is not just "What are the findings?" but also "How did the process *unfold* that yielded these findings?" Researchers writing an action research thesis or dissertation typically have multiple chapters in which they present findings of the study at different stages to capture the process. They might have a chapter about the findings from the initial phase of planning with the participants. Then they might have two or three chapters that capture different spirals of the action research plan-act-observe-reflect cycle, and a chapter on the final set of findings. Herr and Anderson (2015) provide some excellent advice on what an action research thesis or dissertation might look like, and they include some good examples.

But writing for journal articles is a different matter, because one must deal with the reality of space limitations. How does one set up the problem, deal with the literature, and cover both an action research process and the findings and discussion in the space of 7,500 words? Indeed, this is a dilemma. Some researchers choose to cover only some aspects of the study in one journal article. For example, in a recent action research study that explored the role of community conversations in improving the clinical educational experience of paramedical professionals, the authors focus more on the methodology of community conversations (Hickson, O'Meara, & Huggins, 2014). In essence, they highlight the stages of the process with only general comments on findings (with no supporting quotes). They probably will discuss the actual findings in more depth in another article. As another example, in one article Stuckey (2009) discusses creative expression as a way of knowing for people with diabetes. In another, she and her coauthor focus more on the exploration of the meaning-making process as it unfolded in the participant narratives over time (Stuckey & Tisdell, 2010).

In arts based approaches to research, obviously the write-up of the study is to foreground the art or the artistic process. So if it is a study about an artist and/or visual arts or photography, usually aspects of the participants' art are included as part of the write-up. Zorrilla (2012), for example, in her dissertation study of conceptual artist Luis Camnitzer, displayed photographs of some of his art, so the reader could follow her line of analysis. In another example, Tyler's (in press) study of the role of storytelling and mosaic making in a community-based organization's ongoing planning and strategic visioning provided a discussion of the process as well as a photograph of the mosaic the community made. Manovski's (2014) book-length autoethnography of how the arts and music related to the development of her identity, features chapters about multiple art forms in relationship to different aspects of her identity formation. If the study is about people making knowledge through poetry, than aspects of the study will include poetry, as in Hanley and View's (2014) study of how people of color create counternarratives through poetry. Obviously, the write-up of arts based research can take a variety of approaches in a way that meets the creative needs of the writer.

SUMMARY

This chapter has focused on the writing of a qualitative study report. Without the important step of reporting and disseminating results, the research process would not be complete. Research in applied fields is important for extending the knowledge base of the field as well as for understanding and improving practice. Research can contribute to both theory and practice, but only if it is communicated beyond the research situation. Suggestions for writing the report were as follows. First, the writer should compile all the relevant data and then determine the intended audience. The next step is to settle on the main message—that is, the focus or theme of the study. An outline reflecting the study's focus is essential for dealing with a large amount of material. The researcher is then ready to write the first draft. The major portion of the chapter focused on the content of a qualitative research report. The essential elements of the study problem, methodology, and findings were reviewed, along with the issues of the placement of component parts, balancing description with analysis, and disseminating the research findings. The chapter closed with a discussion of issues in writing up action research and arts based studies.

Writing the final report is much like the entire process of conducting a qualitative research study: it is as much an art as a science. Although we have examples, guidelines, and other people's experiences to draw upon, the process as well as the end product will reflect the uniqueness, peculiarities, and idiosyncrasies of each research situation. In this book we have provided some guidelines, shared our experiences, and provided numerous examples of how to handle the various components of qualitative research. There is, however, no substitute for actually engaging in the process of shaping a research problem, collecting and analyzing data, and writing up findings. We hope that this book will make your journey easier.

The Methodology Section of a Qualitative Research Study

Sharan B. Merriam

A qualitative research proposal, whether it's a full chapter of a prospective dissertation or an abbreviated methods section of a proposal, must explain to the approving/funding committee the design of the study, how a sample will be selected, how data are to be collected and analyzed, and how trustworthiness will be ensured. The following is a template of the methodology section or chapter (usually the third chapter of a dissertation or thesis) for a *qualitative* research study. *Each section is keyed to a chapter in this book where you will find more detailed coverage of that topic.* This is only a general guideline; each study is unique, and what is included in the methodology chapter or section will vary according to the specialized circumstances of your particular study.

METHODS

The chapter begins with about a half page introduction reminding the reader of the problem and purpose of the study, followed by your research questions. You might also tell the reader what topics you plan to cover in this chapter (that is, design of the study, sample selection, and so on).

Design of the Study (Chapters One and Two)

Here you will tell us that you are doing a qualitative study, what the underlying philosophy is (for example, social constructivism), and what some of the defining characteristics of a qualitative study are. For example, you might tell us that in qualitative research the focus is on process, meaning, and understanding, that the researcher is the primary instrument of data collection and analysis, that it is inductive, and so on. You might tell us why a qualitative design is most appropriate for *your* particular study. If you are doing a basic qualitative study, this is all you need.

If you are using a *particular* type of qualitative design (such as grounded theory, narrative, phenomenological, ethnographic, or case study), here you will describe what this type of qualitative research is all about. Be explicit as to why you selected this particular qualitative methodology to deal with the problem of your study. For example, if your focus is on culture, an ethnographic approach makes sense; if you are doing an in-depth study of a bounded system, case study is appropriate.

Sample Selection (Chapter Four)

In a qualitative study we usually use *purposeful sampling* or *purposive sampling* (sometimes the term *criterion sampling* is used). First, define purposeful sampling, then tell us the *criteria* you will use to select your sample, providing a rationale for each criterion (unless it's very obvious). Is level of education a criterion for who will be eligible to be in your study? If so, why? Years of experience? Age? Sex? Race? In a study of transformational leadership, for example, you would first have to decide what criteria you would use to identify transformational leaders. If your study is about successful businesses, you will have to establish criteria for what businesses qualify as "successful." Finally, tell us precisely how you will go about getting your sample, and approximately how many participants you will have in your study (committees recognize that you cannot determine this precisely ahead of time, but they like to have some idea).

If you are doing a case study, you will have *two* levels of purposeful sampling. First, tell us the criteria for selecting the case(s) (such as a program, an institution, an intervention). Purposefully selecting the case according to preestablished criteria is the first step. Then, unless you plan to interview *all* of the people in the case, or observe all of the activities, or read all of the documents associated with the case, you will also have to tell us how you will select your sample of people, activities, or documents *within* the case. For example, what criteria will you use to select those whom you will interview? You could even use random sampling within the case (such as teachers or students within a large school) if a cross-section of perspectives within the case is desired. More likely, however, persons to be interviewed or activities to be observed will be selected on purpose.

Data Collection (Chapters Five, Six, and Seven)

Begin with an introductory paragraph identifying which data collection method(s) you will use in your study. Then have separate subsections for each method. Of course, if you are going to use only one method, there is usually no need for subsections.

Interviews

Tell us what a research interview is, the different types, and which type you plan to use. Most qualitative studies employ semistructured interviews, but you may also have a section that is structured, perhaps for gathering the same demographic data from everyone; likewise, some part of your interview may be quite unstructured and informal. Briefly describe the interview schedule or guide you plan to use, and refer us to an appendix for the specific questions. Tell us whether the interviews will be in person, via telephone, online, or some mix of the three. Tell us whether interviews will be tape recorded or video recorded and transcripts made. If there may be follow-up interviews, say so.

Often researchers will try out their interview questions with a friend or colleague or even someone who would qualify to be included in the study (or you may have conducted an interview on your topic as part of a research methods course). Tell us about these "pilot" interviews here. Be sure to tell us what you learned from those interviews. In what way(s) has your interview schedule been refined as a result of pilot interviews?

OBSERVATIONS

Researchers who collect data through observations in the field are confronted with choosing the best times to observe, deciding how many sessions to observe, and so on. Many begin with informal visits to the site to become familiar with the context, the people, and the activities. Informal visits would then be followed by intense and targeted observations of the phenomenon of interest. Tell us how you plan to go about conducting observations. How will you gain access to the site(s) of your observations? Who has to approve your being there? Will you first acquaint yourself with the setting, or is this not necessary? What do you plan to observe? What will your role be (complete observer, participant-observer, and so on)? What will be the focus of your observations? (How you focus the observation will be directly related to your research problem.) Will you be using any type of protocol or checklist? If so, explain it and refer the reader to a copy of it in the appendix.

DOCUMENTS

Documents can be the main source of data for your study (see Chapter Seven). If that is the case, in this section you should give us a full and detailed description of the document database. Then tell us whether you plan to examine *all* the documents or whether you'll be selecting a sample of documents. If you are selecting a sample from a particular documentary database, you would use purposeful sampling, establishing criteria to guide your selection.

If you plan to use documents as a data source to supplement interviews or observations, speculate as to what types of documents you might seek out. Official records? Student papers? Photographs? Personal documents (such as diaries, letters, and the like)? Or will you be asking participants to generate documents for the study (like critical incidents, reflections, even scales or measures of the phenomenon)?

ONLINE DATA

There is a great deal of uncertainty as to how to classify data collected online. Will you be "observing" online interactions? Are printouts of online discussions documents? Instead of trying to classify this material (with the exception of online interviews, which are clearly interviews), I suggest you just tell us what the online data consist of and how you plan to get these data. If you are going to do some interviews online, I recommend you handle it under the earlier "interviews" section.

DATA ANALYSIS (CHAPTER EIGHT)

If there's anything a committee is likely to be puzzled about, it's how you intend to analyze your data (and then once you've completed your study, how you *actually* analyzed your data). You begin this section by telling us what your data set will consist of, such as transcribed interviews, field notes, and documents and how you plan to manage and organize your data. For example, will you be using a particular qualitative data analysis software program, or will you adapt your word processing program?

All qualitative data analysis is inductive and comparative in the service of developing common themes or patterns or categories that cut across the data. Qualitative data analysis should also be conducted *along with* (not after) data collection. Tell us your plan to analyze your data as you go along, to the extent possible (data collection logistics sometimes interfere with the ideal here), and confirm that you will employ an overall inductive and comparative analysis strategy. The majority of qualitative theses and dissertations use the constant comparative method (see Chapter Eight). Tell us what this is and cite a couple of references. Tell us *precisely* how you plan to go about doing it. What will you do first? Second? After that? That is, tell the reader your step-by-step plan for analyzing your data. This is where you might talk about coding your data.

Although all qualitative data analysis is ultimately inductive and comparative, there are a number of additional strategies you can employ, depending on the type of qualitative study you are conducting. Phenomenology, narrative analysis, grounded theory, and so on have specific strategies that need to be explained in this section if, indeed, you are doing a particular type of qualitative research. There are also analysis strategies that can be applied to different types of qualitative research, such as discourse analysis, content analysis, and analytic induction. If you chose to use one of these strategies, explain it in detail in this section.

Pilot Study

If you have conducted a pilot study or you intend to do one, tell us about it here. A pilot study entails more than trying out your data collection methods. You will have selected a sample based on some criteria, collected data, and analyzed the data. Tell us what you learned, or expect to learn, from this pilot study.

Validity and Reliability (Chapter Nine)

What strategies will you build into your study to ensure that your study is *trustworthy*—that is, that it is valid and reliable? Triangulation is a common strategy, as is the audit trail and especially member checks. Tell us how to think about external validity (generalizability), because in a qualitative study the reader will not be able to generalize in the statistical sense.

Researcher Bias and Assumptions (Chapter Nine)

In this section, you tell us what you are assuming going into the study. What are your biases? What should we know about you, the researcher, that will help us understand how you are approaching this study, how you might be interpreting the data, what you are going to be sensitive to, and so forth? What is your relationship to the topic under investigation?

Translation Issues

If you are collecting data in a language other than English, you will need to tell us how you will handle translating the data into English.

There are typically two strategies students employ who interview in another language. In one strategy, a transcript can be prepared in the language and then translated verbatim into English; data analysis is then done in English. In the other, you work in the original language, including data analysis, and then translate the findings and supporting evidence into English. In either case, you will have to build in a "back translation" strategy as a check on your translation; that is, a bilingual person will be asked to translate some of your English back into the original language. The closer it comes to the original, the more reliable is your translation.

REFERENCES

Abramson, P. R. (1992). *A case for case studies.* Thousand Oaks, CA: Sage.

Adler, P. A., & Adler, P. (1998). Observational techniques. In N. K. Denzin & Y. S. Lincoln (Eds.), *Collecting and interpreting qualitative materials* (pp. 79–109). Thousand Oaks, CA: Sage.

Allen, W. (2013). Rewarding participation in social media enabled communities of practice. In *International AAAI Conference on Weblogs and Social Media.* Retrieved from http://www.aaai.org/ocs/index.php/ICWSM/ICWSM13/paper/view/6257

Al Lily, A. E. (2014). The tribe of educational technologies. *Higher Education Studies, 4*(3), 19–37. Retrieved from http://search.proquest.com/docview/1539696663?accountid=13158

Alston, G. D. (2014). *Cross-cultural mentoring relationships in higher education: A feminist grounded theory study.* Unpublished doctoral dissertation, Texas State University.

Alston, G. D., & Ellis-Hervey, N. (2014). Exploring the nonformal adult educator in twenty-first century contexts using qualitative video data analysis techniques. *Learning, Media and Technology.* doi: 10.10080/17439884.2014,968168

Altheide, D. L., & Schneider, C. J. (2013). *Qualitative media analysis* (2nd ed.). Thousand Oaks, CA: Sage.

Anfara, V. A. Jr., & Mertz, N. T. (2015). Introduction. In V. A. Anfara Jr. & N. T. Mertz (Eds.), *Theoretical frameworks in qualitative research* (2nd ed.). (pp. xiii–xxxii). Thousand Oaks, CA: Sage.

Ardévol E., & Gómez-Cruz, E. (2014). Digital ethnography and media practices. In F. Darling-Wolf (Ed.), *The international encyclopedia of media studies: Research methods in media studies* (pp. 498–518). San Francisco: Wiley.

Armstrong, D., & Ogden, J. (2006). The role of etiquette and experimentation in explaining how doctors change behavior: A qualitative study. *Sociology of Health and Illness, 28,* 951–968.

Auster, C. J. (1985). Manuals for socialization: Examples from Girl Scout handbooks 1913–1984. *Qualitative Sociology, 8*(4), 359–367.

Bailey, N., & Van Harkein, E. (2014). Visual images as tools of teacher inquiry. *Journal of Teacher Education, 65*(3), 241–260.

Ballenger, C. (2009). *Puzzling moments, teachable moments. Practicing teacher research in urban classrooms.* New York: Teachers College Press.

Banerjee, A. (2013). *Leadership development among scientists: Learning through adaptive challenges.* Unpublished doctoral dissertation, University of Georgia, Athens.

Barbour, R. (2008). *Doing focus groups.* Thousand Oaks, CA: Sage.

Barone, T., & Eisner, E. (2012). *Arts based research.* Thousand Oaks, CA: Sage.

Bateson, M. C. (1990). *Composing a life.* New York: Penguin Books.

Beale, C. (2013). Keeping the story together: A holistic approach to narrative analysis. *Journal of Research in Nursing, 18,* 692–704.

Becker, H. S. (1993). Theory: The necessary evil. In D. J. Flinders & G. E. Mills (Eds.), *Theory and concepts in qualitative research: Perspectives from the field* (pp. 218–229). New York: Teachers College Press.

Becker, H. S. (2007). *Writing for social scientists: How to start and finish your thesis, book, or article* (2nd ed.). Chicago: University of Chicago Press.

Bierema, L. L. (1996). How executive women learn corporate culture. *Human Resource Development Quarterly, 7*(2), 145–164.

Blankenship, J. C. (1991). *Attrition among male nursing students.* Unpublished doctoral dissertation, University of Georgia, Athens.

Boellstorff, T., Nardi, B., Pearce, C., & Taylor, T. (2012). *Ethnography and virtual worlds: A handbook of method.* Princeton, NJ: Princeton University Press.

Bogdan, R. C., & Biklen, S. K. (2011). *Qualitative research for education: An introduction to theories and methods* (5th ed.). Boston: Pearson.

Bogdan, R. C., & Taylor, S. (1975). *Introduction to qualitative research methods.* New York: Wiley.

Bohannan, L. (1992). Shakespeare in the bush. Reprinted in J. M. Morse (Ed.), *Qualitative health research* (pp. 20–30). Thousand Oaks, CA: Sage.

Borg, W. R., & Gall, M. D. (1989). *Educational research* (5th ed.). White Plains, NY: Longman.

Bracken, S. (2011). Understanding program planning theory and practice in a feminist community-based organization. *Adult Education Quarterly, 61*(2), 121–138.

Braun, V., & Clarke, V. (2013). *Successful qualitative research: A practical guide for beginners.* Thousand Oaks, CA: Sage.

Brinkmann, S., & Kvale, S. (2015). *InterViews: Learning the craft of qualitative research interviewing* (3rd ed.). Thousand Oaks, CA: Sage.

Brockenbrough, E. (2012). Agency and abjection in the closet: The voices (and silences) of black queer male teachers. *International Journal of Qualitative Studies in Education, 25*(6), 741–761.

Buckner, T. M. (2012). *Engaging moments: Adult educators reading and responding to emotion in the classroom.* Unpublished doctoral dissertation, University of Georgia, Athens.

Bullingham, L., & Vasconcelos, A. (2013). "The presentation of self in the online world": Goffman and the study of online identities. *Journal of Information Science, 39,* 101–112.

Burbules, N. C. (1986). *Tootle:* A parable of schooling and destiny. *Harvard Educational Review, 56*(3), 239–256.

Burgess, R. G. (Ed.). (1991). *Field research: A source book and field manual.* New York: Routledge.

Carney, G., Dundon, T., & Ní Léime, A. (2012). Participatory action research *with* and *within* community activist groups: Capturing the collective experience of Ireland's community and voluntary pillar in social partnership. *Action Research, 10*(3), 313–330.

Carr, W., & Kemmis, S. (1995). *Becoming critical: Education, knowledge and action research.* London: Hyperion Books.

Charmaz, K. (2000). Grounded theory: Objectivist and constructivist methods. In N. K. Denzin & Y. S. Lincoln (Eds.), *Handbook of qualitative research* (2nd ed.). (pp. 509–535). Thousand Oaks, CA: Sage.

Charmaz, K. (2011). Grounded theory methods in social justice research. In N. K. Denzin & Y. S. Lincoln (Eds.), *The Sage handbook of qualitative research* (4th ed.). (pp. 359–380). Thousand Oaks, CA: Sage.

Charmaz, K. (2014). *Constructing grounded theory* (2nd ed.). London: Sage.

Chein, I. (1981). Appendix: An introduction to sampling. In L. H. Kidder (Ed.), *Selltiz, Wrightsman & Cook's research methods in social relations* (4th ed.). (pp. 418–441). Austin, TX: Holt, Rinehart and Winston.

Cho, J., & Trent, A. (2006). Validity in qualitative research revisited. *Qualitative Research, 6*(3), 319–340.

Clandinin, D. J. (Ed.). (2007). *Handbook of narrative inquiry: Mapping a methodology.* Thousand Oaks, CA: Sage.

Clandinin, D. J., & Connelly, F. M. (1998). Personal experience methods. In N. K. Denzin & Y. S. Lincoln (Eds.), *Collecting and interpreting qualitative methods* (pp. 150–178). Thousand Oaks, CA: Sage.

Clark, G. K. (1967). *The critical historian.* Portsmouth, NH: Heinemann Educational Books.

Clarke, A. E. (2005). *Situation analysis: Grounded theory after the postmodern turn.* Thousand Oaks, CA: Sage.

Coady, M. (2013). Adult health learning and transformation: A case study of a Canadian community-based program. *Adult Education Quarterly, 63*(4), 321–337.

Cochran-Smith, M., & Lytle, S. (Ed.). (2009). *Inquiry as stance: Practitioner research in the next generation.* New York: Teachers College Press.

Coffey, A., & Atkinson, P. (1996). *Making sense of qualitative data.* Thousand Oaks, CA: Sage.

Collins, J. (2001). *Good to great: Why some companies make the leap and others don't.* New York: HarperCollins.

Collins, J., & Hansen, M. T. (2011). *Great by choice: Uncertainty, chaos, and luck—why some thrive despite them all.* NY: HarperCollins.

Connelly, F. M., & Clandinin, D. J. (1990). Stories of experience and narrative inquiry. *Educational Researcher, 9*(5), 2–14.

Cooper, H. M. (1984). *The integrative research review: A systematic approach.* Thousand Oaks, CA: Sage.

Cooperrider, D., Whitney, D., & Stavros, J. (2008). *The appreciative inquiry handbook: For leaders of change* (2nd ed.). Brunswick, OH: Crown Publisher House.

Corbin, J., & Strauss, A. (2015). *Basics of qualitative research: Techniques and procedures for developing grounded theory* (4th ed.). Thousand Oaks, CA: Sage.

Cortazzi, M. (1993). *Narrative analysis.* London: Falmer Press.

Courtenay, B. C., Merriam, S. B., & Reeves, P. M. (1998). The centrality of meaning-making in transformational learning: How HIV-positive adults make sense of their lives. *Adult Education Quarterly, 48*(2), 102–119.

Cranton, P., & Merriam, S. B. (2015). *A guide to research for educators and trainers of adults* (3rd ed.). Malabar, FL: Krieger.

Creswell, J. W. (2013). *Qualitative inquiry & research design* (3rd ed.). Thousand Oaks, CA: Sage.

Creswell, J. W. (2015). *A concise introduction to mixed methods research.* Thousand Oaks, CA: Sage.

Creswell, J., & Plano Clark, V. (2011). *Designing and conducting mixed methods research* (2nd ed.). Thousand Oaks, CA: Sage.

Cronbach, L. J. (1975). Beyond the two disciplines of scientific psychology. *American Psychologist, 30,* 116–127.

Crosby, J. L. (2004). *How learning experiences foster commitment to a career in teaching English as a foreign language.* Unpublished doctoral dissertation, University of Georgia, Athens.

Crotty, M. (1998). *The foundations of social research.* London: Sage.

Crowe, T. V. (2003). Using focus groups to create culturally appropriate HIV prevention material for the deaf community. *Qualitative Social Work, 2*(3), 289–308.

Daiute, C. (2014). *Narrative inquiry: A dynamic approach.* Thousand Oaks, CA: Sage.

D'Andrade, R. G. (1992). Afterword. In R. G. D'Andrade & C. Strauss (Eds.), *Human motives and cultural models.* Cambridge, England: Cambridge University Press.

Davidson, J., & diGregorio, S. (2013). Qualitative research and technology. In N. K. Denzin & Y. S. Lincoln (Eds.), *Collecting and interpreting qualitative materials* (4th ed.). (pp. 481–511). Thousand Oaks, CA: Sage.

Davidson, S. M. (2006). Exploring sociocultural borderlands: Journeying, navigating, and embodying a queer identity. *Journal of Men's Studies, 14*(1), 13–26.

Davis, C. A. (2014). Unraveled, untold stories: An ethnodrama. *Adult Education Quarterly, 64,* 240–259.

De Fina, A., & Georgakopoulou, A. (2012). *Analyzing narrative: Discourse and sociolinguistic perspectives.* Cambridge, UK: Cambridge University Press.

deMarrais, K. (2004). Qualitative interview studies: Learning through experience. In K. deMarrais & S. D. Lapan (Eds.), *Foundations for research* (pp. 51–68). Mahwah, NJ: Erlbaum.

Denzin, N. K. (1978). *The research act: A theoretical introduction to sociological methods* (2nd ed.). New York: McGraw-Hill.

Denzin, N. K. (1989). *Interpretive biography.* Newbury Park, CA: Sage.

Denzin, N. K. (2014). *Interpretive autoethnography.* Thousand Oaks, CA: Sage.

Denzin, N. K., & Lincoln, Y. S. (2000). *Handbook of qualitative research* (2nd ed.). Thousand Oaks, CA: Sage.

Denzin, N. K., & Lincoln, Y. S. (2011). *The Sage handbook of qualitative research* (4th ed.). Thousand Oaks, CA: Sage.

Denzin, N. K., & Lincoln, Y. S. (2013). *Collecting and interpreting qualitative materials* (4th ed.). Thousand Oaks, CA: Sage.

Dewey, J. (1933). *How we think.* Lexington, MA: Heath.

Dexter, L. A. (1970). *Elite and specialized interviewing.* Evanston, IL: Northwestern University Press.

Dey, I. (1993). *Qualitative data analysis: A user friendly guide for social scientists.* London: Routledge.

Donmoyer, R. (1990). Generalizability and the single-case study. In E. W. Eisner & A. Peshkin (Eds.), *Qualitative inquiry in education: The continuing debate* (pp. 175–200). New York: Teachers College.

Donnelly, M. K. (2014). Drinking with the derby girls: Exploring the hidden ethnography in research of women's flat track roller derby. *International Review for the Sociology of Sport, 49* (3/4), 346–366. doi: 10.1177/1012690213515664

Eisner, E. W. (1998). *The enlightened eye: Qualitative inquiry and the enhancement of educational practice.* Upper Saddle River, NJ: Prentice-Hall.

Ember, C. R., & Ember, M. (2012). *A basic guide to cross-cultural research.* http://hraf.yale.edu/wp-content/uploads/2013-12/

English, L. M. (2005). Third-space practitioners: Women educating for justice in the global south. *Adult Education Quarterly, 55*(2), 85–100.

Enomoto, E. K., & Bair, M. A. (1999). The role of the school in the assimilation of immigrant children: A case study of Arab Americans. *International Journal of Curriculum and Instruction, 1,* 45–66.

Erickson, F. (1986). Qualitative methods in research on teaching. In M. C. Whittrock (Ed.), *Handbook of research on teaching* (3rd ed.). (pp. 119–161). Old Tappan, NJ: Macmillan.

Erickson, F. (2012). Qualitative research methods for science education. In B. J. Fraser, K. Tobin, & C. J. McRobbie (Eds.), *Second international handbook of science education* (pp. 1451–1469). New York: Springer.[1]

Fadiman, A. (1997). *The spirit catches you and you fall down.* New York: Farrar, Strauss and Giroux.

Fear, W. (2012). Discursive activity in the boardroom: The role of the minutes in the construction of social realities. *Group and Organization Management, 37,* 486–520.

Fernandez, M. E., Breen, L. J., &. Simpson, T. A. (2014). Renegotiating identities: Experiences of loss and recovery for women with bipolar disorder. *Qualitative Health Research, 24*(7), 890–900.

Fielding, N. G. (2008). *Interviewing II* (4-volume set). Thousand Oaks, CA: Sage.

Fielding, N. G. (2014). Qualitative research and our digital futures. *Qualitative Inquiry, 20*(9), 1064–1073.

Firestone, W. A. (1987). Meaning in method: The rhetoric of quantitative and qualitative research. *Educational Researcher, 16*(7), 16–21.

Flick, U. (2014). Mapping the field. In U. Flick (Ed.), *The Sage handbook of qualitative data analysis* (pp. 3–18). Thousand Oaks, CA: Sage.

Fontana, A., & Frey, J. J. (2005). The interview. In N. K. Denzin & Y. S. Lincoln (Eds.), *The Sage handbook of qualitative research* (3rd ed.). (pp. 695–727). Thousand Oaks, CA: Sage.

Foster, J. (1994). The dynamics of gender in ethnographic research: A personal view. In R. G. Burgess (Ed.), *Studies in qualitative methodology 4: Issues in qualitative research.* Greenwich, CT: JAI Press.

Foucault, M. (1980). *Power/knowledge: Selected interviews and other writings, 1972–1977* (edited by Colin Gordon). New York: Harvester Press.

Frankenberg, R. (1982). Participant observers. In R. G. Burgess (Ed.), *Field research: A sourcebook and field manual* (pp. 50–52). London: Allen & Unwin.

Gabrys, J. (2013). *Digital rubbish: A natural history of electronics.* Ann Arbor, MI: University of Michigan Press.

Gaffney, D. A., DeMarco, R. F., Hofmeyer, A., Vessey, J. A., & Budin, W. C. (2012). Making things right: Nurses' experiences with workplace bullying—a grounded theory. *Nursing Research and Practice, 2012* (243210). doi: 10.1155/2012/243210

Galvan, J. L. (2012). *Writing literature reviews: A guide for students of the social and behavioral sciences* (5th ed.). Glendale, CA: Pyrczak.

Gans, H. J. (1982). The participant observer as a human being: Observations on the personal aspects of fieldwork. In R. G. Burgess (Ed.), *Field research: A sourcebook and field manual* (pp. 53–61). London: Allen & Unwin.

Gatson, S. (2011). The methods, politics, and ethics of representation in online ethnography. In N. K. Denzin & Y. S. Lincoln (Eds.), *The Sage handbook of qualitative research* (4th ed.). (pp. 513–527). Thousand Oaks, CA: Sage.

Gee, J. P. (2014). *An introduction to discourse analysis: Theory and method* (4th ed.). London: Routledge.

Geertz, C. (1973). *The interpretation of cultures: Selected essays.* New York: Basic Books.

Gibbs, G. R. (2013). Using software in qualitative analysis. In U. Flick (Ed.), *The Sage handbook of analyzing qualitative data.* London: Sage. Accessed at http://eprints.hud.ac.uk/14873/

Glaser, B. G. (1978). *Theoretical sensitivity.* Mill Valley, CA: Sociology Press.

Glaser, B. G., & Strauss, A. (1967). *The discovery of grounded theory: Strategies for qualitative research.* Chicago: Aldine.

Glesne, C., & Peshkin, A. (1992). *Becoming qualitative researchers: An introduction.* White Plains, NY: Longman.

Gold, R. (1958). Roles in sociological field observations. *Social Forces, 36,* 217–223.

Grady, J. (2008). Visual research at the crossroads. *Forum Qualitative Sozialforschung/Forum: Qualitative Social Research, 9*(3). Retrieved from http://www.qualitative-research.net/index.php/fqs/article/view/1173

Gray, D. E. (2014). *Doing research in the real world* (3rd ed.). Thousand Oaks, CA: Sage.

Grbich, C. (2013). *Qualitative data analysis* (2nd ed.). Thousand Oaks, CA: Sage.

Grenier, R. S. (2009). The role of learning in the development of expertise in museum docents. *Adult Education Quarterly, 60*(5), 142–157.

Guba, E. G. (1978). Toward a methodology of naturalistic inquiry in educational evaluation. *CSE Monograph Series in Evaluation, 8.* Los Angeles: Center for the Study of Evaluation, University of California.

Guba, E. G., & Lincoln, Y. (1981). *Effective evaluation.* San Francisco: Jossey-Bass.

Gubrium, J. F., Holstein, J., Marvasti, A. B., & McKinney, K. D. (2012). *The Sage handbook of interview research: The complexity of the craft* (2nd ed.). Thousand Oaks, CA: Sage.

Hahn, C. (2008). *Doing qualitative research using your computer: A practical guide.* Thousand Oaks, CA: Sage.

Hanley, M., & View, L. (2014). Poetry and drama as counternarrative. *Cultural Studies ↔ Critical Methodologies, 14*(6), 558–573.

Harper, D. (2002). Talking about pictures: A case for photo elicitation. *Visual Studies, 17*(1), 13–26.

Harper, D. (2003). Reimagining visual methods: Galileo to Neuromancer. In N. K. Denzin & Y. S. Lincoln (Eds.), *Collecting and interpreting qualitative materials* (2nd ed.). (pp. 176–198). Thousand Oaks, CA: Sage.

Hawkins, G. (2006). *The ethics of waste: How we relate to rubbish.* Lanham, MD: Rowman & Littlefield Publishers.

Hennink, M. M. (2014). *Focus group discussions.* New York: Oxford University Press.

Herr, K,. & Anderson, G. (2015). *The action research dissertation: A guide for students and faculty* (2nd ed.). Thousand Oaks, CA: Sage.

Hewson, C., Yule, P., Laurent, D., & Vogel, C. (2003). *Internet research methods: A practical guide for the social and behavioural sciences.* London: Sage.

Hickson, H., O'Meara, P., & Huggins, C. (2014). Engaging in community conversation: A means to improving the paramedicine student clinical placement experience. *Action Research, 12*(4), 410–425.

Hill Collins, P. (2008). *Black feminist thought: Knowledge, consciousness, and the politics of empowerment.* New York: Routledge.

Hodder, I. (2003). The interpretation of documents and material culture. In N. K. Denzin & Y. S. Lincoln (Eds.), *Collecting and interpreting qualitative materials* (2nd ed.). (pp. 155–175). Thousand Oaks, CA: Sage.

Hohl, S. D., Gonzalez, C., Carosso, E., Ibarra, G., & Thompson, B. (2014). "I did it for us and I would do it again": Perspectives of rural Latinos on providing biospecimens for research. *American Journal of Public Health, 104*(5), 911–916. Retrieved from http://search.proqust.com/docview/1524713438?accountid=13158

Hollenbeck, C. R. (2005). Online anti-brand communities as a new form of social action in adult education. In R. J. Hill & R. Kiely (Eds.), *Proceedings of the 46th annual adult education research conference* (pp. 205–210). Athens, GA: University of Georgia.

Holstein, J. A., & Gubrium, J. F. (2012). *Varieties of narrative analysis.* Thousand Oaks, CA: Sage.

Honigmann, J. J. (1982). Sampling in ethnographic fieldwork. In R. G. Burgess (Ed.), *Field research: A sourcebook and field manual* (pp. 79–90). London: Allen & Unwin.

Hookway, N. (2008). "Entering the blogosphere": Some strategies for using blogs in social research. *Qualitative Research, 8*, 91–113.

Horton, M., & Freire, P. (1990). *We make the road by walking: Conversations on education and social change* (edited by Brenda Bell, John Gaventa, and John Peters). Philadelphia: Temple University Press.

Hughes, J. (Ed.). (2012). *Sage visual methods* (Vols. 1–4). Thousand Oaks, CA: Sage.

Husserl, E. (1970). *The crisis of European sciences and transcendental phenomenology.* Evanston, IN: North University Press.

Hyde, P. (2006). A case study of unconscious processes in an organization. In L. Finlay & C. Ballinger (Eds.), *Qualitative research for allied health professionals: Challenging choices* (pp. 218–231). West Sussex, England: Wiley.

Imel, S. (2011). Writing a literature review. In T. Rocco & T. Hatcher (Eds.), *The handbook of scholarly writing and publishing* (pp. 145–160). San Francisco: Wiley.

James, N., & Busher, H. (2012). Internet interviewing. In J. Gubrium et al. (Eds.), *The Sage handbook of interview research: The complexity of the craft* (2nd ed.). (pp. 177–192). Thousand Oaks, CA: Sage.

Janesick, V. J. (1994). The dance of qualitative research design: Metaphor, methodolatry, and meaning. In N. K. Denzin & Y. S. Lincoln (Eds.), *Handbook of qualitative research* (pp. 209–235). Thousand Oaks, CA: Sage.

Jarecke, J. (2011). *Teacher-learner beliefs in medical education: A mixed methods study of the third-year experience.* Unpublished dissertation, The Pennsylvania State University.

Johnson-Bailey, J. (2004). Enjoining positionality and power in narrative work: Balancing contentious and modulating forces. In K. Desmarrais & S. Lapan (Eds.), *Foundations for research: Methods of inquiry in education and the social sciences* (pp. 123–138). New York: Erlbaum.

Jonassen, D. H., & Hernandez-Serrano, J. (2002). Case-based reasoning and instructional design: Using stories to support problem solving. *Educational Technology Research and Development, 50*(2), 65–77.

Josselson, R., Lieblich, A., & McAdams, D. P. (Eds.). (2007). *The meaning of others: Narrative studies of relationships.* Washington, DC: American Psychological Association.

Jowett, M., & O'Toole, G. (2006). Focusing researchers' minds: Contrasting experiences of using focus groups in feminist qualitative research. *Qualitative Research, 6*(4), 453–472.

Kelle, U. (2004). Computer-assisted qualitative data analysis. In C. Seale, G. Gobo, J. R. Gubrium, & D. Silverman (Eds.), *Qualitative research practice* (pp. 473–489). Thousand Oaks, CA: Sage.

Kemmis, S., McTaggert, R., & Nixon, R. (2014). *The action research planner: Doing critical participatory action research.* New York: Springer.

Kerrigan, M. (2014). Understanding community colleges' organizational capacity for data use: A convergent parallel mixed methods study. *Journal of Mixed Methods Research, 8*(4), 241–362.

Kilbourn, B. (2006). The qualitative doctoral dissertation proposal. *Teachers College Record, 108*(4), 529–576.

Kim, S. J. (2014). The career transition process: A qualitative exploration of Korean middle-aged workers in postretirement employment. *Adult Education Quarterly, 64*(1), 3–19.

Kincheloe, J. L., & McLaren, P. (2000). Rethinking critical theory and qualitative research. In N. K. Denzin & Y. S. Lincoln (Eds.), *Handbook of qualitative research* (2nd ed.). (pp. 279–314). Thousand Oaks, CA: Sage.

Kincheloe, J. L., McLaren, P., & Steinberg, S. (2011). Critical pedagogy and qualitative research: Moving to bricolage. In N. K. Denzin & Y. S. Lincoln (Eds.), *The Sage handbook of qualitative research* (pp. 163–178). Thousand Oaks, CA: Sage.

Knowles, J. G., & Cole, A. L. (2007). *Handbook of the arts in qualitative research: Perspectives, methodologies, examples, and issues.* Thousand Oaks, CA: Sage.

Koro-Ljungberg, M. (2012). Methodology is movement is methodology. In S. Sternberg & G. Cannella (Eds.), *Critical qualitative research reader* (pp. 82–90). New York: Peter Lang.

Kozinets, R., Dolbec, P., & Earley, A. (2014). Netnographic analysis: Understanding culture through social media data. In U. Flick (Ed.), *The Sage handbook of qualitative data analysis* (pp. 262–276). Thousand Oaks, CA: Sage.

Krippendorff, K. H. (2013). *Content analysis: An introduction to its methodology.* Thousand Oaks, CA: Sage.

Krueger, R. A., & Casey, M. A. (2015). *Focus groups: A practical guide for applied research* (5th ed.). Thousand Oaks, CA: Sage.

Kuhne, G., & Quigley, B. A. (1997). Understanding and using action research in practice settings. In B. A. Quigley & G. Kuhne (Eds.), *Creating practical knowledge through action research* (pp. 23–40). New Directions for Adult and Continuing Education, no. 73. San Francisco: Jossey-Bass.

Labov, W. (1982). Speech actions and reactions in personal narrative. In D. Tannen (Ed.), *Analyzing discourse: Text and talk* (pp. 354–396). Washington, DC: Georgetown University Press.

Lachal, J., Speranza, M., Taïeb, O., Falissard, B., Lefèvre, H., Moro, M. R., & Revah-Levy, A. (2012). Qualitative research using photo-elicitation to explore the role of food in family relationships among obese adolescents. *Appetite, 58,* 1099–1105.

Lather, P. (1992). Critical frames in educational research: Feminist and post-structural perspectives. *Theory into Practice, 31*(2), 87–99.

Lather, P. (2006). Paradigm proliferation as a good thing to think with: Teaching research in education as a wild profusion. *International Journal of Qualitative Studies in Education, 19*(1), 35–58.

Lather, P., & St. Pierre, E. A. (2013). Post-qualitative research. *International Journal of Qualitative Studies in Education, 26*(6), 629–633.

Leavy, P. (2015). *Method meets art: Arts-based research practice* (2nd ed.). New York: Guilford Press.

LeCompte, M. D., & Preissle, J., with Tesch, R. (1993). *Ethnography and qualitative design in educational research* (2nd ed.). Orlando, FL: Academic Press.

LeCompte, M. D., & Schensul, J. J. (2010). *Designing and conducting ethnographic research: An introduction* (2nd ed.). Lanham and New York: AltaMira Press.

Lee, R. M. (2000). *Unobtrusive methods in social research.* Philadelphia: Open University.

Levinson, D. J., & Levinson, J. D. (1996). *The seasons of a woman's life.* New York: Ballantine.

Lichtman, M. V. (2013). *Qualitative research in education: A user's guide.* Thousand Oaks, CA: Sage.

Lightfoot, S. L. (1983). *The good high school.* New York: Basic Books.

Lincoln, Y. S. (1995). Emerging criteria for quality in qualitative and interpretive research. *Qualitative Inquiry, 1*(1), 275–289.

Lincoln, Y. S. (2010). "What a long, strange trip it's been . . .": Twenty-five years of qualitative and new paradigm research. *Qualitative Inquiry, 16*(1), 3–9.

Lincoln, Y. S., & Guba, E. G. (1985). *Naturalistic inquiry.* Thousand Oaks, CA: Sage.

Lincoln, Y. S., Lynham, S. A., & Guba, E. G. (2011). Paradigmatic controversies, contradictions, and emerging confluences, revisited In N. Denzin and Y. S. Lincoln (Eds.), *The Sage handbook of qualitative research* (pp. 97–128). Thousand Oaks, CA: Sage.

Lindlof, T., & Taylor, B. (2011). *Qualitative communication research methods.* Thousand Oaks, CA: Sage.

Liu, W., Manias, E., & Gerdtz, M. (2012). Medication communication between nurses and patients during nursing handovers on medical wards: A critical ethnographic study. *International Journal of Nursing Studies, 49*(8), 941–952.

Lodico, M., Spaulding, D., & Voegtle, K. (2010). *Methods in educational research: From theory to practice* (2nd ed.). San Francisco: Jossey-Bass.

Lofland, J. (1974). Styles of reporting qualitative field research. *American Sociologist, 9,* 101–111.

Lofland, J., & Lofland, L. H. (1995). *Analyzing social settings: A guide to qualitative observation and analysis* (3rd ed.). Belmont, CA: Wadsworth.

Lofland, J., Snow, D., Anderson, L., & Lofland, L. H. (2006). *Analyzing social settings: A guide to qualitative observation and analysis* (4th ed.). Belmont, CA: Wadsworth/Thomas Learning.

Lopez, C. J. (2013). *Early intensive behavior treatment for children with autism: A multiple case study of long term outcomes.* Unpublished dissertation, California State University, Stanislaus.

Lorenz, L. S. (2010). Brain injury survivors: Narratives of disability and healing. *Disability in society.* R. Berger (Series Ed.). Boulder, CO, and London: Lynne Riener.

Macnaghten, P., & Myers, G. (2004). Focus groups. In C. Seale, G. Gobo, J. F. Gubrium, & D. Sliverman (Eds.), *Qualitative research practice* (pp. 65–79). Thousand Oaks, CA: Sage.

Madison, D. S. (2012). *Critical ethnography: Method, ethics, and performance* (2nd ed.). Thousand Oaks, CA: Sage.

Manovski, M. (2014). *Autoethnography and music education: Singing through a culture of marginalization.* Boston: Sense Publishing.

Margolis, E., & Pauwels, L. (Eds.). (2011). *The Sage handbook of visual research methods.* Thousand Oaks, CA: Sage.

Marotzki, W., Holze, J., & Verständig, D. (2014). Analysing virtual data. In U. Flick (Ed.), *The Sage handbook of qualitative data analysis* (pp. 450–464). Thousand Oaks, CA: Sage.

Marshall, C., & Rossman, G. B. (2015). *Designing qualitative research* (6th ed.). Thousand Oaks, CA: Sage.

Martin, D., & Yurkovich, E. (2014). "Close-knit" defines a healthy Native American Indian family. *Journal of Family Nursing, 20*(1), 51–72.

Matteucci, X. (2013). Photo elicitation: Exploring tourist experiences with researcher-found images. *Tourism Management, 35,* 190–197.

Maxwell, J. A. (2013). *Qualitative research design: An interactive approach* (3rd ed.). Thousand Oaks, CA: Sage.

Mayfield-Johnson, S., Rachal, J. R., & Butler, J. III. (2014). "When we learn better, we do better": Describing changes in empowerment through photovoice among community health advisors in a breast and cervical cancer health promotion program in Mississippi and Alabama. *Adult Education Quarterly, 64*(2), 91–109.

McAdams, D. P., Josselson, R., & Lieblich, A. (Eds.). (2013). *Turns in the road: Narrative studies of lives in transition.* Washington, DC: American Psychological Association.

McCulloch, G. (2004). *Documentary research in education, history and the social sciences*. London: RoutledgeFalmer.

McLean, S. (2013). Public pedagogy, private lives: Self-help books and adult learning. *Adult Education Quarterly, 63*(4), 373–388.

Merriam, S. B. (1988). *Case study research in education: A qualitative approach*. San Francisco: Jossey-Bass.

Merriam, S. B. (1989). The structure of simple reminiscence. *The Gerontologist, 29*(6), 761–767.

Merriam, S. B. (2015). Transformational learning and HIV-positive young adults. In V. A. Anfara Jr. & N. T. Mertz (Eds.), *Theoretical frameworks in qualitative research* (2nd ed.) (pp. 80–95). Thousand Oaks, CA: Sage.

Merriam, S. B., & Muhamad, M. (2013). Roles traditional healers play in cancer treatment in Malaysia: Implications for health promotion and education. *Asian Pacific Journal of Cancer Prevention, 14*(6), 3593–3601.

Merton, R., Riske, M., & Kendall, P. L. (1956). *The focused interview*. New York: Free Press.

Mertz, N. T., & Anfara, V. A. Jr. (2015). Conclusion: Closing the loop. In V. A. Anfara Jr. & N. T. Mertz (Eds.), *Theoretical frameworks in qualitative research* (pp. 227–235). Thousand Oaks, CA: Sage.

Michel, A. (2014). Participation and self-entrapment: A 12-year ethnography of Wall Street participation practices' diffusion and evolving consequences. *Sociological Quarterly, 55*(3), 514–536. doi: 10.1111/tsq.12064

Miles, M. B., Huberman, A. M., & Saldaña, J. (2014). *Qualitative data analysis: A methods sourcebook* (3rd ed.). Thousand Oaks, CA: Sage.

Mishler, E. G. (1995). Models of narrative analysis: A typology. *Journal of Narrative and Life History, 5*(2), 87–123.

Mishoe, S. C. (1995). The effects of institutional context on critical thinking in the workplace. *Proceedings of the 36th Annual Adult Education Research Conference* (pp. 221–228). University of Alberta, Edmonton, Alberta, Canada.

Montuori, A. (2005). Literature review as creative inquiry: Reframing scholarship as a creative process. *Journal of Transformative Education, 3*, 374–393.

Moon, P. (2011). Bereaved elders: Transformative learning in late life. *Adult Education Quarterly, 61*(1), 22–39.

Moss, G., & McDonald, J. W. (2004). The borrowers: Library records as unobtrusive measures of children's reading preferences. *Journal of Research in Reading, 27*(4), 401–412.

Moustakas, C. (1990). *Heuristic research: Design, methodology, and applications*. Thousand Oaks, CA: Sage.

Moustakas, C. (1994). *Phenomenological research methods*. Thousand Oaks, CA: Sage.

Muncey, T. (2010). *Creating autoethnographies.* Thousand Oaks, CA: Sage.

Murdock, G. P. (1983). *Outline of world cultures* (6th ed.). New Haven, CT: Human Relations Area Files.

Murdock, G. P., Ford, C. S., Hudson, A. E., Kennedy, R., Simmons, L. W., & Whitney, J. M. (2008). *Outline of world cultures* (6th rev. ed. with modifications). Human Relations Area File. New Haven, CT: Yale University.

Norman, D. A. (1993). *Things that make us smart: Defending human attributes in the age of the machine.* Reading, MA: Addison-Wesley.

Ntseane, P. G. (1999). *Botswana rural women's transition to urban business success: Collective struggles, collective learning.* Unpublished doctoral dissertation, University of Georgia, Athens.

Ntseane, P. G. (2004). Botswana rural women's transition to urban small business success: Collective struggles, collective learning. *Gender and Development, 12*(2), 37–43.

Ntseane, P. G. (n.d.). Interview transcript. University of Georgia, Athens.

Ozanne, J. L., Adkins, N. R., & Sandlin, J. A. (2005). Shopping [for] power: How adult literacy learners negotiate the marketplace. *Adult Education Quarterly, 55*(4), 251–268.

Padgett, D. K., Smith, B. T., Derejko, K. S., Henwood, B. F., & Tiderington, E. (2013). A picture is worth . . . ? Photo elicitation interviews with formerly homeless adults. *Qualitative Health Research, 23*(11), 1435–1444.

Parmentier, G., & Roland, S. (2009). Consumers in virtual worlds: Identity building and consuming experience in Second Life. *Recherche et Applications en Marketing* (English edition), *24*(3), 43–55.

Patton, M. Q. (1978). *Utilization-focused evaluation.* Beverly Hills, CA: Sage.

Patton, M. Q. (1981). *Practical evaluation.* Beverly Hills, CA: Sage.

Patton, M. Q. (1985, April). Quality in qualitative research: Methodological principles and recent developments. Invited address to Division J of the American Educational Research Association, Chicago.

Patton, M. Q. (2002). *Qualitative research and evaluation methods* (3rd ed.). Thousand Oaks, CA: Sage.

Patton, M. Q. (2015). *Qualitative research and evaluation methods* (4th ed.). Thousand Oaks, CA: Sage.

Paulus, T., Lester, N., & Dempster, P. (2014). *Digital tools for qualitative research.* Thousand Oaks, CA: Sage.

Perry, H. (2008). Integrating adult education and public health policy: A case study of policy formation in Uganda. Unpublished dissertation, University of Georgia, Athens.

Peshkin, A. (1988). In search of subjectivity—one's own. *Educational Researcher, 17*(7), 17–22.

Piersol, L. (2014). Listening place. *Australian Journal of Outdoor Education,* *17*(2), 43–53. Retrieved from http://search.proquest.com /docview/1511026278?accountid=13158

Pillow, W. (2003). Confession, catharsis, or cure? Rethinking the uses of reflexivity as methodological power in qualitative research. *Qualitative Studies in Education, 16*(2), 175–196.

Pink, S. (2012). *Advances in visual methodology.* Thousand Oaks, CA: Sage.

Pink, S. (2013). *Doing visual ethnography* (3rd ed.). Thousand Oaks, CA: Sage.

Plano Clark, V., Schumacher, K., West, C., Edrington, J., Dunn, L., Harzstark, A., . . . Miaskowski, C. (2013). Practices for embedding an interpretive qualitative approach within a randomized trial. *Journal of Mixed Methods Research, 7*(3), 219–242.

Plunkett, R., Leipert, B., Ray, S. L., Olson, J. K. (2014). Healthy spaces in meaningful places: The rural church and women's health promotion. *Journal of Holistic Nursing,* 1–12. doi: 10.1177/0898010114546191

Prasad, P. (2005). *Crafting qualitative research: Working in the postpositivist traditions.* Armonk, NY: M.E. Sharpe.

Preissle, J. (2006). Envisioning qualitative inquiry: A view across four decades. *International Journal of Qualitative Studies in Education, 19*(6), 685–695.

Preissle, J., & Grant, L. (2004). Fieldwork traditions: Ethnography and participant observation. In K. deMarrais & S. D. Lapan (Eds.), *Foundations for research: Methods of inquiry in education and the social sciences* (pp. 161–180). Mahwah, NJ: Erlbaum.

Preston, R. (1995). *The hot zone.* New York: Random House.

Probst, B., & Berenson, L. (2014). The double arrow: How qualitative social work researchers use reflexivity. *Qualitative Social Work, 13*(6), 813–827.

Punch, M. (1994). Politics and ethics in qualitative research. In N. K. Denzin & Y. S. Lincoln (Eds.), *Handbook of qualitative research* (pp. 83–97). Thousand Oaks, CA: Sage.

Pyrch, T. (2007). Participatory action research and the culture of fear. *Action Research, 5*(2), 199–216.

Ramaswamy, A. (2014). Natya yoga therapy: Using movement and music to create meditative relief in schizophrenia (based on ashtanga yoga). *Action Research, 12,* 237–253.

Ratcliffe, J. W. (1983). Notions of validity in qualitative research methodology. *Knowledge: Creation, Diffusion, Utilization, 5*(2), 147–167.

Rathje, W. L. (1979). Trace measures. In L. Sechrest (Ed.), *Unobtrusive measurement today.* New Directions for Methodology of Social and Behavioral Science, No. 1 (pp. 75–91). San Francisco, CA: Jossey-Bass.

Rathje, W. L., & Murphy, C. (2001). *Rubbish: The archaeology of garbage.* Tucson, AZ: University of Arizona Press.

Richards, L. (2015). *Handling qualitative data* (3rd ed.). London: Sage.

Richards, T. J., & Richards, L. (1998). Using computers in qualitative research. In N. K. Denzin & Y. S. Lincoln (Eds.), *Collecting and interpreting qualitative materials* (pp. 211–245). Thousand Oaks, CA: Sage.

Richardson, L. (2000). Writing: A method of inquiry. In N. K. Denzin & Y. S. Lincoln (Eds.), *Handbook of qualitative research* (2nd ed.). (pp. 923–948). Thousand Oaks, CA: Sage.

Richardson, L., & St. Pierre, E. A. (2005). Writing: A method of inquiry. In N. K. Denzin & Y. S. Lincoln (Eds.), *The Sage handbook of qualitative research* (3rd ed.). (pp. 959–978). Thousand Oaks, CA: Sage.

Richer, M., Ritchie, J., & Marchionni, C. (2009). "If we can't do more, let's do it differently!": Using appreciative inquiry to promote innovative ideas for better health care work environments. *Journal of Nursing Management, 17*(8), 947–995.

Richer, M., Ritchie, J., & Marchionni, C. (2010). Appreciative inquiry in health care. *British Journal of Healthcare Management, 16*(4), 164–172.

Riessman, C. K. (2007). *Narrative methods for the human sciences.* Thousand Oaks, CA: Sage.

Roach, C. M. (2014). "Going native": Aca-fandom and deep participant observation in popular romance studies. *Mosaic, 47*(2), 33–49.

Roberson, D. N. Jr., & Merriam, S. B. (2005). The self-directed learning process of older, rural adults. *Adult Education Quarterly, 55*(4), 269–287.

Robertson, R. V., Bravo, A., & Chaney, C. (2014, online first). Racism and the experiences of Latino/a college students at a PWI (predominantly white institution). *Critical Sociology,* 1–21.

Rossiter, M. (1999). Understanding adult development as narrative. In M. C. Clark & R. S. Caffarella (Eds.), *An update on adult development theory: New ways of thinking about the life course.* New Directions for Adult and Continuing Education, no. 84. San Francisco: Jossey-Bass.

Roulston, K. (2010). *Reflective interviewing: A guide to theory and practice.* London and Thousand Oaks, CA: Sage.

Ruona, W.E.A. (2005). Analyzing qualitative data. In R. A. Swanson & E. F. Holton (Eds.), *Research in organizations: Foundations and methods of inquiry* (pp. 223–263). San Francisco: Berrett-Koehler.

Ruth-Sahd, L. A., & Tisdell, E. J. (2007). The meaning and use of intuition in novice nurses: A phenomenological study. *Adult Education Quarterly, 57*(2), 115–140.

Ryan, J., Rapley, M., Dziurawiec, S. (2014). The meaning of coping for psychiatric patients. *Qualitative Health Research, 24*(8), 1068–1079.

Saldaña, J. (2013). *The coding manual for qualitative researchers* (2nd ed.). Thousand Oaks, CA: Sage.

Salmons, J. (2015). *Qualitative online interviews* (2nd ed.). Thousand Oaks, CA: Sage.

Schatzman, L., & Strauss, A. L. (1973). *Field research.* Englewood Cliffs, NJ: Prentice Hall.

Schensul, J. J., & LeCompte, M. D. (2013). *Essential ethnographic methods: A mixed methods approach. Ethnographer's toolkit, book 3* (2nd ed.). Lanham, MD: AltaMira Press.

Schiffrin, D., Tannen, D., & Hamilton, H. E. (Eds.). (2001). *The handbook of discourse analysis.* Malden, MA: Blackwell.

Schram, T. H. (2003). *Conceptualizing qualitative inquiry.* Upper Saddle River, NJ: Merrill Prentice Hall.

Schreier, M. (2014). Qualitative content analysis. In U. Flick (Ed.), *The Sage handbook of qualitative data analysis* (pp. 170–183). Thousand Oaks, CA: Sage.

Schultz, J. G. (1988). Developing theoretical models/conceptual frameworks in vocational education research. *Journal of Vocational Education Research, 13*(3), 29–43.

Schwandt, T. A. (1993). Theory for the moral sciences; Crisis of identity and purpose. In D. J. Flinders & G. E. Mills (Eds.), *Theory and concepts in qualitative research* (pp. 5–23). New York: Teachers College Press.

Seale, C. (1999). *The quality of qualitative research.* London: Sage.

Seale, C. (2008). Using computers to analyse qualitative data. In D. Silverman & A. Marvasti, *Doing qualitative research* (pp. 233–256). Thousand Oaks, CA: Sage.

Seidman, I. (2013). *Interviewing as qualitative research* (4th ed.). New York: Teachers College Press.

Selltiz, C., Jahoda, M., Deutsch, M., & Cook, S. W. (1959). *Research methods in social relations.* Austin, TX: Holt, Rinehart and Winston.

Siha, A. (2014). Power to the students: Using critical pedagogy to develop and sustain adult basic writing skills. In C. Boden-McGill & K. P. King (Eds.), *Developing and sustaining adult learners* (pp. 51–68). Charlotte, NC: Information Age.

Smith, E. F., Gidlow, B., & Steel, G. (2012). Engaging adolescent participants in academic research: The use of photo-elicitation interviews to evaluate school-based outdoor education programmes. *Qualitative Research, 12*(4), 267–287. doi: 10.1177/1468794112443473

Smith, L. M. (1978). An evolving logic of participant observation, educational ethnography, and other case studies. In L. Shulman (Ed.), *Review of research in education* (pp. 316–377). Itasca, IL: Peacock.

Snelson, C. (2015, online first—September 26, 2013). Vlogging about school on YouTube: An exploratory study. *New Media and Society*, *17*(3), 321–339.

Spiegelberg, H. A. (1965). *The phenomenological movement* (Vol. 2). The Hague, Netherlands: Martinus Nijhoff.

Spradley, J. S. (1979). *The ethnographic interview*. New York: Holt, Rinehart and Winston.

Sprow Forté, K. (2013). Educating for financial literacy: A case study with a sociocultural lens. *Adult Education Quarterly*, *63*(3), 215–235.

Stake, R. E. (1988). Case study methods in educational research: Seeking sweet water. In R. M. Jaeger (Ed.), *Complementary methods for research in education* (pp. 253–278). Washington, DC: American Educational Research Association.

Stake, R. E. (1995). *The art of case study research*. Thousand Oaks, CA: Sage.

Stake, R. E. (2005). Qualitative case studies. In N. K. Denzin & Y. S. Lincoln (Eds.), *The Sage handbook of qualitative research* (3rd ed.). (pp. 443–466). Thousand Oaks, CA: Sage.

Stake, R. E. (2006). *Multiple case study analysis*. New York: The Guilford Press.

Stake, R. E. (2010). *Qualitative research: Studying how things work*. New York: The Guilford Press.

Stanley, M. (2006). A grounded theory of the wellbeing of older people. In L. Finlay & C. Ballinger (Eds.), *Qualitative research for allied health professionals: Challenging choices* (pp. 63–78). West Sussex, England: Wiley.

Steinbeck, J. (1941). *Sea of Cortez*. New York: Viking Penguin.

Steinberg, S., & Cannella, G. (Eds.). (2012). *Critical qualitative research reader*. New York: Peter Lang.

Stellefson, M., Chaney, B., Ochipa, K., Chaney, D., Haider, Z., Hanik, B., Chavarria, E., & Bernhardt, J. (2014). YouTube as a source of chronic obstructive pulmonary disease patient education: A social media content analysis. *Chronic Respiratory Disease*, *11*(2), 61–71.

Stewart, D. W., & Shamdasani, P. N. (2015). *Focus groups: Theory and practice* (3nd ed.). Thousand Oaks, CA: Sage.

Stewart, K., & Williams, M. (2005). Researching online populations: The use of online focus groups for social research, *Qualitative Research*, *5*(4), 395–416.

Strauss, A. L. (1987). *Qualitative analysis for social scientists*. Cambridge, England: Cambridge University Press.

Strauss, A. L., & Corbin, J. (1994). Grounded theory methodology: An overview. In N. K. Denzin & Y. S. Lincoln (Eds.), *Handbook of qualitative research*. Thousand Oaks, CA: Sage.

Strauss, A., Schatzman, L., Bucher, R., & Sabshin, M. (1981). *Psychiatric ideologies and institutions* (2nd ed.). New York: Wiley.

Stringer, E. (2014). *Action research* (4th ed.). Thousand Oaks, CA: Sage.

Stuckey, H. L. (2009). Creative expression as a way of knowing in diabetes adult health education: An action research study. *Adult Education Quarterly, 60*(1), 46–64.

Stuckey, H. L., & Tisdell, E. J. (2010). The role of creative expression in diabetes: An exploration into the meaning making process. *Qualitative Health Research, 20*, 42–56.

Taylor, E. W. (2006). Making meaning of local nonformal education: Practitioner's perspective. *Adult Education Quarterly, 56*(4), 291–307.

Taylor, S. J., & Bogdan, R. (1984). *Introduction to qualitative research methods* (2nd ed.). New York: Wiley.

Tedlock, B. (2011). Braiding narrative ethnography with memoir and creative nonfiction. In N. K. Denzin & Y. S. Lincoln (Eds.), *Handbook of qualitative research* (4th ed.). (pp. 331–339). Thousand Oaks, CA: Sage.

Terkel, S. (2001). *Will the circle be unbroken? Reflections on death, rebirth, and hunger for a faith.* New York: Ballantine.

Tesch, R. (1990). *Qualitative research: Analysis types and software tools.* New York: Falmer.

Thaker, S. (2008). *Understanding the role of culture in the health-related behaviors of older Asian Indian immigrants.* Unpublished dissertation, University of Georgia, Athens.

Thaker, S. (n.d.). Interview transcript. University of Georgia, Athens.

Thomas, W. I., & Znaniecki, R. (1927). *The Polish peasant in Europe and America.* New York: Knopf.

Thornton, S. J. (1993). The quest for emergent meaning: A personal account. In D. J. Flinders & G. E. Mills (Eds.), *Theory and concepts in qualitative research* (pp. 68–82). New York: Teachers College Press.

Tierney, W. G. (1993). The cedar closet. *Qualitative Studies in Education, 6*(4), 303–314.

Timmermans, S., & Oh, H. (2010). The continued social transformation of the medical profession. *Journal of Health and Social Behavior, 51*, S94–S105.

Tinkler, P. (2013). *Using photographs in social and historical research.* Thousand Oaks, CA: Sage.

Tisdell, E. J. (2003). *Exploring spirituality and culture in adult and higher education.* San Francisco: Jossey-Bass.

Tisdell, E. J., Taylor, E. W., & Sprow Forté, K. (2013). Community-based financial literacy education in a cultural context: A study of teacher beliefs and pedagogical practice. *Adult Education Quarterly, 63*(4), 338–356.

Tobin, J., & Tisdell, E. J. (2015, online first). "I know down to my ribs": A narrative research study on the embodied adult learning of creative writers. *Adult Education Quarterly*, pp. 1–17.

Tracy, S. J. (2013). *Qualitative research methods*. West Sussex, UK: Wiley-Blackwell.

Treadwell, J. (2012). From the car boot to booting it up? Ebay, online counterfeit crime and the transformation of the criminal marketplace. *Criminology and Criminal Justice, 12,* 175–191.

Trotman, D. (2006). Interpreting imaginative lifeworlds: Phenomenological approaches in imagination and the evaluation of educational practice. *Qualitative Research, 6*(2), 245–265.

Tuttas, C. (2015). Lessons learned using web conference technology for online focus groups. *Qualitative Health Research, 25,* 122–133.

Tyler, J. (in press). From spoke to hub: Transforming organizational vision and strategy with story and visual art. *Adult Education Quarterly*.

Uldam, J., & McCurdy, P. (2013). Studying social movements: Challenges and opportunities for participant observation. *Sociology Compass, 7* (11), 941–951.

Underberg, N., & Zorn, E. (2013). *Digital ethnography*. Austin, TX: University of Texas Press.

Valente, J. S. (2005). *The role of self-directed learning in older adults' health care*. Unpublished doctoral dissertation, University of Georgia, Athens.

Van Maanen, J. (1979). Reclaiming qualitative methods for organizational research: A preface. *Administrative Science Quarterly, 24*(4), 520–526.

Van Maanen, J. (1982). Fieldwork on the beat. In J. Van Maanen, J. M. Dabbs, & R. R. Faulkner (Eds.), *Varieties of qualitative research* (pp. 103–151). Beverly Hills, CA: Sage.

Van Maanen, J. (2011). *Tales of the field: On writing ethnography* (2nd ed.). Chicago: University of Chicago Press.

Van Manen, M. (2014). *Phenomenology of practice: Meaning-giving methods in phenomenological research and writing*. Walnut Creek, CA: Left Coast Press.

Vicars, M. (2012). Toward a rhizomatic methodology: How queer! In S. Sternberg & G. Cannella (Eds.), *Critical qualitative research reader* (pp. 468–478). New York: Peter Lang.

Wainwright, S. P., Williams, C., & Turner, B. S. (2006). Varieties of habitus and the embodiment of ballet. *Qualitative Research, 6*(4), 535–558.

Waldron, J. (2013). YouTube, fanvids, forums, vlogs, and blogs: Informal music learning in a convergent on- and offline music community. *International Journal of Music Education, 31*(1), 91–105.

Walford, G. (2001). *Doing qualitative educational work: A personal guide to the research process*. London and New York: Continuum.

Ward, A. (2011). "Bringing the message forward": Using poetic representation to solve research dilemmas. *Qualitative Inquiry, 17*(4), 355–363.

Webb, E., Campbell, D. T., Schwartz, R. D., & Sechrest, L. (1966). *Unobtrusive measures: Nonreactive research in the social sciences.* Chicago: Rand McNally.

Webb, E., Campbell, D. T., Schwartz, R. D., & Sechrest, L. (1981). *Nonreactive measures in the social sciences* (2nd ed. of *Unobtrusive measures*). Boston: Houghton Mifflin.

Webb, E., Campbell, D. T., Schwartz, R. D., & Sechrest, L. (2000). *Unobtrusive measures: Nonreactive research in the social sciences* (revised ed.). Thousand Oaks, CA: Sage.

Weeks, S. (n.d.). Interview. Unpublished transcript, University of Georgia, Athens.

Wenger, E. (1998). *Communities of practice: Learning, meaning, and identity.* New York: Cambridge University Press.

Werner, O., & Schoepfle, G. M. (1987). *Systematic fieldwork: Ethnographic analysis and data management* (Vol. 2). Thousand Oaks, CA: Sage.

Wilensky, A. S., & Hansen, C. D. (2001). Understanding the work beliefs of nonprofit executives through organizational stories. *Human Resource Development Quarterly, 12*(3), 223–239.

Wiles, J. L., Rosenberg, M. W., & Kearns, R. A. (2005). Narrative analysis as a strategy for understanding interview talk in geographic research. *Area, 37*(1), 89–99.

Wolcott, H. F. (1992). Posturing in qualitative inquiry. In M. D. LeCompte, W. L. Millroy, & J. Preissle (Eds.), *The handbook of qualitative research in education* (pp. 3–52). Orlando, FL: Academic Press.

Wolcott, H. F. (1994). *Transforming qualitative data: Description, analysis, and interpretation.* Thousand Oaks, CA: Sage.

Wolcott, H. F. (2003). *The man in the principal's office: An ethnography* (updated ed.). Walnut Creek, CA: AltaMira Press.

Wolcott, H. F. (2005). *The art of fieldwork* (2nd ed.). Walnut Creek, CA: AltaMira Press.

Wolcott, H. F. (2008). *Ethnography: A way of seeing* (2nd ed.). Walnut Creek, CA: AltaMira Press.

Wolcott, H. F. (2009). *Writing up qualitative research* (3rd ed.). Thousand Oaks, CA: Sage.

Wright, R. R. (2008). Research as quest: An autoethnographic exploration of embodied class, intellectual obsession, and the academy. *Journal of Curriculum and Pedagogy, 5*(2), 69–94.

Wright, R. R., & Sandlin, J. (2009). Popular culture, public pedagogy, and perspective transformation: *The Avengers* and adult learning in living rooms. *International Journal of Lifelong Education, 28*(4), 533–551.

Wuthnow, R. (2012). *The God problem: Expressing faith and being reasonable.* Los Angeles: University of California Press.

Yin, R. K. (1984). *Case study research: Design and methods.* Newbury Park, CA: Sage.

Yin, R. K. (2014). *Case study research: Design and methods* (5th ed.). Thousand Oaks, CA: Sage.

Zeki, S. (2000). *Inner vision: An exploration of art and the brain.* New York: Oxford University Press.

Zorrilla, A. (2012). *More than meets the eye: Adult education for critical consciousness in Luis Camnitzer's art.* Unpublished doctoral dissertation, Penn State University-Harrisburg.

NAME INDEX

A

Abramson, P. R., 167, 277
Adkins, N. R., 278
Al Lily, A. E., 33, 89
Allen, W., 76
Alston, G. D., 218, 228, 231
Altheide, D. L., 178, 179
Anderson, G., 4, 50–51, 53, 145, 234–235, 239, 289
Anderson, L., 30, 230, 273
Anfara, V. A., Jr., 85, 88
Ardévol, E., 158, 160
Atkinson, P., 232
Augustine, Saint, 181–182
Auster, C. J., 164

B

Bailey, N., 65
Bair, M. A., 283
Ballenger, C., 54
Banerjee, A., 55
Barbour, R., 114
Barone, T., 65, 66, 69
Bateson, M. C., 108
Beale, C., 231
Becker, H. S., 90, 242, 273, 274
Berenson, L., 64, 249
Bierema, L. L., 78–79, 97
Biklen, S. K., 6–7, 8, 40, 142–143, 144, 150, 163, 166, 168, 170, 197, 211–212, 221, 271–272, 286
Blankenship, J. C., 216–218
Boellstorff, T., 158, 159
Bogdan, R. C., 6–7, 8, 40, 127–128, 142–143, 144, 150, 163, 166, 168, 170, 197, 211–212, 221, 263, 271–272, 286
Bohannan, L., 16
Braun, V., 6
Bravo, A., 62
Breen, L. J., 25
Brinkmann, S., 107
Brockenbrough, E., 36
Bucher, R., 119
Budin, W. C., 229
Bullingham, L., 177
Burbules, N. C., 61–62
Burgess, R. G., 166–167
Busher, H., 114, 159
Butler, J., III, 170
Byrd, R. E., 166

C

Camnitzer, L., 69–70
Campbell, D. T., 163, 172, 182, 262
Cannella, G., 62
Carney, G., 58

323

Subject Index

A

ABR. *See* Arts based research

Accuracy: of documents, 176–177; of personal documents, 181–182

Action research, 4–5, 49–58; AI in, 4, 55–56; coding for, 235; data analysis for, 52–53, 234–235; data collection for, 52–53; in-depth interviews for, 53; participants in, 4, 49, 51; postmodernism and, 11; principles of, 50–53; reports for, 288–290; researcher in, 49–52; types of, 53–58. *See also* Critical action research; Participatory action research

Adobe Connect, 115, 116

AI. *See* Appreciative inquiry

Ambiguity: in interviews, 130; in observations, 147; in qualitative research, 18; in theorizing, 216

Analysis section, in ethnography, 229–230

Analytical coding, 206

Anchored interviews, 139

Anonymity: on Internet, 188; in reports, 264

Anthropologists, 6; artifacts and, 171; case studies by, 37; nonprobability sampling by, 96. *See also* Ethnography

Applied research, 3–5; data collection for, 4; types of, 4–5

Appreciative inquiry (AI), 4–5; in action research, 4, 55–56

Artifacts: anthropologists and, 171; of culture, 171; data collection from, 53, 106, 162–193; defined, 162; limitations and strengths of, 180–183; as mute evidence, 171; for qualitative research, 175–180; by researcher, 173–175; types of, 163–175

Arts based research (ABR), 65–72; about artists and artistic processes, 69–72, 71*fig*; autoethnography and, 70; data collection for, 66–69; reports for, 288–290

Asynchronous interviews, 115–116

ATLAS.ti, 223, 225*t*

Audience conjuring, for reports, 268–270

Audit trail: for data collection, 252–253, 259*t*; for reliability, 252, 259*t*

Authenticity: of documents, 176–177, 181–183; of personal documents, 181–182; in qualitative research, 238–239; researcher and, 252

Autoethnography, 29; ABR and, 70; with critical research, 60